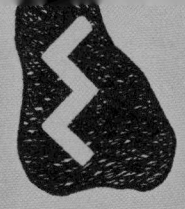

THE BOOK OF WITCHCRAFT

THE BOOK OF WITCHCRAFT

Semra Haksever

DK

CONTENTS

INTRODUCTION

Hello, and welcome to *The Book of Witchcraft*. I am pretty sure it is no accident that you have picked up this book… You have connected, in one way or another, to the energy of the witch.

Perhaps you are a little bit curious about witchcraft, or there is a calling within to explore the mystical or unseen. Maybe you are wondering what makes someone a witch. Is it their connection to nature, their intuition, or the ability to see magic in the everyday? Or is it a political statement, reclaiming a title that was once used to persecute those – usually women – who lived outside of societal norms? To me, it's all of this and more.

Connecting to the energies of the Universe and calling myself a witch has always felt like second nature to me. It's not something I question; it's more an inner trust I have that magic flows through absolutely everything. I have over 30 years of magical practice behind me, something that I've dropped, picked up, doubted, and returned to time and time again.

I find that trying to explain the mystical can sometimes strip it of its magic, so instead I invite you to quite simply trust it and have faith in its power. Know that this trust is the foundation of all magic. Allow yourself to believe in the miracle of everything, see the extraordinary in the ordinary and the magic in the mundane, and accept that your practice is allowed to evolve and take detours. As you step into your witch energy, believe in yourself and the interconnectedness of all things, and you'll find that the magic will flow and reveal itself to you everywhere.

My intention with this book is to introduce you to practices and rituals that will awaken and inspire the magic within you. My wish is that it will assist in building your confidence and help you trust in your power to create spells and rituals of your own. Whether you're here to deepen your understanding or take your first steps into witchcraft, know that the magic you seek is already a part of you.

Love,

Semra X

CHAPTER ONE

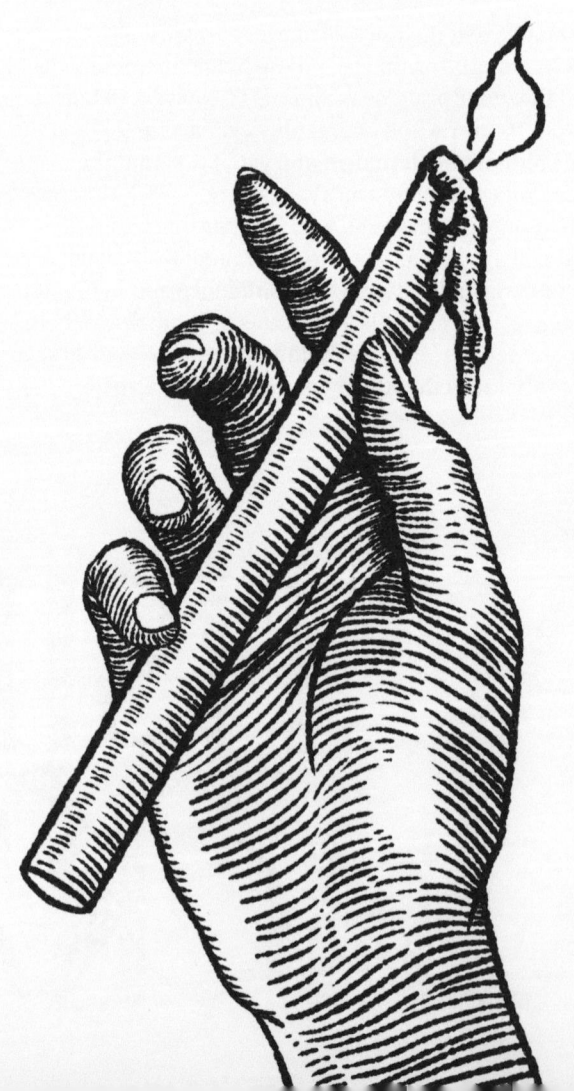

PRACTISING WITCHCRAFT

these words, place your hands on your heart. Feel the life force within you; recognize the absolute wonder of your heartbeat ticking away, of the intricate system that is working to keep you alive, and truly experience this very moment of your existence.

Spend time looking around at the trees, the changing seasons, the sun, the moon, and the entire ecosystem that holds it all together. By noticing the magical energy that flows through everything, you begin to align yourself with the magic around you.

START HERE

Magic is about what resonates with you personally. Perhaps you feel a connection to the moon and its phases, or you find meaning in the elements – Earth, Air, Fire, and Water. Start with what draws your interest: light a candle, hold a crystal, listen to the wind. These small acts are the seeds of your practice.

WITCHING WAYS

There are many ways of being a witch and practising witchcraft. Some may join a coven (see p.16), while others prefer to remain solitary. You may hear of green witches or hedge witches, who draw their power from the natural world (see p.17); cosmic witches, for whom the Tarot (see pp.204–235) and astrology (see pp.262–274) are central to their practice; hearth witches, who focus on spellcraft (see pp.46–91) in the home; or crystal witches, whose key interests lie, as you may expect, in crystals (see pp.152–165). But how you identify as a witch – if you choose to label yourself at all – is entirely up to you.

Being curious and open-minded is crucial. Read about different traditions (see pp.14–15), but feel free to adapt and blend them in ways that feel right for you and respectful of those traditions. For me, this exploration has been deeply tied to my ancestry. With Turkish and Polish heritage, I've found that my strongest connections often emerge when working with herbs native to these lands. Olive leaves, for example, serve as an equivalent to sage in Turkish folk magic, used for cleansing and protection. In Polish traditions, mugwort has long been used for its power in divination and protection spells. When you tap into these ancestral ingredients, it adds a personal touch, and is a powerful reminder that magic is not just learned, but remembered.

Magic is not one-size-fits-all – it is as unique as the individual who is involved. Experiment with different techniques, whether it's visualization, meditation, or creating a sacred space. Pay attention to how these practices make you feel and the changes they bring into your life. Think of this book as a roadmap, guiding the way – but feel free to go off the beaten track, explore, and find your own route.

BRIEF HISTORY OF WITCHCRAFT

Once upon a time, everyone was guided by folklore. It shaped the daily lives, beliefs, and practices of ancient communities. Within these societies lived individuals who went by various names – wise folk, healers, herbalists, magic practitioners, and, yes, witches – and their services were highly prized.

These were the go-to people for everything from curing illnesses to protecting crops and warding off evil. They were the keepers of knowledge that had been practised and passed down through time.

But then came the dark times. As organized religion and politics took over societies in the Middle Ages, these women (and some men) became targets. Demonstrating independent spirit, special knowledge, or even just being a bit different meant you could be labelled as a witch. The fear was stoked further by the *Malleus Maleficarum* (*The Hammer of Witches*), a 15th-century witch-hunting manual written by a German clergyman named Heinrich Kramer. This nasty little book framed witchcraft as a dangerous crime, particularly targeted women, and gave so-called authorities a step-by-step guide to hunting, torturing, and executing suspected witches. It became one of the most influential tools in justifying the mass persecution that followed.

King James VI of Scotland (later James I of England) took things to the next level when he decided that a storm that nearly sank his ship must have been caused by witches plotting against him. This led him to write *Daemonologie* in 1597, a manual that turned fear into law, giving everyone permission to persecute and kill witches. Witch trials exploded, first in Europe before spreading to colonial America. The witch trials weren't really about magic, they were about control. Communities turned on those who held the kind of power that didn't come from Church or King.

Others were just unlucky, caught in the wrong place at the wrong time, or were victims of grudges. Thousands of innocent people lost their lives – mostly women, and anyone marginalized or othered within a community, whether this was due to their race, religion, age, physical characteristics, or neurodiversity. Those who were accused and executed are a reminder of a time when fear and ignorance was out of control. Let this very sad time in history remind you to always stay informed, use your voice, be an activist, and use your freedom within your magic: it is important to honour those who had it stolen from them. Many witches today align their spiritual practices with causes such as social justice and environmentalism, and the figure of the witch remains a powerful symbol of resistance against oppression.

The mid-20th century brought a revival of interest in folk magic, and the New Age movement at the end of the century saw the resurgence of divination, crystal magic, and astrology, together with other witchcraft practices. Modern witchcraft blends traditions from various cultures, with a focus on personal empowerment, connection to nature, and spirituality rather than adhering to one particular teaching. The internet has also played a big part in growing a global community of witches, with platforms like Instagram and TikTok making "witchtok" trend, where witches share spells and rituals. Today, we can see a renewed respect for witchcraft as a beautiful and magical practice, rather than a dangerous one.

MAGIC OR MAGICK?

The term "magick" was coined by Aleister Crowley, a prominent English occultist, in the early 20th century. Crowley introduced the "k" at the end to differentiate spiritual and occult practices from stage magic performed by illusionists. While "magick" was intended to clarify the distinction, its association with Crowley is problematic due to his controversial nature, with allegations of his sexism and fascination with extreme ideologies. As a result, many practitioners, including myself, choose to not use the "k" in our magic.

WITCHCRAFT TRADITIONS

As you choose your path you may find yourself drawn to certain practices more than others, feeling a connection to specific traditions. While it's natural to be inspired by the magic of different cultures, it is important to approach these with respect.

As witches, we don't have a strict doctrine that dictates our craft; it is a deeply personal journey. As your practice develops, you'll naturally gravitate towards areas that resonate with you, and this is exactly as it should be. Your magic will evolve as you do. Over time, your beliefs may shift, the spells you create may change, and the focus of your magic may transform. This growth is not only natural but is also an essential and important part of your magical journey. Still, it's important to understand the most common witchcraft traditions.

ETHICAL PRACTICE

In witchcraft, an open practice is accessible to all, like herbal magic and astrology. A closed practice belongs to particular cultures or traditions (such as Hoodoo and Indigenous ceremonies). Practising closed traditions without initiation or permission is considered cultural appropriation. Always research and respect spiritual boundaries, ensuring ethical engagement with magical traditions.

PAGANISM

Paganism is a spiritual path that is rooted in nature and concerned with honouring the cycles of life. It originated in prehistoric times, and archaeological evidence dates back as early as 8000 BCE. This path is often polytheistic, meaning there is no one divine being, with many Pagans worshipping or working with a variety of deities and celebrating the interconnectedness of all living things. It is guided by the turning of the seasons, the phases of the moon, and the cycles of life, death, and renewal.

WICCA

Wicca is a modern Pagan religion that was founded in the mid-20th century by the English author and anthropologist Gerald Gardner. It is a mix of ancient folklore, ceremonial magic, and occult traditions, with an emphasis on nature and living in harmony with the Earth and its cycles. At its core, Wicca celebrates the duality of divine forces, often personified as a goddess and a god, representing the feminine and masculine aspects of nature and creation.

HOODOO

Hoodoo is an African-American spiritual tradition that blends together African, Native American, and European influences. It focuses on practical magic, ancestor veneration, and the use of herbs, roots, and charms to manifest intentions and offer protection. Traditional Hoodoo magic is known as a "closed practice", meaning that its magical traditions are reserved only for members of the Indigenous communities and the African diaspora, and those who have been formally initiated or invited in. Engaging with these practices without permission or understanding their significance can be seen as disrespectful or appropriative.

SYMPATHETIC MAGIC

This type of magic works with the rule of "like attracts like" by using symbols or objects to represent your desired outcome. This might be using a poppet to represent yourself or another person (see p.80) or choosing a candle with a corresponding colour in your spells (see p.110). For example, in a spell to attract a favourable financial outcome you might choose a green candle, because the colour green corresponds with money.

CHAOS MAGIC

Chaos magic is often experimental and personal to you. It doesn't follow any particular system, with its core belief centring on your own intent. It focuses on tapping into your subconscious mind's power to manifest your conscious desires – think of symbols (see p.168), sigils (see p.182) and servitors (see p.86). Because there are no rigid rules here, you can work with whatever symbols resonate and use them to focus your mind and direct your energy.

FORMS OF PRACTICE

Just as with the witchcraft traditions that you choose to follow, how you enact your magical practice is entirely up to you. The following are just a few of the ways that witches have carried out their craft over the centuries, and continue to do so today.

COVENS

This is a group of witches who gather to practise magic, share wisdom, and support one another in their spiritual journeys. Coven members typically work together to perform rituals, ceremonies, and spellwork, amplifying their collective energy to achieve greater results. This shared space allows witches to exchange knowledge, learn from one another, and form deep connections rooted in mutual respect and shared purpose.

Some covens require initiation and training, while others are more open. Check online forums, social media, and local metaphysical shops for coven listings, or visit festivals or Pagan Pride events. If something feels off, trust your instincts and don't join – true spiritual groups would never put you under any sort of pressure.

SOLITARY WITCH

A solitary witch practises alone, creating their own rituals and exploring their path without the guidance or influence of a coven. This approach allows for personal freedom and introspection, often tailored to your own unique beliefs and experiences.

The book you hold is your perfect starting point. Begin your journey by creating a book of shadows (see p.42), your personal journal for recording spells, rituals, correspondences, and experiences.

ECLECTIC WITCH

Eclectic witches draw from multiple traditions, practices, and belief systems to create a personalized form of magic and witchcraft. Eclectic witches are not confined to a single path but instead choose and work with elements that they feel the most connected to.

Create your own bespoke practice, blending planetary magic (see Chapter 10), candle magic (see pp.64–69), divination (see pp.200–203), sigils and symbols (see Chapter 7).

HEDGE WITCH

Hedge witches' practice involves working with the physical and spiritual realms. They practise "hedge jumping", a form of journeying or travelling between worlds to gain insight or to communicate with spirits. Their magic is intuitive and personal, often focusing on healing and transformation.

Try honing your intuition (see pp.188–199), and practise communing with your ancestors and spirit guides (see p.295) to seek insight.

GREEN WITCH

Green witches are deeply connected to the Earth and its energy. They are drawn to plants, trees, and flowers of all kinds, and connect their magic purely to plants, herbs, oils, resins, barks, seeds, fruit, and flowers.

Check out the Wheel of the Year (see Chapter 11) to align your magical practice to the cycles of the seasons, and the Witch's Apothecary (see Chapter 5) to understand how to use nature's ingredients in your spellwork.

KITCHEN WITCH

Kitchen witches find magic in everyday life, particularly in cooking and home care. They see the kitchen as a sacred space, using food and cooking rituals to create spells and intentions. Their focus is on nurturing the body and spirit through the act of cooking, turning each recipe into a magical moment of enchantment.

Consult the Witch's Apothecary (see Chapter 5) for healing ingredients to use in your rituals, and follow the rhythms of the seasons (see pp.276–279).

CHAPTER TWO

MAGICAL BEGINNINGS

GETTING STARTED

The success of any ritual, whether you're following a spell from this book or creating your own, is largely dependent on the setup. You're carving out sacred time for yourself, and it is a beautiful act of conscious meditation and self-care, rooted in practices that have been passed down for thousands of years.

Generations ago, your ancestors might have prepared herbal ointments and remedies; this could well be part of your cultural heritage. These ointments may have been intended to heal or to offer protection. Take a moment to think about this. Tune in to the ancient knowledge of the past and allow it to inspire you.

From the moment you shop for a bag of patchouli and corresponding-coloured candles, buy a bunch of lavender from a florist, or even pick out the outfit you want to wear during your ritual, you are mentally preparing for magic and the spell has unofficially begun. You may find that some spells instantly spark excitement, while others might feel less natural to you, and that is perfectly fine. My advice is to make it your own. Have fun with it, adapt it to fit your own personal vibe and requirements, and, most importantly, trust in the process. The magic lies in your intention and belief, so let go of perfection and focus on connecting deeply with your ritual.

Over the following pages you will find a step-by-step guide to getting started in your magical practice, from preparing yourself and setting up your altar to stepping into your personal power, performing a ritual, and understanding the ethics of magic. You can use this as a guide for carrying out the spells in this book, and also for creating your own spells.

Before you begin any spell or ritual, ensure you are practising safely. Only light candles in an area where it is safe to do so, and keep a damp cloth handy just in case (never throw water over a lit candle). Familiarize yourself with any risks of herbs or tools you plan to use, especially anything you will imbibe or use on your skin. Clear up everything when you're finished to protect your environment and others who share the space. Remember: it's never worth putting yourself or others at risk.

START HERE

Before diving into practical magic, take a moment to ask yourself why you are drawn to witchcraft, and what you are looking for? Think about what type of practice resonates with you, and consider the consequences of spellwork. Begin with simple practices like meditation and moon tracking. Reach out to the community for guidance, if you would like, joining online groups or researching local covens, but always trust your intuition – witchcraft is deeply personal.

A MAGICAL MINDSET

Preparation creates the right conditions for witchcraft, making your practice more effective and aligned with your intentions. You can get ready to perform rituals and spells in a number of ways, which we will explore over the following pages.

Your aim is to create an environment that feels energetically clean and inviting, clearing whatever it is that needs to be removed to make room for what you are calling in. It is also important to start your ritual with a calm, clear mind. You want to feel grounded and centred to ensure that your energy is aligned and focused. Before you start to practice, do the following:

✳ **TAKE A BATH OR SHOWER WITH EPSOM SALTS, AND HERBS SUCH AS LAVENDER AND ROSEMARY TO HELP RELAXATION, SETTING AN INTENTION TO WASH AWAY NEGATIVITY**

✳ **TIDY THE SPACE WHERE YOU WILL BE WORKING YOUR MAGIC, AND CLEANSE IT TO PURIFY THE ENERGY**

✳ **GROUND YOURSELF TO CONNECT TO THE EARTH'S ENERGY (SEE P.37)**

As you cleanse yourself, visualize old energy leaving your body and being replaced with light and the energy that you are calling in. When cleansing your space, focus on your intention: this is the core desire or goal that fuels your magic and directs the energy towards a specific outcome. Your intention should feel achievable, be clear and specific, and presented as though it has already happened: for example, "I radiate love and attract healthy relationships".

CLEAR YOUR MIND

There are a number of ways to clear your mind before you begin a magical ritual. See what feels right for you.

PERFORM Do a short meditation, or simply take a few deep breaths.

LISTEN Play relaxing music or sounds; you could create a magical playlist filled with songs that make you feel powerful, inspired, or connected to your intention.

MOVE Activate your body with stretches, dancing, or a yoga session.

CLEANSE THE ENERGY

Before engaging in witchcraft, it's important to cleanse the space where you will be working and the tools you'll be using. This removes lingering, stagnant energy that may get in the way of your intention. You can do this in any of the following ways:

SMOKE CLEANSING Create an incense blend of corresponding herbs and burn it on a charcoal disc (see p.123). Let the smoke disperse throughout your room, and pass magical tools through it, allowing them to bathe in the purifying smoke.

SOUND CLEANSING Use bells, chanting, or clapping to break up heavy energy, or ring a tuning fork or clap next to your tools.

WATER CLEANSING Sprinkle salt water or water that has been charged under the moon (see p.128) around your space, and submerge your tools in it (ensure they're water-safe first).

SETTING UP AN ALTAR

An altar is a physical space that is dedicated to focusing your energy when performing spellwork, rituals, meditating, or even journalling. It might be an intricate, permanent setup, a space that is set aside for specific magical workings, using only what is needed, or you may create a shrine to honour and call in the power of a specific deity, god, or goddess.

Altars date from prehistoric times and have been used across many cultures and religions as spaces for worship, making offerings, and communicating with the divine. Early altars were formed of simple stones and earth and used to honour deities, with later altars in churches and tabernacles becoming more complex and decorative. Celtic Druids placed altars outdoors in sacred groves, by standing stones, or near water to call in the elements, and these Pagan altars were largely destroyed as Christianity swept through Europe.

During the persecution of the Middle Ages, witches often made hidden altars and practised their craft in secret. These days, modern witches adapt altars to their personal beliefs. Altars can be indoors or outdoors, minimal or elaborate, and reflect an individual witch's connection to nature, ancestors, or particular deities.

KEEP IT SIMPLE

Remember with this that you don't need to go big: any small shelf, corner, or windowsill can become a sacred space. The beauty of an altar lies in its adaptability. Keep it simple, meaningful, and flexible. You might want to swap items on your altar with the changing seasons, add personal tokens, and refresh offerings as needed.

COMPONENTS OF AN ALTAR

As with every aspect of magic, your altar should be personal to you. However, there are some ritual tools that are used to create a traditional altar setup, with each of these representing the energy of an element: Earth, Air, Fire, and Water, and what is known in witchcraft as the fifth element, Spirit – the bridge between the spiritual world and the physical word, your body and soul.

ATHAME A ceremonial knife (or sword), these are used for directing energy and pointing in all directions to cast a circle for your spell, (see p.33). They symbolically bring strength and power to your altar and represent the element of Fire. They should be placed facing south on your altar.

CHALICE Symbolizes Water and is used in rituals or offerings. Fill it with water to represent an abundance of magical energy. Place the chalice on the side that faces west on your altar.

CAULDRON Or any heat-proof vessel, such as a ceramic bowl, for burning incense and petitions. When we burn items on the altar, the smoke represents the fifth element of Spirit. This can sit to the west of your altar, or in the centre while you are using it.

WAND Represents focus and intention. These can be used to guide smoke from an incense spell into the Universe, or to tap something and bless it. They can be made with a specific wood, feathers, and crystals. They represent the element of Air and should be placed in the area facing east on your altar.

PENTACLE/PENTAGRAM Represents Earth and is a grounding tool. The five points symbolize a connection between the spirit world and the physical world (representing Air, Water, Fire, Earth, and Spirit). Place at the centre of your altar, and make this energy the anchor of your ritual.

You can also choose other objects to symbolize the elements and place them in the directions that they are connected to, as follows:

EARTH Crystals, stones, salt, soil; these should face north.

AIR Feathers, incense, or a bell (bells can also be used to cleanse the energy, and represent the opening and closing of a ritual); face east.

FIRE Candles, a small cauldron/heat-proof vessel with burning herbs; face south.

WATER Bowl of water (you might charge this under the moon, or in certain weather conditions: see pp.130–131); face west.

SPIRIT A favourite scent; face west.

For an instant altar, a scented candle can be used to represent all of the elements: the flame represents Fire, melting wax stands for Water, the wax itself represents Earth, and the aroma is Air/Spirit.

You may also choose to decorate your altar with other corresponding, personal, and symbolic items, including:

* **SEASONAL FLOWERS, OR THOSE THAT HAVE SPECIAL MEANING FOR YOU**

* **HERBS (PP.136–151)**

* **COLOURED CANDLES (WE'LL EXPLORE THE SIGNIFICANCE OF CERTAIN COLOURS ON PP.110–113)**

* **PHOTOS OF LOVED ONES**

* **PICTURES OF GODS OR GODDESSES**

* **PHOTOS OF TREASURED MEMENTOS**

* **DRAWINGS OF SYMBOLS THAT ARE CONNECTED TO YOUR INTENTIONS (SEE PP.170–181)**

* **FOOD, DRINK, OR SYMBOLIC ITEMS PRESENTED AS OFFERINGS FOR DEITIES OR ANCESTORS**

* **CRYSTALS (PP.158–165)**

* **TAROT CARDS (PP.209–223)**

* **SIGILS (PP.182–185)**

* **WRITTEN INTENTIONS (P.55)**

 NOTE: You'll see that the elements play a huge role in magic, since they represent the fundamental forces of nature and existence, and they will come up again and again throughout this book.

DEDICATED ALTARS

A traditional altar can become the focal point for all of your spells and rituals. But you may want to create an altar with a more specific purpose – either instead of or as well as your more traditional altar – as these can help to clarify your goals and intentions.

ANCESTRAL ALTAR

|||||||||||||||||||||||||||||

This serves as a powerful focal point for honouring and connecting with your ancestors. Create an ancestral altar on a dark moon (see p.244), a time when the veil – the imperceptible barrier that separates the living from the spirits of the deceased – between our world and the unseen is thinnest. You might call upon the strength of your ancestors, or thank them during a time of good fortune.

You will need

* ❋ **PEN AND PAPER**
* ❋ **DRINK OR FOOD AS AN OFFERING FOR YOUR ANCESTOR**
* ❋ **MEMENTOS AND PHOTOS OF ANCESTORS**
* ❋ **5 WHITE CANDLES**
* ❋ **1 YELLOW CANDLE**
* ❋ **HERBS CONNECTED TO YOUR ANCESTORS, PERHAPS USED IN TRADITIONAL COOKING**
* ❋ **PLANTS THAT THEY MAY HAVE LOVED AND GROWN**
* ❋ **MUGWORT TEA TO SIP**

1. Create a family tree. Write your name at the bottom of the paper, and above it write your parents' names, with a line to connect you to each. Do the same above their names for their parents (your grandparents), and on and on as far back as you know. A family tree can be as simple as that, or you can add more detail, including siblings and other important people in your ancestry.

2. Take the time to prepare a dish or beverage to offer up to your ancestors. This could be something that reminds you of your culture, or a recipe handed down through generations. It could be something as simple as a plate of shop-bought biscuits that you know your grandparents would have enjoyed.

3. As you build your altar, think about the people whose own lives and choices made you who you are today, bringing you to this present moment.

4. Meditate on your ancestors as you sip mugwort tea, or speak to them if you like, asking questions or invoking their guidance whenever you need it.

BRING PEACE TO YOUR HOME

This helps to establish a calming, protective, and harmonious energy in your home. White corresponds with tranquillity, quartz brings harmony, selenite is associated with peace, and the herbs carry powerful purification properties.

You will need

* 11 WHITE CANDLES
* CLEAR QUARTZ CRYSTALS
* SELENITE
* FRESH ROSEMARY
* FRANKINCENSE

1. Arrange the items in a way that feels soothing and balanced to you.

2. Light a candle to set the mood, and say an intention or prayer, for example:

"MAY THIS HOME BE FILLED WITH PEACE, LOVE, AND HARMONY."

3. Meditate in front of the altar, breathing in the scent of the herbs and focusing on inviting peace.

4. Light a candle each night over 11 nights. This number is associated with inner wisdom in numerology. Spend a few minutes daily near the altar, visualizing a peaceful light spreading through the home.

LOVE ALTAR

Use this altar to call in love, whether you want to find a romantic connection or bolster the love that already exists in your life. Remember the ethics of magic: focus on yourself and what you desire, rather than encroaching on another person's free will.

You will need

* 2 PINK CANDLES
* FRESH RED ROSES
* A PICTURE OF YOURSELF, OR YOUR FULL NAME WRITTEN ON A PIECE OF PAPER
* A MAGNET OR LODESTONE
* CORRESPONDING CRYSTALS: RED JASPER FOR PASSION, ROSE QUARTZ FOR LOVE, AQUAMARINE FOR PEACE AND COMMUNICATION

1. Arrange your altar with the items and dress the base of the candles with the roses.

2. Place your picture on the altar with the lodestone or magnet on top of it.

3. Light the candles over three nights, each night returning to your altar and calling in your love.

RAISE PSYCHIC VISIONS

|||||||||||||||||||||||||||||||||||

Create a sacred space that enhances intuition, clarity, and spiritual connection. Purple corresponds with divination and can help awaken your psychic energy, while seven is the number of introspection, associated with spiritual insight.

You will need

* ❋ **7 PURPLE CANDLES**
* ❋ **1 WHITE CANDLE**
* ❋ **MUGWORT AND ROSEMARY INCENSE**
* ❋ **CHARCOAL DISC**
* ❋ **CAULDRON OR HEAT-PROOF VESSEL**
* ❋ **BIG BOWL OF WATER**

1. Find a quiet space where you won't be disturbed and set up your altar with your candles, water, and herbs.

2. Light the candles, and as you do so, focus on their flames, visualizing them igniting your inner sight.

3. Gently burn a small amount of incense on a charcoal disc, or rub it between your fingers to release its scent.

4. Gaze into the water, keeping your mind open, allowing any images or feelings to naturally arise.

5. Once finished, write down any visions, words, or sensations you received.

For instruction on burning incense see p.123.

MINI ELEMENTAL ALTARS

You can bring all of the elements to your home or workspace by creating mini altars dedicated to each element and placed in its corresponding direction. These elemental touchstones are reminders for reflection and manifestation, and connect you to the forces that work in the background to support your magical flow.

By aligning these altars with the cardinal directions, you will create a subtle yet powerful energetic grid that grounds and protects your space. As you pass these altars throughout the day, take a moment to breathe in their energy, set intentions, or express gratitude.

NORTH: EARTH

ENERGY: Stability, grounding, prosperity, growth
WISHES TO CALL IN: Financial abundance, security, health, protection
ALTAR IDEAS: Bowl of soil or salt; stones or crystals like green aventurine and tourmaline; small houseplants; wooden objects; a pentacle symbol; a coin if manifesting abundance

EAST: AIR

ENERGY: Inspiration, intellect, clarity, new beginnings
WISHES TO CALL IN: Mental sharpness, creativity, fresh starts, communication skills
ALTAR IDEAS: Feathers; incense; bells; paper with written affirmations; light-coloured stones like citrine or clear quartz

SOUTH: FIRE

ENERGY: Passion, transformation, courage, willpower
WISHES TO CALL IN: Motivation, strength, confidence, love, personal power
ALTAR IDEAS: Candles; red or orange crystals like carnelian or garnet; a piece of charcoal; a symbol of the sun; a spicy herb like chilli

WEST: WATER

ENERGY: Emotion, intuition, healing, flow
WISHES TO CALL IN: Emotional balance, love, spiritual connection, dreamwork
ALTAR IDEAS: Bowl or cup of water, or add a vial of water from the ocean, a sacred spring, or somewhere that is meaningful to you; seashells; a chalice; blue stones like aquamarine or moonstone; essential oils; a small mirror

PRACTICAL MAGIC

Once you have prepared yourself both mentally and physically, and have set up your altar, it's time to begin your magical practice. The following pages will provide guidance on how to create a sacred space and open and close a ritual.

While magical practices can differ, depending on the tradition and your own personal preferences, by and large most rituals and spells follow a similar structure:

* ✳ **SET YOUR INTENTION, CLEARLY DEFINING YOUR GOAL OR PURPOSE FOR THE RITUAL OR SPELL**
* ✳ **CHOOSE THE TIMING (SEE P.238)**
* ✳ **GATHER YOUR TOOLS, OR SET UP YOUR ALTAR (SEE P.24)**
* ✳ **REMOVE ANY LINGERING NEGATIVE ENERGY (SEE P.23)**
* ✳ **OPEN THE RITUAL BY CASTING A CIRCLE (SEE OPPOSITE)**
* ✳ **USE INCANTATIONS AND SYMBOLIC ACTIONS (SEE P.40–41)**
* ✳ **CLOSE THE RITUAL AND GROUND YOURSELF (SEE P.37)**

Throughout this book, we will deep dive into all of these aspects of magical practice. First we will look at casting a circle, using three different ways to create this sacred space: using a sigil, invoking your ancestors, and calling in the directions.

CASTING A CIRCLE

Casting a circle is a way to create a protected space for your ritual. It concentrates your energy and keeps out distractions or disruptive forces. There are many ways to cast a circle, and, as with all magic, choose what resonates with you, bringing your own personal power to the spell. You can go all out here, or it can be as simple as lighting a candle. Here are some ideas, from easy-peasy to more focused ways to open your circle.

USE A SIGIL

1. Make a sigil (see p.183) that encompasses all that a magic circle means to you, draw it on a bay leaf and burn it at the beginning of a ritual.

2. Carve elemental symbols onto white candles (see p.111) and surround yourself with them, or place in corresponding directions on your altar.

3. You can also physically surround yourself with items that represent the elements, or place them on your altar (see right).

* CANDLE IN THE SOUTH CORNER TO REPRESENT FIRE
* BOWL OF WATER IN THE WEST TO REPRESENT WATER
* INCENSE BURNING IN THE EAST TO REPRESENT AIR
* BOWL OF SALT, SAND, OR SOIL IN THE NORTH TO REPRESENT EARTH

INVOKE YOUR ANCESTORS

1. First create some protective water. To do this, hold a bowl of water and imagine it being infused with shielding light.

2. Dip your fingers in the bowl and sprinkle it around you as you visualize a protective circle forming.

3. Stand in the centre of this circle and call upon your ancestors or spirit guide:

4. If you sense a presence, acknowledge it and invite them to stay. Remember to thank and release them when closing your ritual.

"ANCESTORS OF MY BLOOD, MY SPIRIT, AND MY PATH, I CALL UPON YOU.

COME FORTH AND STAND BY ME IN THIS SACRED SPACE."

CALL IN THE DIRECTIONS

Invoke the energies of each elemental direction with a chant or affirmation to draw in their strength, protection, and guidance. As you face each of the directions you can point using the tip of your finger, a selenite crystal (see p.165), wand, or athame (see p.26).

Take your time. Stand in the centre of your space and turn to each direction as you speak its corresponding chant. Make this chant your own. Feel free to adapt the wording to suit you, or add specific requests related to how the energy of each element will assist your intention.

NORTH

"GUARDIANS OF THE NORTH, SPIRITS OF EARTH, I CALL UPON YOUR GROUNDING ENERGY. KEEP ME GROUNDED AND GUIDE ME WITH STABILITY AND STRENGTH. I CALL ON YOUR POWER TO PROTECT THIS SACRED SPACE."

EAST

"GUARDIANS OF THE EAST, THE SPIRITS OF AIR, I CALL UPON YOUR CLARITY AND INSPIRATION. BLESS ME WITH IDEAS, INSIGHTS, AND THE WINDS OF CHANGE. GUIDE MY THOUGHTS; BRING ME INSPIRATION AND POSSIBILITY."

SOUTH

"GUARDIANS OF THE SOUTH, I CALL IN THE SPIRITS OF FIRE, I CALL UPON YOUR ENERGY TO AWAKEN MY PASSION AND COURAGE. ADD HEAT AND FUEL MY MAGIC AND INTENTIONS WITH CONFIDENCE. BRING ME LIGHT AND GUIDE ME ON MY PATH."

WEST

"GUARDIANS OF THE WEST, I CALL IN THE SPIRITS
OF WATER, I CALL UPON YOUR INTUITION AND
HEALING. FLOW THROUGH MY EMOTIONS WITH
PEACE, UNDERSTANDING, AND COMPASSION.
CLEANSE MY ENERGY AND NURTURE MY
HEART'S DESIRES."

ABOVE

"GUARDIANS FROM ABOVE, I CALL IN YOUR
COSMIC ENERGY OF THE UNIVERSE, SHINE
YOUR MAGIC AND LIGHT UPON THIS CIRCLE.
BLESS THIS SPACE WITH WISDOM,
GUIDANCE, AND MAGICAL ENERGY."

BELOW

"GUARDIANS FROM BELOW, SPIRITS OF
THE EARTH'S CORE, ANCHOR THIS CIRCLE
WITH YOUR WISDOM AND ANCIENT
ENERGY. PROTECT THIS SPACE WITH
YOUR STRENGTH AND STABILITY."

"THIS CIRCLE IS CAST, PROTECTED,
AND SACRED. SO MOTE IT BE."

"MAY THIS CIRCLE BE
PROTECTED, SACRED,
AND ALIGNED WITH
MY HIGHEST GOOD."

BEGINNING AND ENDING A RITUAL

When you're ready to start, you should clearly state that this is the beginning of your ritual. This can be as simple as saying, "The spell has begun", or marking the moment with a symbolic action like ringing a bell, clapping your hands, or lighting a candle. These gestures help signal to your mind and spirit that the ritual has officially started, bringing focus and intention to your ritual.

Closing a ritual is just as important as beginning it. It signifies that the work is complete and allows you to ground yourself and be back in your body. Because during a ritual we are connecting to different energies and are entering and opening different portals, it is advisable to bring yourself back to earth, grounding and centring yourself. There are various ways to do this:

* When your spell is complete, say words of completion like "And so it is", or "The ritual is complete."

* Extinguish any candles that you lit during the ritual, as a symbolic gesture of closing the energetic space.

* Use sound to seal the ritual: ring a bell, clap your hands three times, or stamp your feet to ground the energy and mark the end of the magical work.

* Gently pat yourself down from the top of your head to your feet, symbolizing the release of excess energy and grounding yourself back into your body. Say your name three times as you do this.

GROUND
AND CENTRE
YOURSELF

‖‖‖‖‖‖‖‖‖‖‖‖‖‖‖‖‖‖‖‖‖‖‖‖‖‖‖‖‖‖‖

After a ritual, it is important to reconnect with the physical world. Perform a grounding meditation by visualizing roots growing from your feet into the earth below, anchoring you to its stability and strength. Alternatively, if you called in the directions during your ritual (pp.34–35) take a moment to thank them and repeat your invocation in reverse, expressing gratitude to each element or guardian for their presence and support.

Once you have completed your ritual, you might find yourself full of energy, pumped up, excited, and unstoppable, or you may feel tired and emotionally drained. Either way, this is a time to nurture yourself. Try the following:

✳ Eat a nourishing meal to ground you and replenish your energy.

✳ Take a bath or shower.

✳ Drink plenty of water or soothing herbal tea.

✳ Relax: the spell is done and now is time to chill.

Be open to messages that appear in your mind, synchronicities, and dreams after performing a ritual; after playing with energy in this way, signs will often present themselves to you.

YOUR PERSONAL POWER

This is a vital component of witchcraft and refers to your inner energy and ability to influence reality through your intentions, rituals, and focus. It is the fundamental force that drives your spellwork and other magical practices. The more that you trust and develop your inner strength, the more powerful your magic becomes.

Your personal power is your greatest magical tool. Unlike external power sources such as deities, spirits, or the elements, this power comes from within and can be enhanced through meditation and practice.

As you hold your intention, notice how it makes you feel. Does it bring a sense of excitement and anticipation, or does it stir up fear or resistance? If it's the latter, this might be because of self-doubt, and this should be explored. For example, in a money spell you might visualize a large amount of money in your bank balance; if this feels overwhelming or unattainable, try starting with an amount that is realistic yet still exciting for you. By aligning your intention with what feels achievable and positive, you will create a clearer, more powerful energetic connection to your desired outcome.

Over the following pages we'll look at how you can connect to the power of your imagination, speak your desires with confidence, and raise your energy to enact rituals that will bring your magic to life.

VISUALIZATION

Before embarking on a spell or ritual, try one of the following visualizations to strengthen your intent and enhance your magic.

✳ Close your eyes and imagine yourself jumping into your future timeline, living out the reality of your spell coming true.

✳ Imagine a day in your life when your intention has manifested, and notice all of the details: what is your morning routine? What are you wearing? What are you eating? Who are you hanging out with when you are living out this intention?

✳ Visualize your intention playing out on a TV screen, as if you are watching a movie of your desired outcome. Sometimes visualization might need a little "tuning in".

✳ To help yourself connect, start with something familiar, like eating a piece of fruit: connect to your senses, imagining the taste, smell, or texture.

✳ Repeat an affirmation while focusing on your intention; as you do this, images may naturally appear in your mind, guiding you towards a clearer vision.

For a small number of people who experience what is known as "aphantasia", an inability to visualize, there's no need to worry. Instead of creating mental images, focus on speaking the words of your desired outcome with conviction, as this can be as powerful.

AFFIRMATIONS AND INCANTATIONS

Speaking your intentions transforms thoughts into vibrations. Words carry powerful energy, and when we state our intentions aloud we activate that energy, sending it out into the Universe. To harness this energy, create an affirmation of your intention. This can be a simple direct statement or even a rhyme, if that feels more magical to you.

* Repeat it out loud with conviction. Speak it three times or select a number that has numerological significance for you (see pp.98– 100). Numbers can add an extra layer of power to your spells.

* Always phrase your affirmation as if your intention has already manifested. Use statements like "I am", "I have", or "I am grateful for", which affirm your belief.

* Avoid phrases like "I want" or "I need", as they suggest lack and can create resistance. For example, instead of saying, "I need financial security", say, "I am financially secure and thriving".

Let your voice carry your intention into the Universe with confidence and trust. This practice not only strengthens your spell but also reinforces your belief in your magic.

For examples of especially powerful words to use in spoken affirmations, see p.54.

ACTIONS

Action is a vital part of collaborating with your magic and bringing your intention to life. It's where you take the energy of your spell and bring it into the physical world by making moves that align with your goal. When you act in alignment with your intention, you are stepping into the energy you want to manifest and reinforcing the magic you've already set in motion.

Taking action shows the Universe, and yourself, that you are committed to your desire. For example, if you are creating a spell to get a new job, you must put this into action and create a resumé, reach out and network, and apply for jobs. Or, if you want to find love, you must figure out the steps you will take to seek it and meet someone. If your spell is for self-love, daily acts of self-care like journalling, taking time to relax, or setting boundaries will align you with the energy you're calling in.

Your actions are a vital signal that you are ready to receive, and sometimes it might be not immediately clear what action to take. In these moments, don't let uncertainty block your progress. Instead, perform a clarity spell (see p.107) to gain insight, or consult tarot cards for guidance (see Chapter 9). Using these tools can help you tune in to opportunities or show you the next steps to take.

The Universe responds to the energy you put out, so when you back up your spellwork with intentional action, you move closer to making your desires a reality.

CREATE A BOOK OF SHADOWS

This is a personal spell book and a place to record all of your magical workings. Creating a book of shadows can serve as a journal and reference guide, helping you to hone your techniques to help you refine your practice over time.

This can also be a place for self-reflection. Use it to document and reflect on your rituals, recording what worked, what didn't, and how you would do something differently next time. By reviewing what you've written, you can pinpoint the techniques that worked best for you and what you could do differently next time to get better results. It also allows you to recreate successful spells and draw inspiration for new ones.

What you put in your book is entirely up to you, but you may consider including any of the following when recording spells:

✳ Write down the exact steps you took, including materials, chants, and actions.

✳ Include astrological and planetary influences: note the planetary alignment, moon phase, and time of day when you performed the spell as these energies can affect the outcome.

✳ Record what emotions arose while creating and casting the spell. Did you feel confident, excited, or hesitant? Reflecting on this helps you understand how your energy impacts your magic.

✳ Results and reflections: include the outcome of the spell, what worked, what didn't, and any signs or synchronicities that happened after the spell.

PERSONAL RESPONSIBILITY

Magic is an extremely powerful tool, and with that power comes the responsibility to use it wisely and compassionately. A core principle is to focus your work on yourself, unless you have permission from someone else to include them in your spellwork: this practice respects the free will and autonomy of others, which is the fundamental rule of ethical magic.

Before casting any spell involving another person, ask yourself: how would I feel if someone performed a spell on me without my knowledge or consent? This simple question can help you gauge whether your actions align with your values and principles.

This rule is especially critical when it comes to love spells. Manipulating someone's feelings or actions through magic can undermine their free will, creating an imbalanced and potentially harmful connection. True love is built on mutual respect, trust, and free choice, not on forced attraction. Instead of casting a spell to draw a specific person to you, focus on spells that attract healthy, genuine love into your life. When you do this, you align yourself with the energy of love while leaving space for the right person to come into your life naturally and of their own free will.

The key touchstones of ethical magic are as follows:

* Take responsibility for your actions, and accept the consequences of your spells.

* Avoid engaging in any magical practice that may cause harm, either to yourself or others.

* Always be respectful and offer gratitude when summoning spirits of deities.

* Avoid cultural appropriation – instead use practices that align with your own traditions, or learn from others respectfully.

Ethical magic not only honours others but also strengthens your own practice. By working within these guidelines, you ensure your intentions remain clear, your energy is balanced, and your spellwork aligns with the highest version of yourself and the greater good.

TRUST AND BELIEF

When it comes down to it, truly trusting and believing in your magic is vital when practising witchcraft. Without trust in its power, your magic is unlikely to work as intended, if it works at all.

The reason why many people can fear magic is because of this very moment of realizing just how much power it holds, and the corresponding responsibility that comes along with it.

Whether you're performing an elaborate ceremonial ritual or simply anointing yourself with an essential oil to tap into a specific energy (see p.126), the key is to trust and believe in what you're doing. Believe, believe, believe! Hold the belief that what is meant for you will always find its way to you, and that nothing that is aligned with your highest good will pass you by.

If you worry that self-limiting beliefs or doubts are blocking your magic, end your spells with the acknowledgement of "this or better". This simple phrase acts as an insurance policy, leaving room for the Universe to deliver something greater than what you can currently imagine. Sometimes the Universe has plans far bigger and better than what we're asking for.

START SMALL

If you're struggling to fully trust your magic, start small; you can choose to create spells in areas where you feel a strong connection and build your confidence over time. A great place to begin is by creating a simple potion with scents that embody the energy or emotion you want to connect with. For example, mix a few drops of essential oils, or carry a tarot card in your bag with the energy that you want to invoke. These small, intentional practices can help you strengthen your belief and build trust in your magical practice.

TRUST IN YOUR INGREDIENTS

As you gather your herbs, oils, and other magical components, remember that each carries unique properties and energy. When you add them to your spells or use in rituals, trust in their purpose and know they are working in harmony to bring your intention to life. Focus on the act of creation with confidence, knowing that your intention is enough to set the magic in motion.

AVOID DOUBT

Avoid falling into the trap of questioning your practice or doubting whether your spell will work. Even worse, "testing" magic – casting a spell with scepticism or as an experiment – can disrupt the energy entirely. Magic thrives on intention, belief, and trust. If you infuse your spellwork with uncertainty, you're creating conflicting energy that could block the very outcome you desire.

COMMITMENT

Fully commit to the process. Trust that the Universe, the tools you're using, and your own power are aligned to help you manifest your intentions. Let go of fear and doubt and allow the energy to flow freely, knowing that you've done your part, and the magic is already at work.

CHAPTER THREE

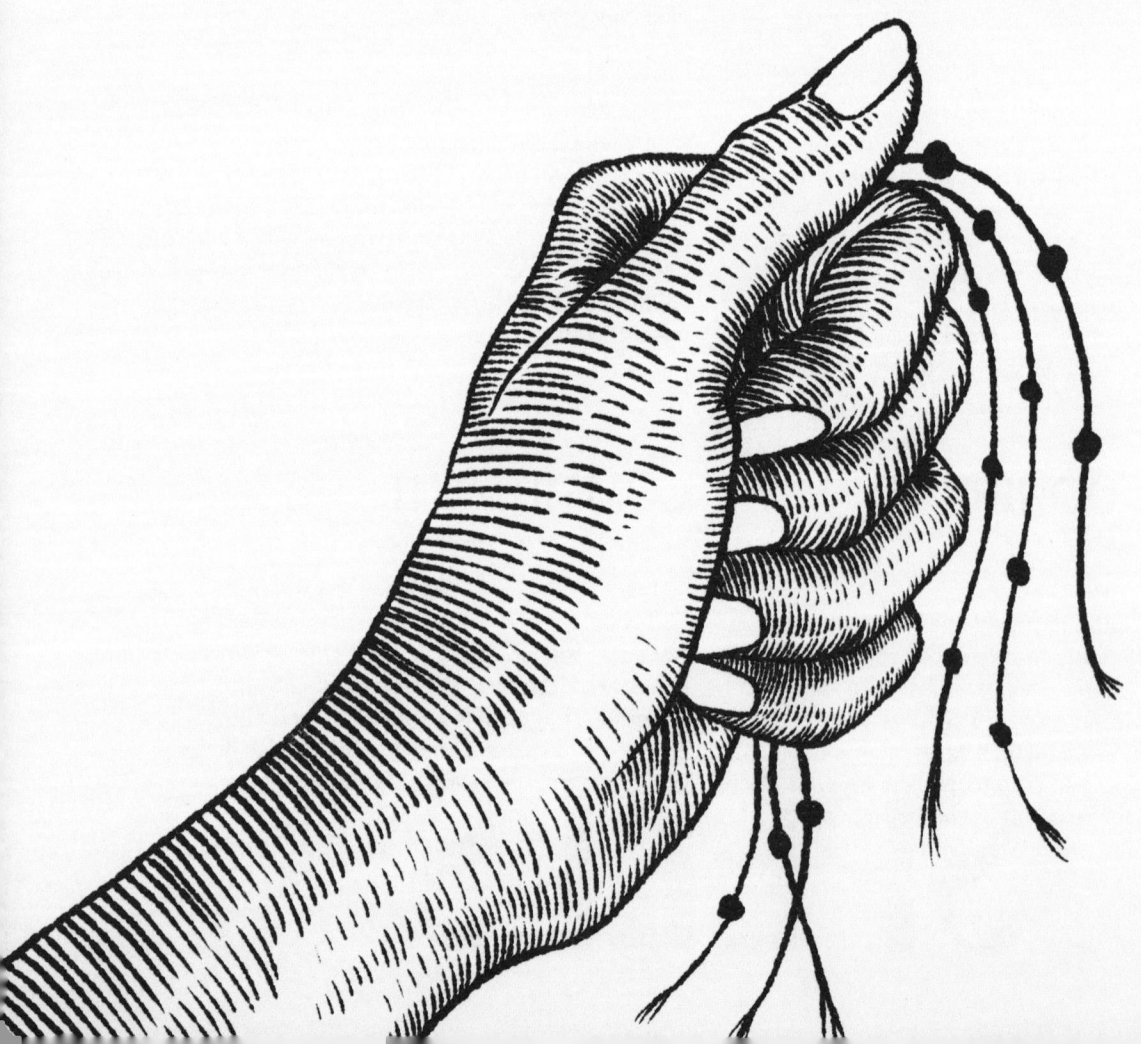

SPELLS

WHAT IS A SPELL?

Simply put, a spell is a manipulation of energy. Essential learning for any witch, spells provide a hands-on way of engaging in witchcraft. You might cast spells to provide protection against harm or misfortune, encourage favourable outcomes, to heal wounds or heartbreak, to facilitate communication – either with spirits or people – and gain insight into the future.

When we create any magical ritual, we are intentionally harnessing the vibrational frequency that we want our energy to operate at. We will explore magical energies in more detail in the next chapter. Whether you are creating an easy daily practice, like repeating affirmations while you drink your morning tea, or crafting an elaborate ritual, a spell's focus is to connect you to the energy you want. Spells can be simple or complex, and they can be performed regularly or as one-offs. Your spellwork is what you make it.

Belief is the fundamental ingredient of any successful spell. If you doubt or question what you're doing, you risk disrupting the energy flow. The energy that you put into a spell impacts its effectiveness, so confidence is key; if you are unsure, then your magic will be too, so step into the power of knowing it's going to work. If you're nervous, do a practice run to familiarize yourself with the steps, allowing you to perform the spell with confidence and focus when the time comes.

Magic often works in mysterious ways, and the results might not always turn out exactly as you envisioned. However, trust that the Universe will align outcomes in a way that is ultimately best for you, even if it's different from what you initially wished for. Remember that spellwork is a collaboration with the energy around you, and like any skill it takes time and patience to master. Respect the process, and most of all, enjoy it.

START HERE

A spell always begins with setting the right scene and cultivating the proper mindset. Planning and preparation are important, and this includes gathering your materials, meditating, and having clarity on your specific intention (see p.22), and making sure that you are in a headspace of belief.

Spells will come up again and again as we move through each chapter of this book. But in this chapter, we'll cover some key components of traditional spells. I'll show you how to use spells in the following ways:

✳ **CHARMS AND TALISMANS: CARRY CORRESPONDING OBJECTS TO ATTRACT LUCK OR OFFER PROTECTION, OR TO ENHANCE YOUR PERSONAL POWER**

✳ **SPELL JARS: FILL WITH INGREDIENTS THAT ALIGN WITH THE INTENTION OF A SPELL, TO CONTINUOUSLY WORK OVER TIME**

✳ **CANDLE MAGIC: USE TO FOCUS ENERGY AND INTENT, CLEANSE, PROTECT, AND HELP WITH INTUITIVE MAGIC**

✳ **KNOT MAGIC: TIE KNOTS TO BIND, RELEASE, OR STORE ENERGY, AND HELP MANIFEST INTENTIONS OR SET SPECIFIC OUTCOMES**

✳ **POPPETS: CREATE A SMALL DOLL TO REPRESENT YOURSELF AND USE IT FOR HEALING, PROTECTION, OR TO ATTRACT PARTICULAR OUTCOMES**

✳ **SERVITORS: CREATE AN ENTITY OUT OF ENERGY TO CARRY OUT YOUR INTENT AND PERFORM SPECIFIC TASKS**

CHARMS

Charms and talismans are objects of power that can hold energy to be used in your magical practice for anything from bringing good fortune to assisting with specific intentions. The great thing about them is their versatility. They can be as simple as a stone or seashell that you carry in your pocket or as elaborate as bags filled with herbs and symbols.

The use of charms can be found in many cultures. Warriors throughout history often carried claws or animal teeth, believing they connected them to the animal's strength. In ancient Egypt scarabs (a type of dung beetle) symbolized protection and rebirth, and in Turkey the nazar, or "eye bead", is an amulet crafted to protect against evil eyes sending negative energy. In medieval times, pouches were filled with protective herbs to ward off evil.

The magic here is about giving something meaning and connecting to that energy. Sometimes, the Universe can present you with a gift that represents a moment in your life. I was once walking along the beach with a friend, sharing stories about transformations we'd experienced, when we spotted a washed-up snake. We couldn't believe our eyes. Snakes are the ultimate symbol of transformation and rebirth. We carefully picked up the dead snake and dried the skin, later using it in charm bags to harness the energy of personal growth and new beginnings.

Charms and talismans are both magical objects, but they have slightly different vibes and purposes. Charms can be thought of as magnets and are usually created to attract something specific, like love, luck, or protection. A talisman is more about holding power or giving you strength. Whatever form your charms come in, they can act as a powerful way to focus intention.

PROGRAMME INTENT

Creating a charm or talisman begins with choosing an object that resonates with the energy you want to harness. It's all about finding something that feels right to you, whether it's a small stone, crystal, or piece of jewellery. Take a moment to meditate on your intention, hold the object in your hands, speak to it, and visualize programming it with how you would like its help in your magic.

LUCKY SOCKS

|||||||||||||||||||||||||||||||||||||||||||||||

When I say that anything can be used as a charm, I mean it. Items of clothing can work as extremely powerful charms. You might already have an existing garment in your wardrobe that makes you feel special, and this can be charged up with intention so that when you wear it you call in that energy. It could be as simple as a pair of socks!

1. To make your socks into a charm, first choose your pair (or any other item of clothing that you want to use for this spell).

2. Hold them in your hands and tell them that they are your lucky socks, that you trust they are going to walk you in the right direction, steer you to chance encounters, and guide you to receive luck.

3. To take this further you can create an incense blend to connect to your intention and bathe the item of clothing in the smoke before you put it on (see p.124 for a lucky incense spell).

CHARM BAGS

|||||||||||||||||||||||||||||||||||||||||||||||

These small pouches are filled with carefully chosen herbs, crystals, and other symbolic items to align with your desired outcome, whether it's protection, love, prosperity, or healing. For these little charm bags, you can use small drawstring pouches in a corresponding colour, or make your own.

1. Select some fabric in a corresponding colour to your spell (see p.110–113).

2. Cut two squares that are 10 x 10 cm (4 x 4 in).

3. Pin the two pieces of fabric together and sew along three edges. Choose thread in a corresponding colour.

4. Turn them inside out.

5. Add herbs (see p.136–151), crystals (see p.158–165), or petitions (see p.55) connected to how you want the charm to work for you.

6. Sew the top together.

7. Carry the charm bag with you, or place it on your altar or in another special place.

CHARM TO AWAKEN PSYCHIC ENERGY

||||||||||||||||||||||||||||||||||||||||||||||||||||||||||||||

This charm can take the form of a crystal, a seashell, a stone, a piece of jewellery, or any other small object. It can be used as your little psychic assistant to guide you through psychic work such as tarot card readings.

1. First choose your charm. Hold it in your non-dominant hand, placing your dominant hand over it so the charm rests against your body.

2. Hold it against your stomach and say,

"I BLESS THIS CHARM WITH THE ENERGY OF MY GUT FEELINGS."

3. Now hold the charm against your heart and say,

"I BLESS THIS CHARM WITH THE WISDOM OF MY HEART. MAY MY HEART ENERGY GUIDE ME WITH LOVE AND COMPASSION."

4. Finally, hold the charm to your third eye and say,

"THIRD EYE, GUIDE ME. MAY THIS CHARM OPEN MY THIRD EYE VISION TO SEE WHAT NEEDS TO BE SEEN."

5. You can choose to anoint the charm with a third eye opening oil (see p.191) or create your own psychic incense blend to bathe it in (see p.123).

6. Once it has been blessed, wear or carry the charm whenever you want to tap into your psychic energy.

SPOKEN CHARMS

||||||||||||||||||||||||||||||

Charms can also be spoken, used in isolation or to bless a spell. The saying, "words are spells" comes from the connection between "spelling" (forming words) and "casting spells" in magical practice. We use words every day to shape our energy. When creating spoken charms, it is important to remember that when we speak we are casting mini spells, whether we are using words to motivate ourselves or those around us, speaking words of love, or releasing rage.

1. Define the intent: what do you want your charm to bring you? Is it for luck, protection, calm, or good fortune?

2. Use powerful words that are evocative and emotionally resonant: short and impactful words work best.

3. You can incorporate repetition, rhythm, and rhyme to amplify the effect and make it easier to remember, though it doesn't have to rhyme; it can be as simple as an affirmation that truly resonates with you.

4. Include symbolic imagery, using metaphors or visual references to nature, protection, or inner power. You might want to invoke the elements using words such as fire, light, wind, and stone.

5. Keep it simple so you can easily recite it from memory.

6. Modulate your tone of voice to match the intent: for example a gentle tone for calming charms and firm for protective ones.

7. Include a personal element, such as your name, a personal symbol, or an affirmation.

8. Repeat the charm regularly, focusing on your intent. The main thing to remember is the power of your words, and to speak them with complete conviction.

Words resonate with specific energies, and I recommend that you use words that work for you, but here are some of my favourites when creating spoken charms.

Manifesting words

* RISE
* FLOW
* SHIFT
* GLOW
* BLOOM
* SHINE
* OPEN
* CHARGE
* GROW
* LIFT

Protection words

* BIND
* SEAL
* SHIELD
* BURN
* CLEAR

Healing words

* HEAL
* CALM
* GUIDE
* SPEAK

PETITIONS

||||||||||||||||||||||||||||||||||||||||

A petition is like a written charm. The process of writing is a way to focus your mind and clarify your intentions. Petitions were originally written on parchment paper made from animal skins, but these days witches choose to write them on paper or baking parchment paper. I advise that you always write out your petitions with a nice pen, so that the ink glides on the paper and makes your handwriting flow.

1. Connect yourself to the paper by tearing along its edges; this way you are "making" the piece of paper yourself, and so you're creating every single element of the spell.

2. Before you begin writing, create a magical incense blend (see p.123) to bless your pen, or bathe your hands in the smoke before writing. You might like to keep this pen especially for your spellwork, and select a colour of ink that corresponds with your intention (see p.110).

3. Write your petition as if you already have it. You may choose to give thanks, for example:

"I AM SO GRATEFUL FOR..........."

"I AM SO HAPPY THAT ....HAPPENED"

Or you can simply write a list, like a to-do list, but avoid writing demands such as "I want..." or "I need..."

4. Your petition can be burnt, sending the message out into the Universe, buried to ground your intention, placed under a candle on your altar, or carried around as a charm.

SPELL JARS

Adding your intentions and various magical ingredients to a jar is a potent way to preserve all of the energy that you want to include in your spell. Using jars in witchcraft can be traced back to folk traditions from around the world as well as Hoodoo practices; all share the same methods and beliefs of adding ingredients to a vessel to hold the energy that you wish to manifest.

In 16th-century Europe, jars were often used in protection spells and filled with items like sharp objects, herbs, and bodily fluids to guard against harm or curses. Similarly, Hoodoo practitioners in the American South used jar spells, known as "container spells", to protect, attract, or banish, combining African spiritual practices with European and Indigenous influences.

Jars have long been a common household item, which is why they are the perfect accessible tools for making magic with. They serve as symbolic containers, holding and preserving the energy you put into your spell, and represent a sacred space where your intentions can be safely stored and nurtured.

Whether left on your altar, buried in the earth, or carried around with you, a jar acts as a reminder of your magic. The act of filling, sealing, and charging a jar is a focused practice that connects you to your desired outcome. As with sigils (see p.182) and knot magic (see p.71), there is real power in creating a tangible representation of the energy that you are wanting to summon.

INGREDIENTS OF A SPELL JAR

Here are some of the components that you can use in a spell jar to invoke various intentions. You can find more information about the symbolic meanings of all of these in the related sections of the book on symbols (see pp.168–175), herbs (pp.136–151), and crystals (pp.158–165). Once you have added your chosen elements, seal your jar with candle wax in a corresponding colour (pp.110–113).

ABUNDANCE

* SUGAR
* COFFEE GROUNDS
* COINS
* KEYS
* HERBS: CINNAMON, BASIL, MINT, CHAMOMILE, PATCHOULI, MARIGOLD
* CRYSTALS: PYRITE, CITRINE, EMERALD, JADE, GREEN AVENTURINE

LUCK

* COFFEE GROUNDS
* SUGAR
* FEATHERS
* KEYS
* HORSESHOE
* HERBS: PATCHOULI, ALL SPICE, BASIL, MINT, NUTMEG
* CRYSTALS: GARNET, PERIDOT, PYRITE, EMERALD, MOONSTONE, LODESTONE

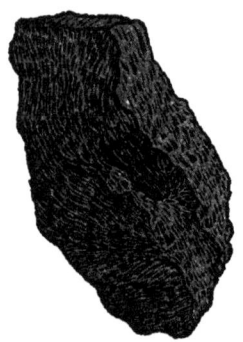

PROTECTION

* SALT (SEA SALT, HIMALAYAN, OR BLACK SALT)
* BLACK PEPPER
* GARLIC
* EGGSHELLS
* VINEGAR
* ASH
* NAILS AND SCREWS
* PINS AND NEEDLES
* BONES
* DIRT
* HERBS: SAGE, ROSEMARY, CAMPHOR, BAY LEAVES, RUE
* CRYSTALS: BLACK TOURMALINE, SELENITE, OBSIDIAN, LABRADORITE, SMOKY QUARTZ

ROMANCE, LOVE, AND SWEETENING SITUATIONS

* HONEY
* SUGAR
* FEATHERS
* SEASHELLS
* HERBS: ROSE, CHAMOMILE, CINNAMON, LAVENDER, PATCHOULI, LEMON BALM

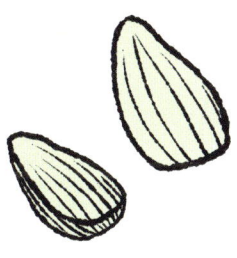

PERSONAL ITEMS

You can use these in any spell jar, whatever the intention, to bind yourself with the spell.

* URINE
* SPIT
* BLOOD
* SALIVA
* FINGERNAILS
* STRAND OF HAIR
* PHOTOS
* PETITIONS AND WRITTEN AFFIRMATIONS
* KNOT SPELLS
* SIGILS

MAKING
A SPELL JAR

||||||||||||||||||||||||||||||||||||||||||

Start by thinking of your intention, focusing on what you want your spell jar to bring you, then gather together all the ingredients that correspond with your intention.

1. First cleanse your jar and ingredients. I find smoke cleansing is the best here, so use some rosemary, sage, or camphor (see p.23). Cleanse the inside of your jar so that it is filled with smoke, and cleanse all the items that you are putting inside the jar.

2. Start adding the ingredients. As you add each item to the jar, hold it in your hands and say out loud why you are putting it inside the jar, programming it and infusing it with your energy.

3. To finalize the spell, use a candle of a corresponding colour (see pp.110–113) to seal the lid. Light the candle and stand it on top of the jar, allowing the wax to melt over the lid.

MONEY JAR

|||||||||||||||||||||||||||||||||||||||||||||||||

These are the base elements of a money spell jar, but you may wish to add extra ingredients to personalize this spell. For example, if you feel that you are not making money because you lack courage, you could add cloves, or if you feel you need to call in guidance for moneymaking ideas, add thyme.

You will need

✳ JAR

✳ 1 BAY LEAF

✳ PEN

✳ 2 CINNAMON STICKS

✳ 8 PINCHES OF DRIED BASIL

✳ 8 PINCHES OF MINT

✳ 1 PYRITE CRYSTAL

✳ 8 COINS

✳ GREEN, GOLD, OR YELLOW THREAD

✳ YOUR NAME ON A PIECE OF PAPER

✳ GREEN CANDLE

1. Cleanse the inside of your jar and all the items that you are putting inside (see p.23).

2. Draw a money symbol on the bay leaf and burn it so that the jar fills with its smoke.

3. Tie the cinnamon sticks together eight times. One cinnamon stick represents you and the other represents the money that you are calling in.

4. Continue to add the herbs and magical ingredients.

5. Before you seal the jar, hold it in your hands and say out loud eight times:

"MONEY COMES TO ME FROM EXPECTED AND UNEXPECTED PLACES."

6. Light the green candle and drip some of the melted wax over the lid to seal the spell, then fix the candle on top of the jar.

7. As it burns, visualize checking your bank balance and seeing the amount that you are manifesting in your account, or visualize yourself counting cash.

8. Let the candle burn until the end. Store the candle by a door or the entrance to your home, or on your altar.

9. Remember, magic works in mysterious ways, so take note of any unexpected moneymaking ideas that pop into your head while the spell is being cast.

WITCH BOTTLE PROTECTION SPELL

||||||||||||||||||

This is inspired by the original "witch bottles" that were buried outside houses during the Middle Ages. I always find it ironic that these were made to ward off witches, yet creating them is undeniably an act of witchcraft in itself. When making a witch bottle, the idea is to include personal items that will lure and fool any negative energy that is coming towards you, and sharp objects to trap and neutralize it.

You will need

* **BOTTLE OR JAR**
* **YOUR URINE OR SALIVA**
* **FINGERNAIL OR TOENAIL CLIPPINGS**
* **RUSTY NAILS**
* **BROKEN GLASS (OR ANY OTHER SHARP OBJECTS)**
* **SOME ASH**
* **PINCH OF SALT**
* **SPRIG OF ROSEMARY**
* **1 BLACK CANDLE**

1. Cleanse the inside of your jar so that it is filled with smoke, and cleanse all of the items that you are putting inside.

2. Start adding all of the ingredients, telling each ingredient that it is serving to protect you.

3. Fasten the lid on to the bottle or jar.

4. Light the black candle and drip some of the melted wax over the lid to seal the spell. As you do this say:

5. Fix the candle to the lid of the bottle or jar and let it burn until the end.

6. This bottle can then be buried by your front door, or if you have a plant pot by your door it can be buried in that. If you don't have a garden or a plant, place it in the back of the cupboard beneath your kitchen sink.

"NEGATIVE ENERGY, STAY AWAY, BOUND AND TRAPPED, YOU CANNOT HARM ME. THIS SPELL IS COMPLETE, SO MOTE IT BE."

SWEETENER JAR SPELL

||||||||||||||||||||||||||||||||||

These jars can be used for a variety of reasons, and they are great for inviting sweetness into any situation. Use them for relationships, business deals, liaisons with landlords, bank managers, and bosses (to name a few!), for court cases, self-love, and to invite kindness, joy, and harmony into your life.

You will need

* JAR
* SUGAR (YOU CAN USE SYRUP OR HONEY, TOO)
* PEN AND PAPER

1. Cleanse the inside of your jar so that it is filled with smoke.

2. Fill the jar halfway with sugar then top it up with hot water.

3. Put the lid on and give it a shake so that the sugar dissolves in the water.

4. Write your name on a piece of paper and then write what it is that you wish to bring sweetness to. Fold the paper so that your name is facing whatever you have written.

5. Put the folded paper in the jar, seal the jar, and shake it, swirling the sugar water around. As you do this, say:

6. Place this spell somewhere visible so that it can serve as a daily reminder of the sweetness that you are inviting into your life.

7. To really boost its energy, charge the spell jar under a full moon (see p.129).

8. If your sweetening jar has been potent in your magical practice, you can keep building on its magic by adding new petitions of things that you want to bring sweetness to.

*"MAGIC SWEETENER DO YOUR THING
AN ABUNDANCE OF SWEETNESS YOU SHALL BRING.
MAY HARMONY FLOW AND KINDNESS GROW
BRINGING SWEETNESS WHEREVER I GO."*

CANDLE MAGIC

The light of a candle demands your presence; its flickering flame can bring a dramatic energy to magic rituals, and this theatrical energy can add a real sense of power to your spellwork. Candles can be used on their own or in multiples to represent the different energies you are working with.

Candles have long been used in many different spiritual traditions, with their light often representing divine energies. In ancient Egypt, candles and lamps symbolized eternal life and were associated with Ra, the sun god; in ancient Greece and Rome, candles were used as offerings to gods and goddesses; and in Christian mysticism, candles represent Christ, "the light of the world".

The element of Fire shows us the power of transformation. For example, when we burn a petition and see it turned to ash, this symbolizes the changes and energy shifts that we can call into our own lives. Fire's energy is exciting and powerful, adding oomph to your manifestations and banishing and burning away what no longer serves you. Candles represent all the elements: Fire is the flame, Earth is the candle wax, Water is the melted wax pool, and Air is the scent or the smoke of the candle.

* ANOINT A CANDLE WITH CORRESPONDING OILS AND IGNITE TO RELEASE YOUR INTENTION INTO THE WORLD (SEE P.126)

* THE FLICKER CAN REVEAL MESSAGES OR THE PRESENCE OF SPIRITS, AND WAX DRIPPINGS CAN BE READ FOR SYMBOLS AND MESSAGES (SEE P.203)

* LET A CANDLE BURN DOWN COMPLETELY TO SEE A GOAL THROUGH TO COMPLETION

* ALIGN BURNING YOUR CANDLE WITH PHASES OF THE MOON OR DAYS OF THE WEEK (SEE PP.244–245)

* USE TO BANISH NEGATIVE ENERGY AND CREATE A SACRED SPACE

* TRANSFORM INTENT INTO ACTION BY CARVING PETITIONS OR SIGILS ON TO A CANDLE AND BURNING IT (SEE PP.182–185)

* GAZING AT A FLAME CAN ENHANCE CONCENTRATION AND FACILITATE VISUALIZATION

CREATING A CANDLE SPELL

When performing a ritual with candle magic, you focus on the flame and tune in to its energy to guide you through your intentions. A lit candle creates a connection to the mystical realms through the flame, which is seen as a living presence.

1. Start by setting an intention: how would you like this candle spell to work for you?

2. Choose a candle in a corresponding colour (see pp.110–113). White can be used as a neutral.

3. Select a number of candles based on the principles of numerology, depending upon what you want to represent in your ritual (see pp.96–100).

4. You can carve your candle with sigils (see pp.182–185) or any other symbols that connect to your intention (see pp.170–175).

5. To add another layer of energy, anoint your candle with oil (see p.126), choosing an essential oil on its own or as part of a blend. This could be a scent that corresponds or the magical element that the scent represents.

6. You might also choose herbs that align with your spell and combine them with a carrier oil or essential oil, dressing the candle with the blend by pouring the mixture onto a plate and rolling the candle in it.

7. When you light your candle, state your intention. Focus on the flame, gaze at it, and speak to it; visualize your outcome and meditate with it.

8. If you are burning the candle in one go, sit with it uninterrupted until the candle has completely blown out. If you choose to perform this spell over multiple days, then sit with the candle for as long as you need to and continue to relight it until the spell is complete.

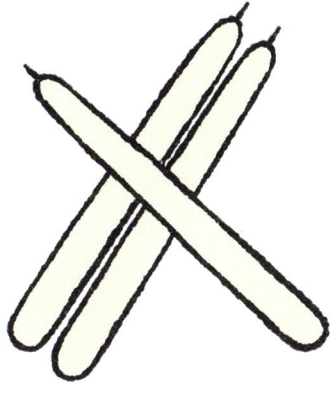
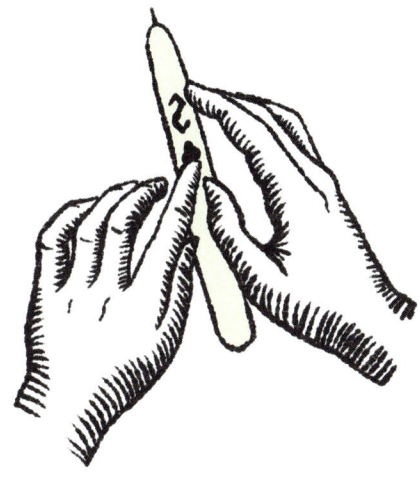

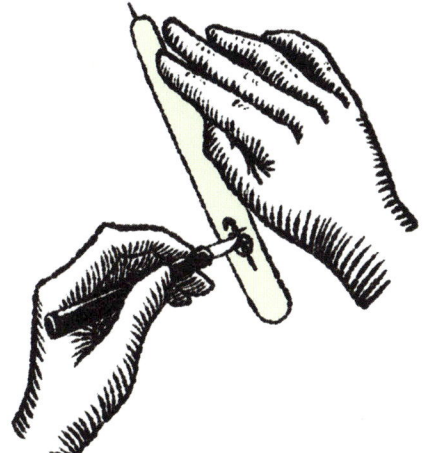
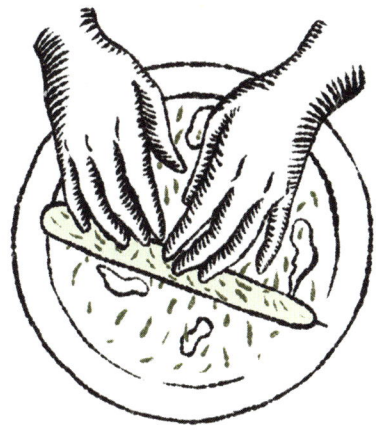

 NOTE: When you anoint the candle (or anything in magic, including your body) you may want to say something like: "With this oil I bless you with ...." (whatever your intention may be). This works as an extra layer of power for your spell.

TRANSFORM NEGATIVE ENERGY

||||||||||||||||||||||||||

This is a spell for when you have experienced some negative energy or have had a run of bad luck and want to transform the energy, put an end to the misfortune and mishaps, and shift the energy away from feeling bad.

You will need

* ✳ **PEN AND PAPER**
* ✳ **5 ML (1 TSP) OF CARRIER OIL**
* ✳ **PLATE**
* ✳ **1 BLACK CANDLE**
* ✳ **HANDFUL OF SALT**

1. Write out what it is that you want to transform.

2. Set this paper alight and keep the ashes.

3. Blend the ashes with a carrier oil and anoint the black candle with this by rolling it in the mixture.

4. Set the black candle upright and create a ring of salt around it.

5. Light the candle and let it burn until the end as you meditate on your intention.

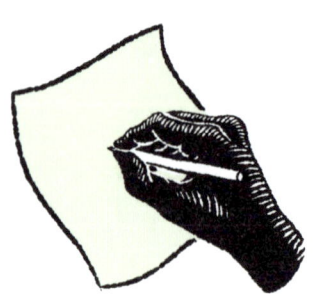

SEVEN WISHES CANDLE SPELL

IIIIIIIIIIIIIIIIIIIIIIIIIIIIIIIIIIIIIIIIIIIIIIIIIIII

This is a manifestation ritual that uses yellow candles to symbolize clarity, joy, and prosperity. If you don't want to do this spell in one sitting, perform it over seven nights, lighting and extinguishing a candle and reciting a wish each night.

You will need

✳ **3 PINCHES OF NUTMEG**

✳ **3 PINCHES OF DRIED BASIL**

✳ **3 PINCHES OF DRIED PATCHOULI OR PATCHOULI ESSENTIAL OIL**

✳ **100 ML (7 TBSP) OF A CARRIER OIL**

✳ **SOME OF YOUR SALIVA**

✳ **7 YELLOW CANDLES**

✳ **PEN AND PAPER**

1. Blend the nutmeg, basil, and patchouli with the oil and a little of your saliva.

2. Hold each candle in your hand and make a wish (make a separate wish for each candle, focusing on positive things you want to attract rather than negative things you want to avoid).

3. Anoint the candles with the magical blend (see p.126) and arrange them in a circle.

4. Write your seven wishes on seven separate strips of paper.

5. As you light each candle, say one of your wishes out loud and place the paper in the centre of the circle.

6. Sit with the spell and visualize your wishes coming true.

7. To finish, either burn the papers with your wishes on or store them as a keepsake. Perhaps place them beneath a crystal on your altar.

4-STRAND PLAIT
Amplifies a spell's power

CELTIC KNOT
Represents infinity

FIGURE OF 8
Brings strength

KNOT MAGIC

Knots are a fantastic and versatile magical tool that can be utilized in pretty much any form of witchcraft. They can be used on their own or be incorporated into poppets, talismans, and spell jars, and you can even wear them as personal charms.

The symbolism and mystical connections of knots have deep historical roots. The Assyrians used knots to bridge connections with the spirit world, the ancient Greeks crafted knots into talismans to ward off negative energies, the Romans wove them into love spells, and Egyptian art often featured symbolic knots representing divine protection. A famous knot named the "witches' ladder", a length of cord with knots and feathers, was discovered in a Somerset attic in the UK in the 19th century. While its exact purpose isn't clear, historians believe it was used in some form of spellwork.

As you loop, twist, and pull the thread to tie a knot, you are metaphorically binding your intention into reality, a completely mindful moment and a symbolic acknowledgement of the intentions that you are setting. You can use knots in your magic in many ways:

* FOR PROTECTION, HANG THEM BY A FRONT DOOR OR WINDOW, OR PLACE THEM UNDER YOUR PILLOW

* CREATE AN INCENSE SPELL AND BATHE THE THREAD IN SMOKE

* ANOINT YOUR THREAD WITH A CORRESPONDING POTION (SEE P.126) OR YOUR SALIVA AS A WAY TO CONNECT TO IT

* CREATE CHANTS OR SPOKEN CHARMS TO ACCOMPANY EACH KNOT AS YOU TIE IT (SEE P.54)

* BRAID KNOTS WITH FEATHERS, HERBS, HAIR, AND CRYSTALS, OR ANY OTHER OBJECTS THAT CONNECT TO YOUR INTENTIONS

CREATING KNOT SPELLS

There are many different styles of knots that can be used to accompany specific spells, each carrying its own symbolic meaning. While these intricate knots can add depth to your magic, they often take practice to get right. Personally, I've always had success with simple, regular knots. For me, the true power in knot magic lies within the focused intention that I tie into them and the use of corresponding colours (see pp.110–113) to connect with the spell's purpose.

1. Start by choosing a thread in a colour that aligns with your intention, or you can also use a neutral colour that covers all spells. In the following spells I refer to "thread", but you can use string, ribbon, twine, or yarn.

2. Choose a number that holds magical significance for your spell (see pp.96–100).

3. Now think of your intention while holding the thread in your hands; close your eyes and focus on your intention.

4. Hold the thread against your heart or your third eye, or breathe into it. As you do this, visualize your desired outcome or say it out loud.

5. Feel the energy fill up your body and then feel it charging up the thread. When you have a good sense of this feeling, start to tie your knots.

6. As you tie the knots, tune in to how you are bringing forth something that is in your mind into a tangible reality that you can see and touch. You are capturing the energy of your desired outcome and sealing the deal.

THREE-KNOT SPELL

||||||||||||||||||||||

This is a classic chant to accompany a three-knot spell. This can be used if you are tying three knots in a thread. If you write out your manifestations on paper you can roll the paper up in a scroll and tie the thread around it, or fold the paper three times and tie the thread around it.

1. Set your intention, clearly defining your goal. Say it aloud or write it down.

2. Tie the first knot to set the spell in motion. As you tie this first knot, say:

"BY KNOT ONE, THE SPELL HAS BEGUN"

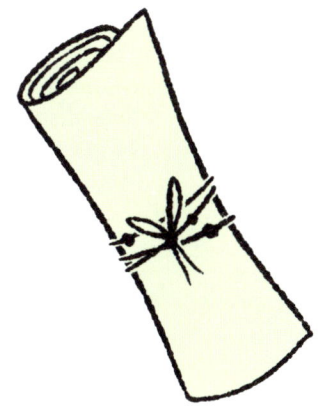

3. Tie the second knot in order to strengthen the spell. As you tie it, say:

"BY KNOT TWO, SO IT IS TRUE"

4. Tie the third knot to seal the spell. As you tie it, say:

"BY KNOT THREE, SO MOTE IT BE"

5. What you do with the thread depends on your intention: you could carry it for love, luck, or protection; bury it in the earth for long-lasting results; burn it for banishing; or tie it around an object to infuse it with energy.

WITCHES' LADDER

The witches' ladder is a magical tool that can be traced back to medieval times. It is made up of nine knots, with each knot representing a step in manifesting a specific intention. As you tie the knots into the thread in this spell, it is important that they are all spread out evenly so that the energy is equally distributed.

1. Tie the first knot on the far left, and the second knot on the far right-hand side of the length of thread.

2. Tie the third knot in the centre. You want the knots to be distributed along the length of your thread as evenly as possible.

3. Continue to tie the rest of the knots. See opposite – the order of the knots would be like this:
1-6-4-7-3-8-5-9-2

4. As you tie these knots, visualize your intention coming true and say this chant aloud as you tie each knot:

"BY KNOT OF ONE, THE SPELL'S BEGUN

BY KNOT OF TWO, IT COMETH TRUE

BY KNOT OF THREE, SO MOTE IT BE

BY KNOT OF FOUR, THIS POWER I STORE

BY KNOT OF FIVE, THE SPELL'S ALIVE

BY KNOT OF SIX, THIS SPELL I FIX

BY KNOT OF SEVEN, EVENTS I'LL LEAVEN

BY KNOT OF EIGHT, IT WILL BE FATE

BY KNOT OF NINE, WHAT'S DONE IS MINE."

WITCHES' LADDER

BY KNOT OF ONE, THE SPELL'S BEGUN

BY KNOT OF TWO, IT COMETH TRUE

BY KNOT OF THREE, SO MOTE IT BE

BY KNOT OF FOUR, THIS POWER I STORE

BY KNOT OF FIVE, THE SPELL'S ALIVE

BY KNOT OF SIX, THIS SPELL I FIX

BY KNOT OF SEVEN, EVENTS I'LL LEAVEN

BY KNOT OF EIGHT, IT WILL BE FATE

BY KNOT OF NINE, WHAT'S DONE IS MINE

FOUR-KNOT PROTECTION SPELL

||||||||||||||||||||||

For this spell, use a black or neutral-coloured thread. It can be anointed with protection oil (see p.126), or you can weave protective herbs such as rosemary and/or sage leaves into the thread once the knots have been tied.

As you tie each knot say out loud:

KNOT 1:

"I AM PROTECTED"

KNOT 2:

"I AM SAFE"

KNOT 3:

"I STAND IN STRENGTH"

KNOT 4:

"NO HARM SHALL COME, UNDER THE MOON AND SUN"

This can then be hung up or buried in any area that you feel needs protection from negativity – by a front door, a window, over your altar, in your car, on your bike, in your pet's collar, or even in your hair if you are feeling unsafe and you need a bit of quick magic on the go.

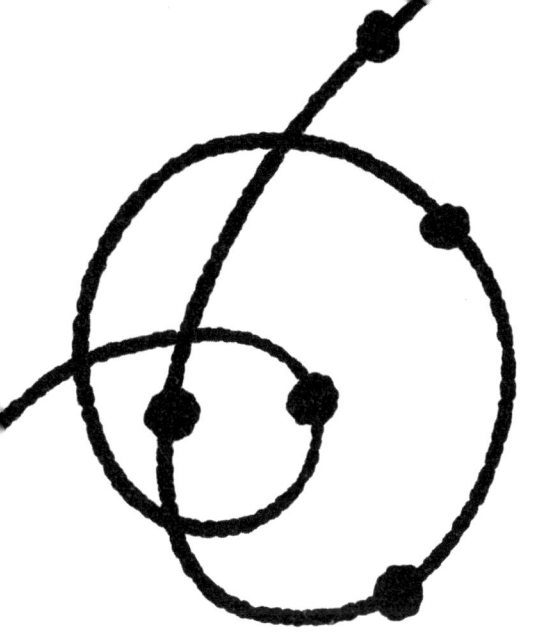

FIVE-KNOT SPELL FOR COURAGE

This spell uses orange or red thread to symbolize strength and power. The number five represents balance and transformation, and calls in the energy of all five elements.

You will need

* ❋ **5 CLOVES**
* ❋ **PESTLE AND MORTAR**
* ❋ **ORANGE OR RED THREAD**
* ❋ **CHARCOAL DISC AND CAULDRON OR HEAT-PROOF VESSEL**

1. Blend the cloves using the pestle and mortar.
2. Hold the thread in your hands and think about how you want this spell to work for you.
3. To summon courageous energy, think about a time when you stood in your power; allow this energy to course through you, then visualize what it is that you need courage for and see yourself in the future, standing in this power.
4. Speak what you wish to summon to the thread and charge it up with this energy (remember that you must be able to feel it in order to summon it!)
5. Burn the cloves over the charcoal disc (see p.123)
6. Tie the knots over the smoke, and as you tie each one, say out loud the words on the left.

KNOT 1:

"I HAVE STRENGTH"

KNOT 2:

"I HAVE COURAGE"

KNOT 3:

"I HAVE NO FEAR"

KNOT 4:

"MY PATH IS CLEAR"

KNOT 5:

"THIS SPELL IS BOUND, MY COURAGE WILL LAST"

HARNESSING ENERGY

||||||||||||||||||||||||||

You might find yourself in a high vibrational frequency if something lucky has just happened, a spell has come to fruition, or you are feeling relaxed. You can take an energetic "snapshot" of the moment and harness this energy in a knot: you can then wear it as a charm, but it could also be stored somewhere safe or on your altar as a reminder of how you felt.

If at some point you wish to release this energy, untie the knot and let its energy flow back into your life or into a spell. Knots can harness planetary energy too, if there is a transit that has brought you blessings or that you feel connected to, or to connect to a specific moon phase (see pp.244–245). For example, if you want to connect to the energy of the full moon and add this to a spell, hold your thread out and charge it up beneath the full moon then tie three knots while saying out loud:

KNOT 1:

"I CAPTURE THE ENERGY OF THIS TIME"

KNOT 2:

"I BIND IT NOW, THIS POWER IS MINE"

KNOT 3:

"HELD IN THIS KNOT, IT SHALL ENTWINE"

This knot can then be untied and its energy unleashed in future spellwork. You may want to keep multiple knot spells like this for each moon phase so you will always be able to connect to a specific moon energy when needed.

BINDING WORRIES INTO A KNOT

||||||||||||||||||||||||||||||||||||||||||||||||

Another powerful way that you can use knots in magic is to connect with the energy of releasing. This practice involves tying your worries into the knot itself. If a situation is causing you stress, unhappiness, or anger, channel those emotions into the thread. A thicker piece of cord is recommended here, as you want to make sure that you can unpick it.

1. Focus on your problem, allowing the feelings to flow through you and charge the thread with their energy as you tie a knot – or multiple knots if you have a few problems that you want to release.

2. As you tie the knot, visualize the concerns you're binding into it.

3. If the situation has brought you to tears, you can anoint the thread with them (see p.126) to infuse the spell with your emotions.

4. Once the knot is tied, set it aside for a short period, and maybe distract yourself with something soothing for at least 20 minutes; you want to return to the spell with a clear mind and calm energy.

5. When you are ready, begin unpicking the knots, focusing on releasing the weight of your worries.

6. Visualize your problems dissolving and no longer having any hold over you. You can also imagine the best possible outcomes and solutions as you untie each knot.

7. Once all the knots are undone, burn the string to make sure that the energy has dissipated completely.

POPPETS

Poppets come in the form of little dolls, and they are used in witchcraft as symbolic representations of a person. These dolls are often associated with the folk magic of the British Isles, or you may be more familiar with Voodoo dolls, which hail from Hoodoo traditions of African-American spiritualism.

Poppets can be filed under the "sympathetic" category in magic, meaning that any interactions with the doll are transferred to the person that the doll represents. I would never condone using them in this way unless you have the full permission of the person you want to make it for (see p.43 for notes on ethics in magic). Many witches, like me, have preferred to use them to represent ourselves.

Poppets are made from, and filled with, corresponding ingredients and act as a vessel for your intention, their focused energies helping bring it to fruition. Poppets can be used in a variety of spells, for protection, and to give our courage a boost. You might want to think of them as your very own personal enchanted avatar. Some common ways that witches use poppets include:

✳ **FILL A POPPET REPRESENTING YOURSELF WITH SELF-LOVE HERBS TO BOOST CONFIDENCE AND ATTRACTION.**

✳ **PUT A POPPET STUFFED WITH HERBS AND CHARGED WITH HEALING ENERGY UNDER A PILLOW TO AID IN RECOVERY OR ATTRACT POSITIVE ENERGY**

✳ **PLACE A POPPET NEAR THE FRONT DOOR TO PROTECT FROM NEGATIVE ENERGY**

✳ **ATTRACT WEALTH, JOB SUCCESS, OR GOOD FORTUNE BY KEEPING A POPPET IN YOUR PURSE OR IN YOUR WORKSPACE**

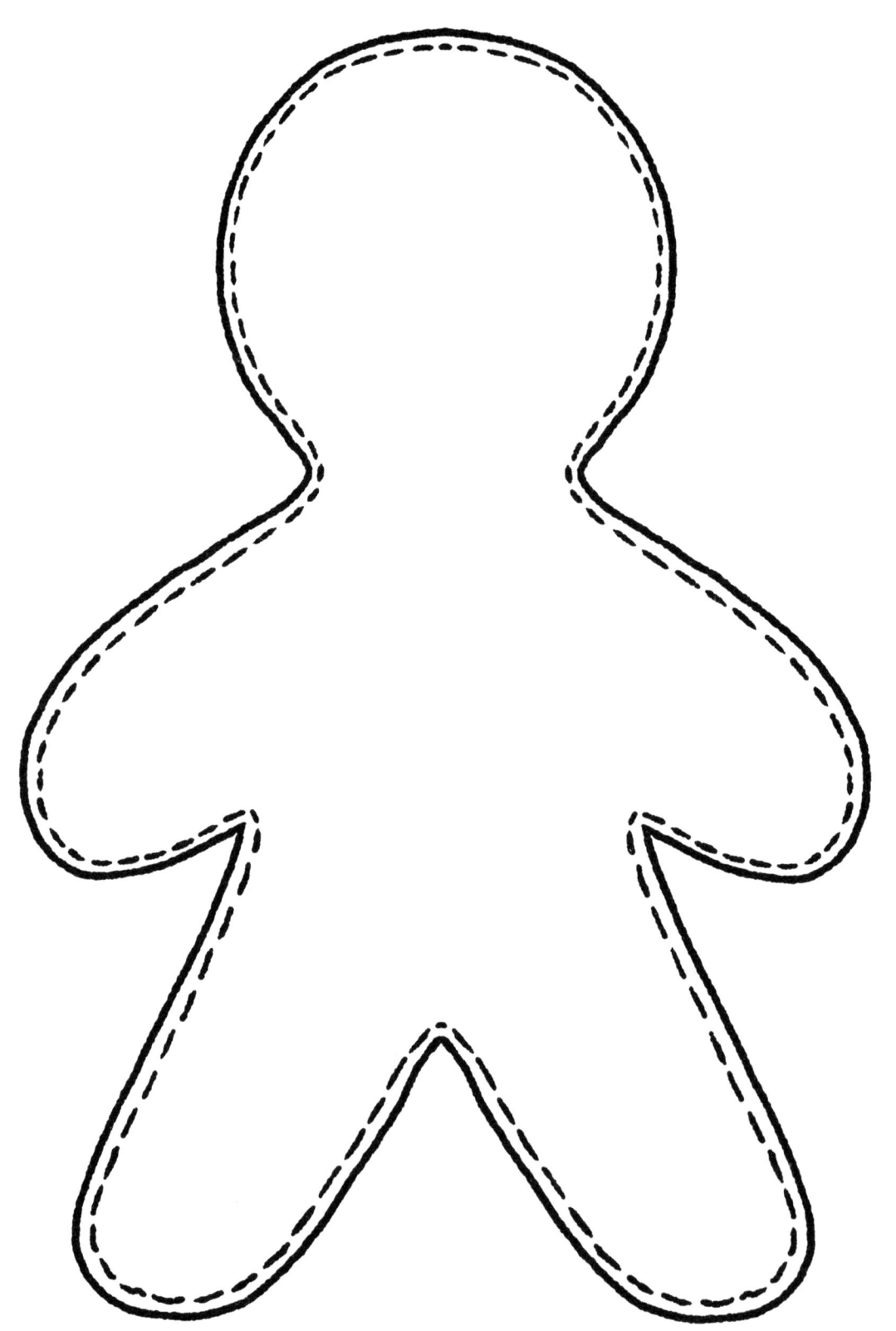

HOW TO MAKE A POPPET

||||||||||||||||||||||||||||||||||

These little figures can be made from a variety of materials, including cloth, paper, wax, wood, clay, corn, and string. Here, I'll show you how to make one from paper or fabric. To amplify your magic, you might want to fill or adorn your poppet with herbs, crystals, or other items aligned with your specific intentions, anoint it with your favourite fragrance, or add personal items such as hair or a photo to connect the poppet to yourself.

Filling your poppet

Read the Correspondences chapter for ideas on what will align with your intention. Some potent ingredients include:

* HEALING: LAVENDER, AMETHYST CRYSTALS, EUCALYPTUS

* COURAGE: CLOVES, THYME, RED JASPER CRYSTAL

* PROTECTION: SAGE, ROSEMARY, AND A TOURMALINE CRYSTAL

* PROSPERITY: COINS

* LOVE: ROSE PETALS OR ESSENTIAL OIL

You will need

* 10 X 10 CM (4 X 4 IN) SQUARE OF FABRIC OR PAPER: I LIKE USING FELT AS IT'S REALLY EASY TO SEW AND HOLDS ITS SHAPE WELL.

* NEEDLE AND THREAD (CHOOSE A CORRESPONDING COLOUR, SEE PP.111–113)

* ITEMS THAT RESONATE WITH YOUR INTENTION: SEE CHAPTERS ON CORRESPONDENCES (CHAPTER 4), HERBS (CHAPTER 5), AND CRYSTALS (CHAPTER 6), AND PERSONAL ITEMS SUCH AS A PHOTO OF YOURSELF, A FAVOURITE PERFUME, OR A LOCK OF HAIR

1. Define your intention: if your poppet represents you, what would you like it to bring? For example, you might be using it for healing, to ward off negative energy, to strengthen relationships, encourage prosperity, or banish bad habits.

2. Trace or copy the pattern from the previous page onto a piece of paper.

3. If you are making a paper poppet, cut out two shapes; cut one to create a template for your fabric poppet.

4. For a fabric poppet, cut 2 pieces of fabric 10 x 10 cm (4 x 4 in), placing them back-to-back. Pin your template on top and cut around it to get your two poppet shapes.

5. Gather your intentions: these might be written petitions (see p.55), corresponding herbs (pp.136–151), charms (p.50), or crystals (pp.158–165).

6. Sew your poppet half way around the edge of your fabric or paper, add your corresponding items, and then sew it all the way up.

7. Embellish with personal items to connect your poppet to you: write your full name on a piece of paper, add a strand of your hair, your favourite perfume, or a photograph of yourself.

8. Cleanse the poppet using smoke from sage, incense, or another cleansing herb to remove any residual energies.

9. Focus on your intent and say out loud an affirmation to bind the poppet to its purpose: for example:

"THIS POPPET NOW REPRESENTS [YOUR NAME]. WHAT IS DONE TO IT IS DONE TO ME. SO IT IS."

10. Use the poppet in a way that symbolizes your desired outcome. For example, for healing, wrap it in healing herbs and say healing affirmations; for protection, surround it with salt or place it in a protective circle; for banishing, bury or burn it to symbolize removing negativity.

11. Once completed, you can leave it on your altar or store it in a special place.

12. If your poppet needs recharging, you can anoint it with a corresponding oil blend (see p.126), or bathe it in an incense spell that aligns with your intention (see p.123).

13. If you wish to dispose of a poppet, do so with care. Dismantle it respectfully and thank it for its workings as you do.

NOTE: It is essential to occasionally recharge spells such as poppets to reinvigorate their energy and ensure they stay aligned with your intention; over time their magical charge can wane due to your connection with it, external influences, and the flow of energy that passes through.

SERVITORS

Servitors are the personification of your own energy and intention. Think of them as being supernatural personal assistants who are at your service to help you with your magical workings and manifestations.

Unlike calling in on the deities or spirit guides, servitors are energetic beings that exist only in connection with you. They are entirely your creation and are designed to serve only you. Servitors are often used in chaos magic (see p.15) and can be called upon for a wide range of purposes, from motivating you to adding magic to your manifestations. They are summoned to serve and offer guidance, and they can help with:

* PERFORMING TASKS, SUCH AS PROVIDING PROTECTION OR ENHANCING CREATIVITY

* FOCUSING YOUR INTENT, ALLOWING YOU TO EXTERNALIZE YOUR MAGICAL INTENTION

* GATHERING INFORMATION TO HELP WITH INTUITIVE OR PSYCHIC TASKS SUCH AS DIVINATION (SEE P.200)

* ACTING AS GUARDIANS TO WARD OFF NEGATIVE INFLUENCES AND PROTECT YOU FROM HARM

* BREAKING BAD HABITS BY PROGRAMMING THEM TO INFLUENCE YOUR SUBCONSCIOUS BEHAVIOUR

* REGULATING YOUR ENERGY, ENSURING IT STAYS BALANCED, AND HELPING WITH MOTIVATION

* ASSISTING WITH MANIFESTATION, ATTRACTING OPPORTUNITIES THAT ALIGN WITH YOUR GOALS

CREATING A SERVITOR

When creating a servitor, the process begins with calling in on the energy of your intentions and the power of your imagination. Ensure that you are connected to the energy you want to manifest.

SET YOUR INTENTION

First think of the intention that you would like your servitor to help you with. It is important to assign a specific role to each servitor and avoid giving the same servitor multiple tasks. You want to keep their purpose focused; when you do this it means that their work will be direct and effective, and it will avoid any confusion with the tasks you are setting them.

DESIGN YOUR SERVITOR

Once their role is clear, you can start envisioning what your servitor looks like and how their energy appears to you. You can really allow your imagination to run free here. They can appear as anything from a dragon or a human to a sparkling orb or even a talking cat! Give your servitor some distinctive traits so that you will have a stronger bond with them, giving their energy extra potency. Think about what their personality is like. Are they serious, playful, calm, or nurturing? Maybe they have an accent, some unusual quirks, amazing fashion sense, or a particular scent.

GIVE THEM A NAME

Your servitor must also be given a name; this might be the first thing that you think of and build their character from there, or you may choose to name them after their task and visual has been created. Choose a name that invokes power and strength – it might be an existing name that resonates with their tasks, or you could invent a name that is totally unique.

WAKE THEM UP

Think about how you want to connect with or wake up your servitor. This can be a chant, whistling a specific tune, a scent, a sigil drawn on a bay leaf (see p.33) and then burnt, or a few taps somewhere on your body. Tapping the side of your hand, known as your karate chop point, is an energy point associated with setting intention and clearing blockages. Tap here 5–7 times, repeating:

"[SERVITOR'S NAME], I AWAKEN YOU NOW. YOU ARE FULLY ALIVE AND CONNECTED TO ME."

When choosing how you will summon your servitor, it is important to consider that this call to action is representative of the energy that you servitor carries. Feel free to experiment with different ways and test actions or gestures. Once awakened, ensure that you communicate clearly, giving your servitor precise tasks aligned with the energy they embody.

CARE FOR THEM

Establish a way to feed your servitor, keeping them energized and focused to help them work their magic. You might feed them with the light of a designated candle, a specific scent, the vibrations of a bell, or a particular song or playlist that is dedicated to them. If your servitor has been set a task to get you motivated, you could feed them by drinking cacao, coffee, or matcha, or if you were calling in your servitor to assist with psychic guidance they might enjoy you drinking mugwort tea.

Because your servitors won't be working full-time, it's important to designate a place where they can rest. This could be an opulent room that you visualize for them to recharge in or a physical vessel that you create for them to live in – think of a genie in a bottle.

CREATE A CONTRACT

Remember: you must establish that you are the boss of your servitor, and the servitor only follows your commands. One way to do this is to incorporate a safe word during the creation process that will signal you no longer need the servitor's energy and allow you to end its existence. You might do this once their work has been completed or if you want to create a new one with more aligned energy. You could pick a word or make a word up and chant it three times, or simply say something like:

"[SERVITOR'S NAME], YOUR WORK IS DONE."

This is vital, as it ensures you are being responsible for the energy you're releasing into the world. Without clear boundaries and strict commands, things could become chaotic, with lots of servitors running amok. Write these down and read aloud with power in your voice.

READY-MADE SERVITORS

Even though I can't stress enough the importance of designing your own personal servitor for the best results, here are some that I have connected with in the past and – with their permission – I am sharing with you to demonstrate the kind of beings that can be summoned. I have deliberately left them un-named, so that you are free to decide where they live and tweak and refine them to suit your specific needs.

HEALING

For healing, I envision an auntie-type character, about 56 years old, who is very bohemian.

* She has wild hair and wears cashmere, crystal jewellery, and is partial to the colour purple.

* She is well-travelled and has spent time learning from powerful healers around the world.

* She has crone wisdom – the deep, intuitive knowledge associated with wise elders in folk magic – a bit of a wild glint in her eye, and a warm smile that reassures you everything is going to be okay.

* She requests that the vessel where she lives is stored somewhere close to your tarot cards and spell books.

NOURISH You can feed her with the scent of patchouli oil, the sound of a cat's purr, and by lighting purple candles that are surrounded with amethyst crystals.

TASKS She may be called upon to assist you with healing physical pain and emotional heartbreak, helping with anxiety, or working on self-love.

PROTECTION

||||||||||||||||||||||||||||||||||||||||||||||||||

I see this protective servitor as a big green dragon:

* About nine feet tall, strong and sturdy
* Silent and powerfully reassuring type of character
* Breathes fire, and blinks slowly and nods to communicate
* Because of their size they move at a sedate pace

NOURISH This dragon likes to be fed with the flame of a red candle that is surrounded with black tourmaline crystals, and feels energized when you drink ginger tea. They would like to be stored in a small box beneath your bed.

TASKS Use as your personal bodyguard to offer you protection. They will do the night shift beside your bed or stand guard outside your front door.

BUSINESS

An ambassador for your business, this woman works as your representative and agent.

* Very well-dressed, wearing sharp tailored suits
* Charming with exceptional manners
* Extremely articulate, able to deliver the perfect pitch to get you seen and your work noticed

NOURISH She likes to be fed on positive affirmations of self-belief that you say aloud while you drink mint tea.

TASKS To deliver sales, drive people towards your business, and work on your public relations. Call on her when you have clear intentions and command her to energetically help you manifest a specific area of your business.

GOOD LUCK

This servitor comes in the form of a cute little kitten who's eager to please you and bring joy to your life.

* Radiates positive energy
* Soft, snowy white fur
* Large, expressive green eyes

TASKS This fluffy feline's command is to work its magic to bring you good fortune, whether finding unexpected opportunities for abundance and success, or to help you work with an intention that you need luck with.

NOURISH Enjoys music and is fed when you make it a playlist of feelgood songs. It likes to curl up on your lap and purr when content.

CHAPTER FOUR

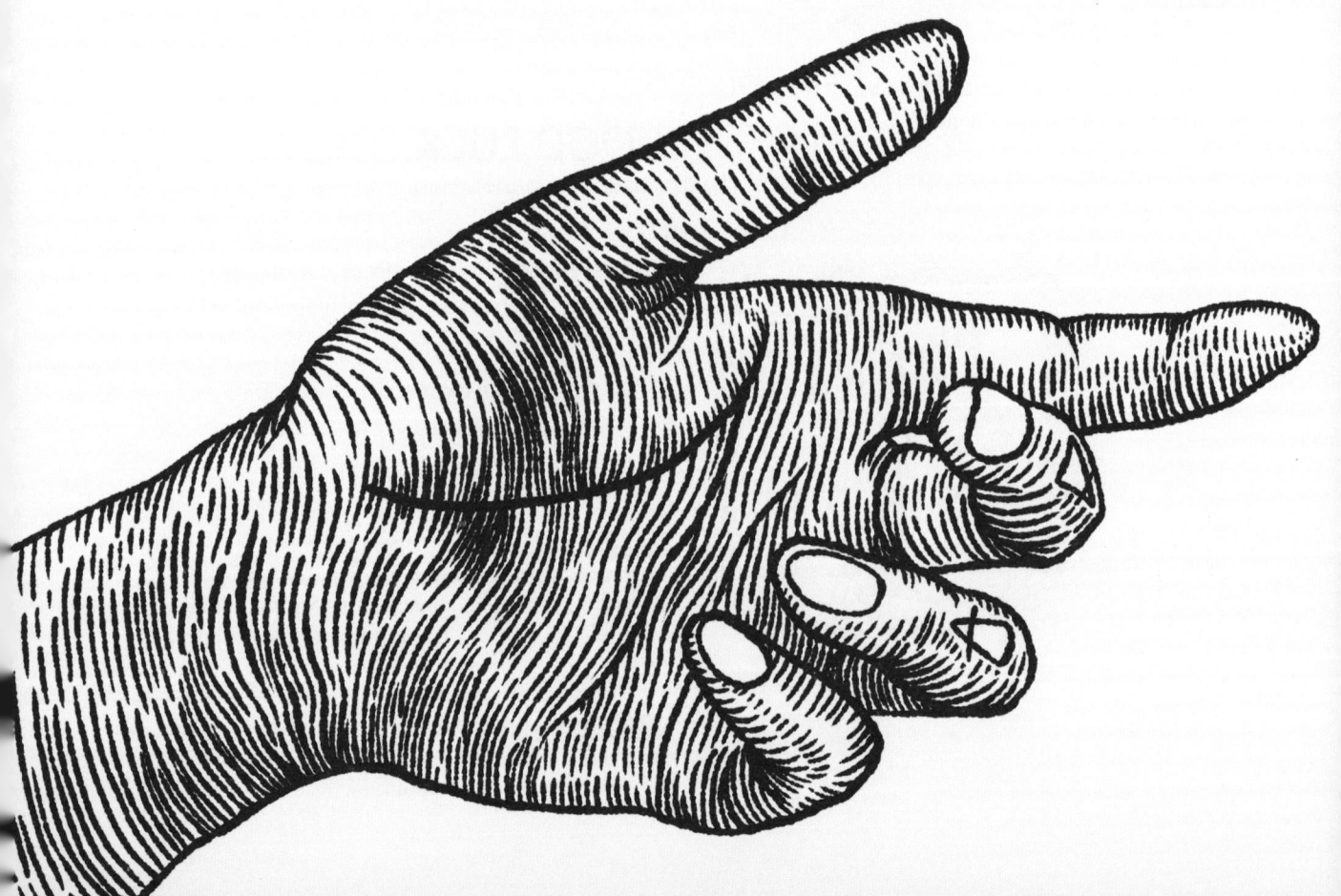

CORRESPONDENCES

CORRESPONDENCES

Everything is made up of energy, which means that every object, thought, and even emotion has a unique vibrational frequency. This is the rate at which something vibrates on an energetic level. In witchcraft, we can harness the vibrational frequency of many things, including colours, numbers, crystals, planets, and elements.

We can use these vibrations to form magical correspondences, creating powerful connections between things that share similar energies. This can enhance our spellwork, shaping energy to match our desires, and allowing us to influence the world around us.

This idea of vibrational energies comes from metaphysical traditions and philosophies such as Hermeticism, which was first practised in ancient Egypt. But it is important to remember that the concept isn't confined to spirituality or magic: in science, everything – sound, light, and matter – has a frequency that can be measured. Colours, for example, are wavelengths of light that vibrate at different speeds: red has a lower frequency and is associated with energy and passion, while blue has a higher vibration and is linked to calmness and communication. Similarly, crystals are often used in magic and healing because they maintain a steady vibrational frequency, making them a powerful amplifier in spellwork.

Everything that we use in witchcraft has some kind of magical correspondence. Some things, such as planets, herbs, and crystals, have their own section in this book. In this chapter, we will focus on numbers, colours, elements, and metals – and look at how these can be interpreted in our magical practice.

START HERE

Think about the personal connections you already have with certain colours, numbers, or elements. Even if this connection doesn't match with what is written in this book, know that your personal connection holds power in these correspondences. Listen to your intuition, and work with the meanings that make most sense to you.

THE IMPORTANCE OF INTENTION

When creating spells and rituals, your intent is the most powerful ingredient – it really is the heart and soul of any spell. An intention is so much more than a thought; it is about focusing all your emotions and beliefs into whatever your goal might be. When you combine focused intent with magical correspondences, whether it's a colour, number, moon phase, crystal, or the magical properties of herbs, you create a powerful alignment of energies that vibrate together to bring about transformations and powerful energetic shifts. Remember: what you put into your spellwork is very much what you get out. For the best outcomes, be sure that your intentions are clear and your energy is focused.

I've already mentioned in the opening chapter how important it is to honour your own personal connections and associations, and this also means you should avoid using any ingredients that don't resonate with you: if it feels bad, then don't use it, for it may work against you.

NUMEROLOGY

Numbers are potent symbols, each carrying its own vibrational frequency that can influence the energies around us. Numerology is the study of numbers as more just than mathematical symbols, acknowledging that they can provide deeper meanings. Aligning with number-specific vibrations and symbols allows you to harness and amplify the energy that you wish to bring to your spellwork.

You may choose a specific number because of a personal connection or its energetic alignment with the spell. You can incorporate this energy into your rituals in various different ways. For example, you can adjust the number of candles used in a spell, the number of pinches of herbs added to an incense blend, and the number of drops of essential oils included in a spell jar (but be careful to stick to the indicated amount for if you will be using a potion on the skin).

You can also use this numerical symbolism to influence your timings. For example, when looking to delve deep within yourself, to uncover buried wisdom or hidden truths, you may decide to perform a spell on the seventh day of the seventh month at 7pm, in order to harness the vibrational frequency of the number seven – associated in numerology with introspection and spiritual insight. You may also adapt the number of days you perform the ritual, the number of times you repeat a chant or incantation, or the number of times that you stir a potion.

Each single-digit number (one to nine) is known as a cardinal number. These form the basis of numerology and each has specific meanings and vibrations, representing different aspects of your personality and life path. We will explore these in more detail over the following pages.

NUMERICAL SYNCHRONICITY

Not only can number energy be used as a correspondence in spellwork, but they can also show up as synchronicities in our lives, often giving us a little nudge or hint that cosmic connections are always there.

These number sequences might be personal to you, like the date of a major life event appearing repeatedly, or numbers you've always felt drawn to. Other times, they can take the form of angel numbers – repeating digits that pop up on clocks, receipts, licence plates, and in random places – whispering messages from the Universe.

Numbers are energy, and when they appear frequently, it's rarely a coincidence; it's a connection with the unseen. The Universe, our spirit guides, or even our higher self can use them to nudge us in the right direction, confirm we're on the right path, or remind us to focus on a particular intention.

One of the most well-known synchronicities is 11:11. Often called the "awakening code" or a portal number, 11:11 is a powerful sign of alignment. Many people instinctively make a wish when they see it, even if they don't fully understand why. This number sequence is thought to signify a moment where the veil between the physical and spiritual worlds is thinner, a reminder that you are co-creating your reality together with the Universe.

When you see repeating numbers, stop and receive them, notice what you were thinking about at the time of seeing them, and then it's up to you to interpret what they mean. It could indicate an energetic reset, or be a message from the Universe after asking a question, or often after performing a spell. Use them as a call to focus on thoughts and intentions, because what you think at that moment will manifest more quickly than usual.

Another belief is that when we see these numbers they are a message from our spirit guides, letting us know they're near and supporting us. Either way, when you see your numbers, take a moment to tune in. Use them as a checkpoint to realign with your desires, express gratitude, or to quite simply acknowledge the magic happening around you.

The more you pay attention, the more you start to recognize the magical language of the Universe is speaking to you.

The number one can symbolize the beginning of something. It is used in witchcraft when initiating something, or to represent a specific intention. It can be used in spells when wanting to break up with someone, or if you wish to act assertively and be more direct in a situation.

Two carries the energy of connections, balance, and relationships. Its frequency inspires collaborative energy and harmony. The number two can be used in spells when calling in love and friendship into your life, or if you are seeking to banish friction.

Three is the number of growth, creativity, and manifestations. It is known as a magic number that can raise vibrations. In magic rituals, actions or incarnations are often repeated three times to raise the vibration and strengthen the spell.

Four carries the energy of stability and solid foundations. Often representing the four elements (Earth, Air, Fire, and Water) and the four directions, it brings a grounding energy to spellwork. This is a protective number, so is good for spells to keep you and your home safe.

Five has a dynamic and energetic vibration, often linked to curiosity, exploration, and the desire for new experiences. It resonates with freedom and change. In spells it can be used to shake up stagnant energy. Use it to call in personal growth or call in courage when you are embarking on new challenges.

Six inspires compassion and service. Connecting with the family, home, and healing. Its vibration inspires harmony within family relationships and compassion for others. Its nurturing energy makes it a powerful number for rituals involving family, community, and the creation of safe and supportive spaces.

NOTE: Numerology is a huge topic, and here we are only scratching the surface of it. If this has whetted your appetite. I've included some resources at the end of the book so that you can delve further into this fascinating aspect of magic.

Nine is the number of completion and transformation. It vibrates with the energy of universal love, making it a potent number in rituals for healing the community or bringing closure to personal lifecycles. When you work with the number nine you align with a wider perspective, focusing not just on yourself, but on a collective energy for the greater good of others too. Use this number to best effect in closure spells, at the end of a romance, for releasing the past, or for communal healing.

Eight is connected to success, infinite abundance, and personal power. It carries the vibrations of material and spiritual wealth. It symbolizes infinity with its continuous loop, which can be associated with career success and financial gain. Use this number in prosperity and wealth spells, and in spells aimed to advance your career, personal achievements, or any area of your life that you wish to grow and bring power to.

Seven holds the vibration of wisdom and spiritual insights. In magic, the number seven is used in rituals that require intuition, divination, or spiritual growth. Seven is the number of introspection, inviting you to explore the unseen. Its energy aligns you with the mystical and hidden aspects of life. This number is powerful in spells involving psychic development, connecting with the higher realms, or seeking answers from the subconscious.

ONE: CALLING IN NEW BEGINNINGS

||||||||||||||||||||||||||||||||||||||

All of the following spells call upon the energetic vibrations, planetary correspondences, and sacred geometry of the numbers one to nine. This first, for number one, is a spell for a fresh start and a complete new beginning.

You will need

* 1 WHITE CANDLE
* CARVING TOOL SUCH AS A TOOTHPICK OR CRAFT KNIFE
* 1 LEMON
* KNIFE
* HANDFUL OF SALT

1. Carve a number one on the candle in a vertical direction.

2. Cut the lemon in half; as you do this, focus on one half of the lemon as being any old ways or things that you don't want to carry into your new beginning, and the other half as representing newness.

3. Squeeze the half that represents newness and anoint the candle (see p.126) with this half of the lemon's juice.

4. Light the candle.

5. Clap your hands over the candle once, to signify the moment that the new beginning starts.

6. Let the candle burn down safely or snuff it out to seal the spell. Throw a handful of salt over the melted wax.

TWO: CALLING IN THE POWER OF CONNECTION

Use the number two in spells to attract something towards you. The formula for a spell like this works with one item representing you and another representing whatever you are calling towards you. This works especially well using two candles.

You will need

* ✳ **2 CANDLES (CHOOSE CORRESPONDING COLOURS)**
* ✳ **PEN**
* ✳ **YOUR SALIVA**
* ✳ **CARVING TOOL SUCH AS A TOOTHPICK OR CRAFT KNIFE**
* ✳ **THREAD (CHOOSE A CORRESPONDING COLOUR)**

1. Write your name on one of the candles and anoint it with your saliva to connect its energy to you.

2. On the second candle, carve whatever it is that you wish to call in; do this in the form of a sigil or sign (see p.182).

3. Choose corresponding colours (see pp.111–113) to chime with the spell. For example, if you are calling in love, use pink candles, pink thread, and draw a heart on the second candle; if attracting money, use green candles, green or gold thread, and draw a money sign on the candle.

4. Tie the candles together twice. As you tie them, focus on what it is that you are calling towards you.

5. Light the candles and let them burn down together; this will strengthen the connection between yourself and what you are calling in.

 NOTE: If you use this as a love spell, only use another person's name if you have their permission – it is highly unethical to use someone's name without them knowing.

THREE: BY THE POWER OF THREE

Three is a powerful number for manifesting with. Here, each point of the triangle represents part of the spell: your intention, action, and completion.

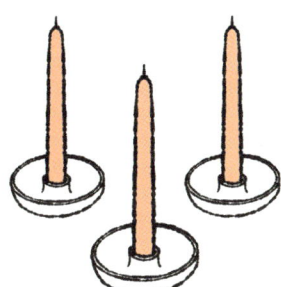

You will need

* **3 CANDLES (CHOOSE CORRESPONDING COLOURS)**
* **PEN AND PAPER**

1. Arrange the candles in a triangle formation.

2. Write out your intention on a piece of paper.

3. Fold the paper three times towards you as follows:

* Fold it in half towards you.

* Turn it a quarter-turn once clockwise, then fold it towards you again.

* Turn it clockwise again, and fold towards you.

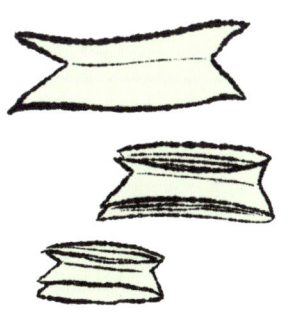

4. Place the paper in the centre of the triangle and light the candles.

5. Hold your hands over the candles and say:

"TRIANGLE OF FIRE,
BRING ME WHAT I DESIRE
I TRUST IN THE POWER OF THREE
SO MOTE IT BE."

6. Allow the candles to burn down safely or snuff them out to seal the spell.

FOUR: A SPELL FOR PROTECTION

||||||||||||||||||||||||||||||||||||||||||

This number represents safety, stability, and protection. This spell uses the energy of number four to create a shield of security around you, your home, or a loved one.

You will need

❋ **4 PINCHES OF DRIED ROSEMARY**

❋ **60 ML (4 TBSP) OF CARRIER OIL**

❋ **PLATE**

❋ **4 WHITE CANDLES**

❋ **PEN AND PAPER**

1. Blend the rosemary and oil together.

2. Tip onto a plate and anoint the candles with the mixture by rolling them in it.

3. Arrange the candles in a square.

4. Write down on paper what needs protecting or where you seek stability (this could be areas where you are needing to feel safe, like a relationship, home, or job).

5. Place the paper in the centre of the square of candles.

6. Light the candles; sit with them and visualize the energy you wish to call in.

7. Allow the candles to burn down safely or snuff them out to seal the spell.

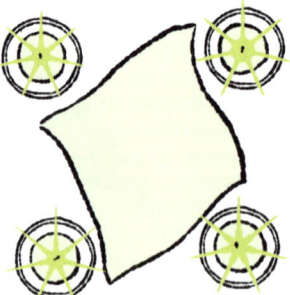

FIVE:
FREEDOM SPELL

||||||||||||||||||||||||||||||||||||||||||||||||||||

Five is perfect for breaking stagnation, attracting new opportunities, and boosting confidence. Use this spell to call in freedom and inspire positive change in your life.

You will need

* ✳ **5 X 30 CM (12 IN) LENGTHS OF THREAD (NEUTRAL OR BLUE)**
* ✳ **1 BLUE CANDLE**
* ✳ **5 HANDFULS OF SALT**

1. Hold the thread in your hands and think about what it is you wish to change. This spell works best when focusing on one thing rather than many things.

2. Light the candle then hold the thread over the flame and again think about what you want to change.

3. As the thread burns, say:

Place any remaining bits of thread at the candle's base and blow the candle out.

4. Throw five handfuls of salt over the candle.

5. Clap your hands five times over the candle, and say,

"THIS THREAD HOLDS WHAT NO LONGER SERVES, I RELEASE AND CREATE THE FREEDOM I DESERVE."

"SO MOTE IT BE, THE SPELL IS DONE."

Repeat this a total of five times.

SIX:
PEACE AND
HARMONY SPELL

This spell connects the nurturing energy of number six to encourage healing and invite balance and harmony into your life.

You will need

✳ **6 PINCHES OF DRIED LAVENDER**

✳ **90 ML (6 TBSP) OF A CARRIER OIL**

✳ **PLATE**

✳ **6 PINK CANDLES (OR YOU CAN USE WHITE)**

✳ **ROSE PETALS**

✳ **ROSE QUARTZ, SELENITE, AND AMETHYST CRYSTALS**

1. Mix the lavender with the carrier oil.

2. Pour this blend onto a plate and anoint the candles by rolling them in it.

3. Create an altar, arranging the candles and adding rose petals and crystals.

4. Light the candles and gaze at your altar; tune in to the candlelight and feel the energy from the spell being sent to all the areas of your life that may require peace and harmony.

5. You can sit with the candles as they continue to burn down, or safely snuff them out and re-ignite them over the following five nights, repeating the ritual for a total of six nights.

SEVEN: AWAKEN PSYCHIC SENSES

Use this spell if you need clarity or to gain insight into a specific question. You can also use it to tune in to your psychic senses.

You will need

* ❋ **1 BAY LEAF**
* ❋ **PEN**
* ❋ **7 STAR ANISE**
* ❋ **CAULDRON OR HEAT-PROOF VESSEL**
* ❋ **SMALL POUCH (WHITE OR PURPLE IS BEST)**

1. Write your question on the bay leaf (if you don't have a specific question you can simply write, "Show me what I need to see").

2. Burn this over the star anise in the cauldron.

3. When cool, put the ash and star anise into the pouch.

4. Sleep with it under your pillow for seven nights and clarity should come to you within this period.

EIGHT: MONEY SPELL

As the number eight represents abundance, it is the perfect number to use in money magic and spells to bring prosperity into your life.

You will need

* ❋ **PEN AND PAPER**
* ❋ **1 GREEN CANDLE**
* ❋ **CARVING TOOL SUCH AS A TOOTHPICK OR CRAFT KNIFE**
* ❋ **3 PINCHES OF DRIED BASIL**
* ❋ **30 ML (2 TBSP) OF CARRIER OIL**
* ❋ **8 COINS**
* ❋ **PLATE**

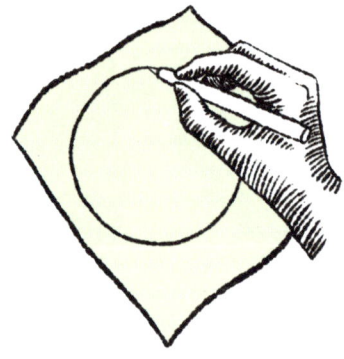

1. Draw a circle on a piece of paper and write your full name in the centre.

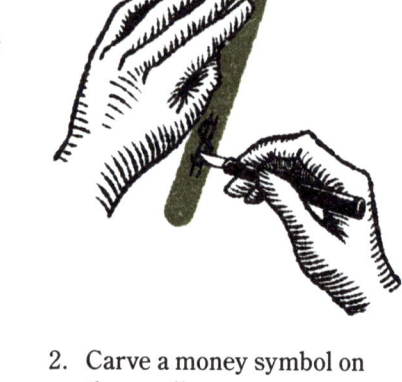

2. Carve a money symbol on the candle.

3. Blend the basil and carrier oil and pour it onto a plate, then roll the candle in the mixture to anoint it.

4. Arrange eight coins around the base of the candle.

5. Light the candle, and as you do this, say,

"PROSPERITY IS MINE."

Repeat this a total of eight times.

6. As you sit with the spell, visualize checking your banking app and seeing the amount that you wish for in your account.

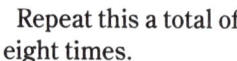

NINE: SPELL FOR ENDINGS

||||||||||||||||||||||||||||||||

As nine signifies completion, use this spell when something has come to an end, or when you need to say goodbye to something in your life.

You will need

✳ **9 BLACK CANDLES**
✳ **PEN AND PAPER**
✳ **3 HANDFULS OF SALT**
✳ **SCISSORS**

1. Light the candles.

2. Cut the paper into nine pieces and write out what it is that you wish to end on each one (it can be different things or the same thing nine times).

3. Burn each piece of paper in the flame of a different candle and as you burn it say:

"BY THE POWER OF NINE, I LEAVE THIS BEHIND."

4. Let the candles burn all the way down.

5. Throw the salt on top of the melted wax and ashes and say out loud:

"AND SO IT IS."

6. Wrap up the remnants of the spell in paper and throw it away, signalling you are done with whatever you wished to be gone from your life.

COLOURS

When you understand and embrace the symbolic power of colour, you can deepen your connection to your intentions and create rituals that are aligned with nature's palette. By choosing colours that resonate with your goals, you can tap into the energetic vibrations that align with love, protection, healing, or manifestation.

As I briefly discussed at the beginning of the chapter, colour has a unique wavelength and vibration: those with shorter wavelengths (higher frequencies), like purple and blue, are associated with spirituality and mental clarity, while those with longer wavelengths (lower frequencies), like red and orange, are linked to passion and physical energy.

Using colour correspondences in witchcraft is a powerful way to enhance your spells and rituals. And there are many ways to harness their energy. You might select specific colours for the candles or crystals in your rituals, the thread you use (see p.72), or even the paper and ink used to write your intentions. The colours of the flowers adorning your altar and the clothing or nail polish you wear while casting your spells can all carry symbolic power.

Visualization is another potent method of working with colour – imagine your intent bathed in colour as you direct energy towards your goal. The unique vibrational frequency of each hue can amplify the energy you're working to manifest.

WHITE Associated with purity and spiritual cleansing. It symbolizes new beginnings, healing, and fresh starts. Use in spells that require cleansing, purification, and protection (see pp.101, 104, 235, and 283).

BLACK Signifies endings and banishing. Use in spells to ward off negative energy and absorb bad vibes, and for spells when you are wishing to put a stop to something (see pp.62, 68, 109, 243, and 293).

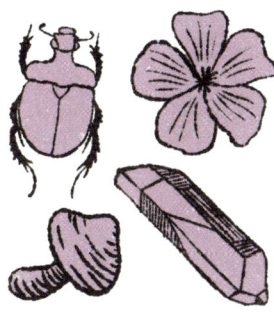

PURPLE Can awaken your psychic energy; this colour is connected to the spirit world and divination. Use when wanting to connect with energies of the spirits or when seeking clarity and psychic downloads (see pp.30 and 257).

RED A real power colour, invoking fire energy, passion, and desire. Red symbolizes physical strength and vitality and can inspire courage and action. Use in spells when wanting to awaken passion or call in bravery, ignite your inner fire, and invoke your personal power (see pp.251 and 281).

PINK Represents nurturing love and kindness. It embodies a healing energy that can comfort and promote compassion. Use in rituals to call in true love, when practising self-love, and for emotional healing (see pp.29, 102, 106, and 249).

GREEN This is the colour of growth and fertility, bringing abundance in all areas. In spellwork it is especially powerful in money spells, and to call in prosperity for your business ventures (see pp.61, 102, and 108).

BROWN This colour has a connection to the Earth and symbolizes feeling grounded and connected to the Earth's energy. Use in spells when you need to feel centred, especially as the seasons are changing (and particularly during autumn equinox), or when needing stability in your life.

BLUE Symbolizes calm, healing, and mental clarity. Blue is connected to inner peace and meditation. The energy of blue creates a tranquil vibration for deep healing. Use it in spells when wanting to gain peace of mind or tune in to your inner guidance for insights, or for emotional healing (see pp.105 and 233).

YELLOW Brings optimism and hope. Use in spells to enhance your creativity, inspire new ideas, break through mental blocks, and awaken self-belief. It is especially powerful in spells to create opportunities and for road opening spells (see pp.69, 234, and 285).

ORANGE Symbolizes abundance, courage, and ambition. Use it in spells when you are manifesting and calling in abundant energy. It can also be utilized to awaken determination, find your voice, and make yourself feel seen and heard. Orange can work as a guiding light for getting through difficult situations (see pp.77, 287, and 293).

ELEMENTS

Elemental spellwork involves using tools, symbols, and rituals corresponding to each element to create sacred space and focus energy. By attuning to the elements, you can deepen your connection to the natural world and dance with nature's energies to help shape your reality.

The four classical elements – Earth, Air, Fire, and Water – play a vital role in magic, each representing a fundamental force of nature. The use of the classical elements has deep roots in much ancient philosophy, alchemy, and magical traditions, where they were seen as the foundational building blocks of the Universe and played a vital role in spiritual practices and witchcraft.

You have already seen how you can call upon the elements to create an altar (see p.31), cast a circle (see p.34–35), and use their energies in various rituals and spells. Some super-simple ways that you can bring their energies into your everyday life include:

* **EARTH: CARRY A STONE OR CRYSTAL IN YOUR POCKET FOR STABILITY**
* **AIR: OPEN YOUR WINDOWS TO INVITE FRESH ENERGY IN**
* **FIRE: LIGHT A CANDLE WITH INTENTION**
* **WATER: DRINK HERBAL TEA FOR EMOTIONAL BALANCE**

EARTH Represents stability, growth, and abundance. This element is invoked when grounding your intentions or manifesting tangible results. Stones, crystals, soil, salt, and plants can be used to channel Earth energy in your workings. You might sprinkle salt to form a protective circle, and walk barefoot in nature to ground yourself.

AIR Represents communication, intellect, and clarity. It brings the energy of movement and transformation to your spells. You might call upon Air when seeking wisdom, inspiration, or calling in energetic changes, using feathers, incense, smoke, or your breath – in spoken affirmations, for example – to connect with this element.

FIRE Embodies passion, transformation, and courage. It's often used in spells involving desire, creativity, or willpower. Lighting candles, working with a fire, burning herbs, and working under the sun can help summon Fire's intense energy. You might write an intention or sigil (see p.183) on a candle to amplify the power of your spell, or burn petitions of something that no longer serves you to release the energy.

WATER Rules our emotions, intuition, and healing. It's ideal for spells related to purification, love, or psychic work. Water can be represented by bowls of fresh water, seashells, or rain, inviting emotional energy into your magic. You can use water for scrying in divination rituals (see p.203), and harvest weather water (see p.130–131) and moon water (see p.128–129) for potions and to use in rituals.

METALS

Using metals in magic connects your practice to the deep, transformative powers of the Earth's resources. Their energies can be integrated into spellwork in several ways. You can charge up jewellery and wear it as a talisman, or you can call on metals you find in your everyday surroundings.

Metals have been used in magic for centuries, revered for their conductivity, durability and deep connection to the elemental forces. Similar to crystals, each metal holds its own powerful energy that you can align with specific magical intentions.

Call upon the energy of metals with the tools you use in rituals; for example, copper is especially useful for creating wands as it is a powerful conductor of energy, helping to channel and amplify the flow of magic during your rituals.

Working with metals also takes you back to ancient times, connecting you to the rich traditions that have been part of human history for thousands of years. Metals have been used in rituals, crafts, and sacred objects, so by working with them, you're tapping into the power of elements that have shaped our world.

GOLD Symbolizing the sun, gold is connected with wealth, success, and personal power. It's often used in spells focused on abundance, confidence, and personal growth. Gold carries a high vibrational frequency that enhances energy flow and draws in prosperity. For spells see pp.289 and 291.

SILVER Connected to the moon, silver is associated with intuition and dreams and is a potent metal for use in psychic work, protection, and healing. Silver's reflective quality makes it ideal for spells involving lunar cycles, introspection, and tapping into the subconscious. For spells see p.243.

COPPER A conductor of energy, making it excellent for spells requiring balance and harmony. Linked to Venus, the planet of love, healing, and fertility, it's used to enhance connections between the spiritual and physical realms. Copper's grounding and amplifying properties make it a staple in both ritual tools and talismans.

IRON Strong and protective, connected to Mars, iron is known for its grounding and safeguarding qualities. It's frequently used in defensive magic, repelling negativity and bringing stability. Iron's earthy strength makes it ideal for protection spells and banishing unwanted energy.

LEAD While toxic, lead has traditionally been associated with transformation and alchemy, though caution is essential when handling it. It's linked to Saturn's energy and is sometimes used in binding spells or for deep internal change.

CHAPTER
FIVE

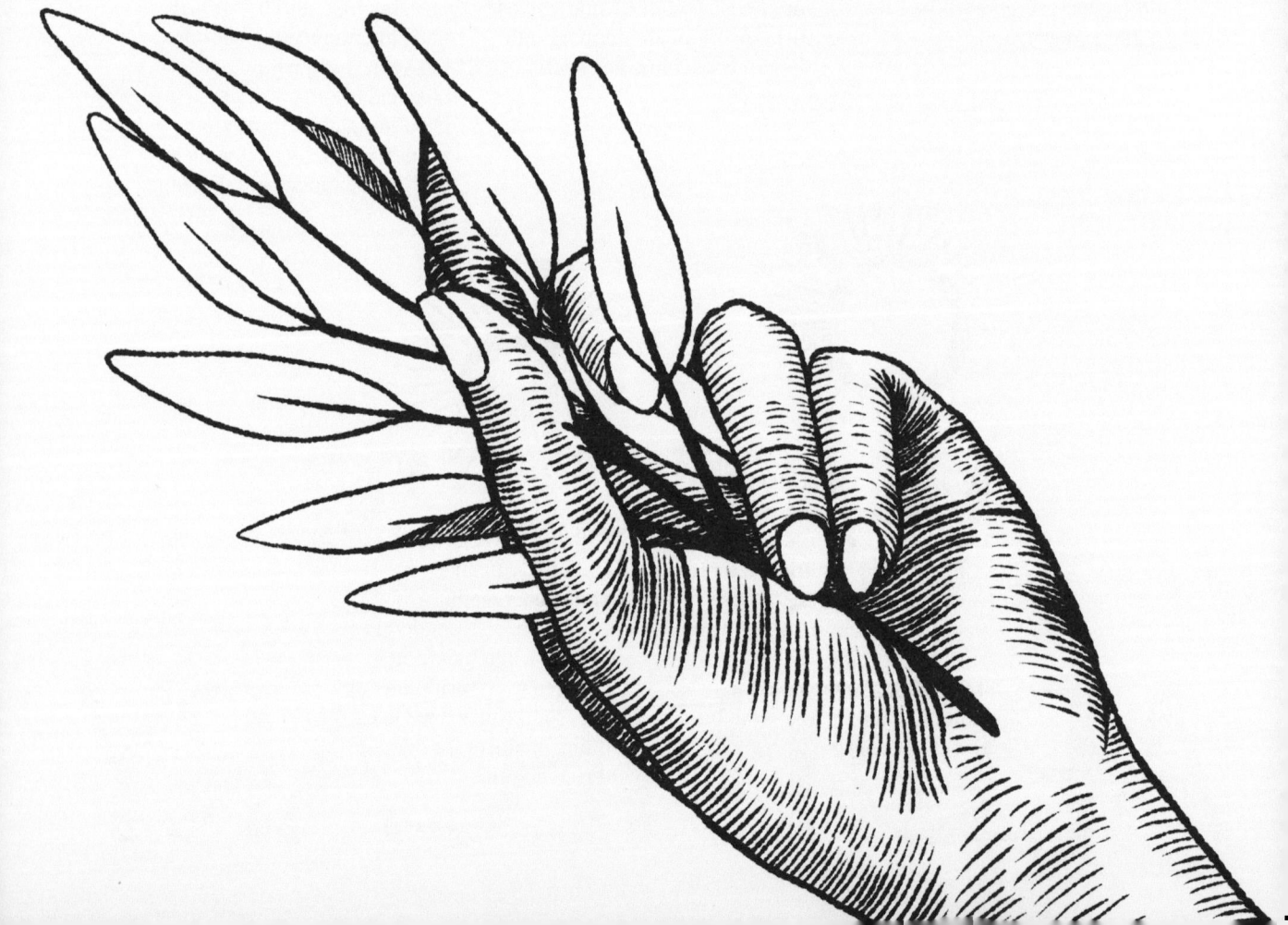

WITCH'S APOTHECARY

AND PLANTS

Herbs carry their own vibrational frequencies, which make them potent tools for connecting with the physical and spiritual realms. Ancient alchemists recognized their power; observing nature showed how certain plants thrived during particular astrological events, moon phases, and seasons. These patterns became a major aspect of aligning spellwork with the cycles of nature.

These magical plants have played a vital role in religious ceremonies, spellcasting, and rituals for centuries, in evidence everywhere from Egyptian temples to Celtic groves. Resins, such as frankincense and myrrh, have been burnt to purify and raise spiritual vibrations, and the healing properties of herbs and oils were known about long before modern medicine. These were the original remedies, offering not only physical relief but also spiritual healing. Some herbal tinctures were prescribed to treat illness, while others were given to cleanse negative energy and offer protection.

Keep the long lineage of the herbs in mind when using them in your spells. I get full-body goosebumps when I burn herbs and resins and think of them being used in rituals 4000 years ago. Connect to herbs and plants that are linked to the land where you live and to your own heritage, and when using those from other cultures, respect and acknowledge their origins.

Over the following pages you will find some spells and recipes to try out for yourself, along with a directory of magical herbs and plants with a description of their properties and best uses.

START HERE

Before using any dried herbs, oils, or resins in magic, first bathe them in a cleansing smoke (see p.23). Camphor, rosemary, and frankincense are best – use them on their own or create an incense blend with equal parts of all three (see p.123).

You can use herbs and plants in many ways in witchcraft, utilizing their unique corresponding energies to enhance your rituals and spells. First charge them by adding them to a bowl and talking to them, telling them how you would like them to work for you. Place your hands in the bowl and visualize what you want them to do, feeling the energy passing to them from your hands.

✳ ENCHANT YOUR INGREDIENTS WITH SIGILS (SEE PP.182–185), CRYSTALS, OR ANYTHING ELSE THAT WILL BLESS THEM WITH THE ENERGY YOU WANT TO INVOKE, AND ADD TO SPELL JARS AND CHARM BAGS (SEE P.52)

✳ CREATE POTIONS AND INCENSE FOR USE IN RITUALS, AND BREW HERBS TO MAKE TEAS

✳ INCORPORATE HERBS INTO RITUAL BATHS FOR THEIR MAGICAL PROPERTIES

✳ ADD CRUSHED HERBS TO OILS AND USE TO BLESS CANDLES IN CANDLE MAGIC (SEE P.66)

INCENSE

Burning incense is a powerful way to release the magical energy of herbs and resins as an offering to the Universe and the spirit world. Smoke represents the element of Air, bringing clarity and communication to your rituals and serving as a powerful channel that carries your intentions out into the world.

For thousands of years, incense has been an important part of spiritual practices. It has been burnt in temples, churches, and sacred spaces to invoke deities, honour ancestors, and purify the environment – from the frankincense and myrrh of the Middle East to sandalwood in India and sage and Palo Santo in Native American ceremonies.

The smoke of incense can cleanse negativity, uplift the spirit, and create the perfect setup for meditation. The scent can purify the air, bring clarity, and work as a powerful offering to the spirits, creating a sacred space for spellwork.

CREATE YOUR OWN BLEND

||||||||||||||||||||||||||||||||||||||||||

Think of your intention, where you would like the smoke to travel, and how you would like it to work for you. When we speak our intentions to the smoke, it carries our messages to the Universe and beyond.

You will need

* ✳ **PESTLE AND MORTAR**
* ✳ **RESINS, HERBS, AND DRIED FLOWERS OF YOUR CHOICE**

1. Blend the herbs and resins; as you blend, think about what the spell will do for you and speak about and visualize your desired outcome as if it has already happened.

2. As you add the ingredients, tell each item what you are adding it for and how you would like it to assist you in your magical workings.

3. As you do this, really connect to the idea that this energy is charging up your blend.

4. Always blend in a clockwise direction when calling things in, and anti-clockwise if you are creating a spell for banishing.

BURN HERBS ON A HOT COAL

||||||||||||||||||||||||||||||||||||||||||

The charcoal gets very hot, very fast, so do not use your hands for this, as burning your fingers before a spell can certainly ruin the vibe (and I am speaking from experience!) If you're doing this spell inside, beware of smoke alarms too.

You will need

* ✳ **SMALL PAIR OF TONGS: IF YOU DON'T HAVE ANY TONGS, SCISSORS OR TWEEZERS WILL ALSO DO THE JOB**
* ✳ **CHARCOAL DISC**
* ✳ **HERBS OR RESINS OF YOUR CHOICE**
* ✳ **CAULDRON OR HEAT-PROOF DISH**

1. Using the tongs, hold the charcoal over a flame until it starts to spark. This usually takes about 10–20 seconds.

2. Place the charcoal disc in the cauldron or heat-proof dish.

3. Add a small pinch of your incense to the charcoal disc. Be careful not to cover it entirely as this can put it out. Continue to add a small pinch at a time. This creates a lot of smoke, so ensure your room is ventilated and watch out for smoke alarms going off.

4. As your smoke rises, speak to it, telling it where you would like it to go and what you want it to do. Imagine it travelling into all the places where you want it to add its magical energy.

CLEANSE EVERYTHING

||||||||||||||||||||||||||||||||||||||||||||

This is one of my personal favourite incense blends for cleansing, and it is a good all-rounder. You can use it to cleanse your home, your magical tools, and yourself. This is also a really good one for using to cleanse second-hand and vintage clothing, bathing them in the smoke.

You will need

* PESTLE AND MORTAR
* 3 BLOCKS OF CAMPHOR
* 3 PINCHES OF DRIED ROSEMARY
* 3 PINCHES OF DRIED SAGE
* CHARCOAL DISC
* CAULDRON OR HEAT-PROOF DISH

1. Blend the ingredients in a clockwise direction using a pestle and mortar.

2. Hold the blend in your hands and visualize a piercing white light coming through the top of your head and travelling through your body.

3. Feel this light coming out of your hands and charging up your incense blend.

4. Burn the incense on a charcoal disc (see p.123).

GOOD FORTUNE BLESSING

||||||||||||||||||||||||||||||||||||

This blend can be used to bless petitions, ingredients for your potions, your home, your body, and your charms. When using this as a house blessing, burn the smoke at the entrance to your home with the front door open to welcome blessings in.

You will need

* PESTLE AND MORTAR
* 3 PINCHES OF SANDALWOOD
* 2 PINCHES OF CINNAMON
* 3 INCHES OF DRIED BASIL
* BOWL
* CHARCOAL DISC
* CAULDRON OR HEAT-PROOF DISH

1. Blend the ingredients in a pestle and mortar in a clockwise direction.

2. As you do so, think about all of the blessings that you have in your life; say them out loud and feel the gratitude that you have for them.

3. Allow this energy of gratitude to flow out of your hands and enchant the ingredients.

4. Tip the blend into a bowl and repeat seven times,

"I WELCOME BLESSINGS AND GOOD FORTUNE."

5. Burn the incense on a charcoal disc (see p.123).

SELF-LOVE

This is a potent recipe to encourage self-love. I store mine in a jar with rose quartz crystals and images of an Indian guru who is known for her ability to inspire unconditional love and inner peace in all who seek her. I feel her energy and presence whenever I use this spell for myself or share it with others.

You will need

- ✳ **PESTLE AND MORTAR**
- ✳ **PEN AND PAPER**
- ✳ **3 CINNAMON STICKS**
- ✳ **3 PINCHES OF DRIED LAVENDER**
- ✳ **3 PINCHES OF DRIED ROSE PETALS**
- ✳ **3 PINCHES OF SANDALWOOD**
- ✳ **9 CLOVES**
- ✳ **GLASS JAR**
- ✳ **ROSE QUARTZ CRYSTALS**

1. Blend all the ingredients in a clockwise direction using a pestle and mortar.

2. Write out affirmations of self-love on separate pieces of paper and place them inside the jar.

3. Add the rose quartz crystals to complete the spell.

4. Keep this on your altar or somewhere safe, and gently shake it whenever you need a boost of self-confidence.

POTIONS

Potions are magical brews that can be made up of oils infused with scent, water that is charged under a full moon, or a liquid empowered with herbs, petitions, and charms. They can be used for a wide range of purposes, and are also ideal for anointing candles, petitions, your body, and charms.

ANOINTING

Focus on your intention and gently apply a few drops of essential oil or potion to your written intentions, objects, or yourself. As you do, speak your purpose aloud, letting the potion serve as a conduit to seal your energy into the items.
For yourself: dab on the forehead, wrists, or heart.
For objects: lightly coat tools, charms, and talismans.
For candles: rub oil from the centre upward (to attract) or downward (to banish).
You may say something like: "With this oil I bless you with protection/love/abundance" (depending on your intention).

Anointing something with a potion is a way of connecting with the magic you've created. It is the act of blessing or charging an object, person, or space using oils or potions. When you apply these to the body, you're not just wearing them as a fragrance; you're inviting the energy and intention behind that potion to bless your skin. This transforms your body into a living talisman, carrying the power of the potion wherever you go and making you a walking embodiment of your intention.

Infused with herbs, oils, or resins, a potion holds the vibrations of its ingredients, which will release their magic as you wear it. Each time you catch a whiff of the scent, it's a nudge from the Universe, reminding you of your magic and its purpose. Speaking affirmations connected to the potion's desired outcome will amplify this magic.

Because potions are a liquid, their energy is connected to the element of Water – known for its transformative properties, bringing with it the power of intuition, healing, and cleansing. Water is often seen as the gateway between the physical and spiritual realms, serving as a powerful channel for energy.

To make a potion, you need to start with an oil or water base. While it is perfectly okay to use filtered or distilled water in your spellwork, extra potency can be added by using moon water (see pp.128–129), weather water (see pp.130–131), or collecting water from its natural source – with each type of water carrying specific properties. When collecting water, always cleanse the vessel that you are collecting it in first (see p.23).

MOON WATER

As its name suggests, moon water is water that has been left out under the moonlight to absorb its energy. The water is charged beneath the moon, capturing the energy from lunar phases to work with your magic.

1. Start by cleansing the vessel that you will be adding the water to (see p.23).

2. Fill a glass jar with filtered, distilled, or spring water, or with water from a river, lake, or ocean.

3. Place the vessel outside in moonlight at night.

4. Leave it out as long as possible and bring it inside when you feel it is ready. Always bring this in before the sun rises to keep the moon energy that you capture pure.

5. Label the jar with the date, the moon phase, weather, and any astrological events to track its energy.

6. Store it in a dark place, away from sunlight, ready for you to use in your spells or rituals when needed.

For more information about lunar cycles and the effects of the different phases of the moon, see pp.244–245.

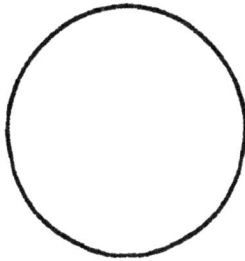

NEW MOON WATER

For new beginnings and setting intentions. Use this water for anything that you are starting or wanting to start. If energy feels a bit stagnant and you want to bless it with new energy, use some new moon energy.

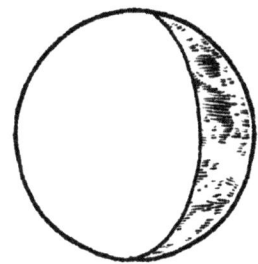

WAXING MOON WATER

This is infused with the strength of the growing moon, ideal for personal growth, expansion, and attraction. Use in manifestation spells, for luck, prosperity, and personal development.

FULL MOON WATER

This is power water. Use it when you need to add energy and strength to spells. When something needs illuminating, anoint your third eye with full moon water to help you see what is needed.

WANING MOON WATER

For removing negative energy, people, and spirits. Use this for areas in your life that require releasing, like breaking bad habits or minimizing problems and annoyances.

DARK MOON WATER

Harness the energy of the invisible moon, a time when we are closest to the spirit realm, and use this water when exploring hidden or unconscious parts of yourself, for justice spells, and for banishments.

WEATHER WATER

Weather water can be collected during rain, storms, snow, or sunshine. Each type of weather brings its own unique energy, which can be harnessed to amplify your magic.

1. To capture weather water, choose a vessel to collect it in and first cleanse with smoke (see p.23).

2. Place the vessel outdoors to collect the rainwater.

3. Label the jar with the date, weather, and any astrological events that occurred.

4. Store in a dark place away from sunlight to preserve its energy, ready to use in spells when needed. You might add it to baths, sprinkle it for protection, or use it to anoint objects or magical tools.

STORM WATER This brings intensity and is associated with raw power, change, and transformation; use it to shake up stagnant energy, release pressure, and to assist with releasing personal rage.

SUN SHOWERS Combines the sun's power of action with rain's power of growth. Use to bring balance and harmony, in sun magic spells, and in healing and manifestation spells. Sprinkle around your home to invite positive opportunities.

SNOW Use to freeze a situation or to calm a heated situation. If you use as snow (rather than melted water) you can use in transformation spells. Write what you wish to transform and put it in the snow; as the snow melts it will energize whatever needs transforming, too.

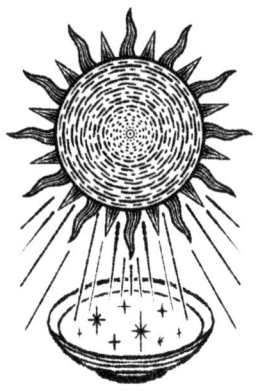

SUN WATER The sun brings life, vitality, and growth. Water blessed with its energy adds power to all spells. Use in happiness, joy, and love spells, and for anointing and blessing petitions with your intentions.

SEAWATER Very powerful due to its connection to the energy of the ocean, a source of deep wisdom. It is naturally salted, which makes it excellent for cleansing, protection, healing, and banishing spells.

RIVER WATER Associated with the flow of life and change. The fast-moving nature of the water makes it ideal for speeding up outcomes of spells, and it's ideal for use in cleansing, purifying, and banishing spells.

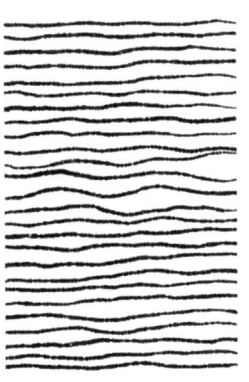

LAKE WATER Blends the qualities of stillness and deep emotional connection. Calm and grounding, this is great for meditation spells and psychic healing. Lake water can inspire true introspection; anoint your journal and pen to help you go deep within.

ECLIPSE WATER Collected during a solar or lunar eclipse, this can help reveal hidden truths and holds powerful transformative energy. It is ideal for using to bring about personal change, energy shifts, and shakedowns.

ICE WATER If you want to freeze something from your life, write it down and put it in the freezer. If you feel stuck in an area of your life, write it down, add it to a vessel of water and freeze it, then smash the ice during a full moon to bring about transformative energy.

SCENTED POTIONS

Fragrance has always been a major part of rituals and witchcraft, and when we blend oils with scent magic it can be used to anoint candles, dress petitions, and bless ourselves, our magical tools, and sacred spaces. Scent has the power to instantly transform us and shift our energy: it can influence our emotions, trigger memories, motivate us, calm us down, and shift our vibrational frequencies.

SAFE PRACTICE

Ensure that the ingredients you use are non-toxic and won't cause irritation when applied to the skin. Never use undiluted essential oils directly on the skin, always mix them with a carrier oil, and test a small amount on your skin before using. Use clean containers, and store in dark glass bottles to preserve their properties, keeping them away from heat or sunlight.

The energy of scent in magic is connected to an unseen presence – we can feel it and have a reaction to it, yet it remains invisible. Our sense of smell is connected to memory, and you might have a strong reaction to a scent without really understanding why. This can be due to an ancestral connection; our DNA carries the memory of up to 255 ancestors and their experiences may influence how we respond to certain smells.

Never make a potion with a scent that you don't like – if you do, the scent can work in the opposite way to your intentions. The following pages provide instruction for making a bespoke scented potion, as well as potions for self-love and vitality.

MAKING A POTION

||||||||||||||||||||||||||||||||

When blending oils that you want to anoint your skin with, always start with a carrier oil such as almond, jojoba, or olive oil and follow this basic ratio to ensure its safety: two drops of essential oil for every 5 ml (1 tsp) of carrier oil, or five drops for every 10 ml (2 tsp) of carrier oil.

You will need

* ✳ **VESSEL TO HOLD YOUR POTION**
* ✳ **PAPER AND PEN**
* ✳ **ROSEMARY, SAGE, OR SALT WATER**
* ✳ **ITEMS THAT CORRESPOND WITH THE ENERGY YOU WANT YOUR POTION TO BRING: THIS CAN INCLUDE OILS, WEATHER WATER, KNOT MAGIC, HERBS, PETITIONS, OR ANY OTHER SYMBOLS AND CHARMS THAT YOU WANT TO CHARGE YOUR POTION WITH**

1. Think of your intention. Write it out so that you are clear on how you want your potion to work.

2. Cleanse your vessel before you add ingredients; this can be in the form of a bay leaf with a protection sigil (see pp.183), the smoke of rosemary or sage, or washing it with salt water.

3. As you add the ingredients, think of all that you want them to bring you and tell each ingredient what you are using it for in order to programme it with your intentions.

4. Charge the potion up by holding it with both hands and visualizing an intention or a memory, summoning the energy that you want it to bring. Feel the energy come through your hands and transfer to the potion.

5. Alternatively, you can read your intentions aloud to the potion, telling it how you want it to work for you.

6. For a really super-powered potion, I recommend that you do both steps 4 and 5.

SELF-LOVE

||||||||||||||||||||||||||||||||||||||

You can treat this as a recipe for practising kindness towards yourself. Use the potion as an anointing oil or add it to a bath, perhaps using it alongside other self-care activities like journalling, meditation, affirmations, or yoga.

You will need

* ❋ **20 ML (4 TSP) OF A CARRIER OIL**
* ❋ **10 DROPS OF ROSE ESSENTIAL OIL**
* ❋ **3 DROPS OF LAVENDER ESSENTIAL OIL**
* ❋ **7 DROPS OF FRANKINCENSE ESSENTIAL OIL**

1. Blend all of the ingredients, and as you do so repeat self-love affirmations out loud:

"I LOVE MYSELF"
"I AM KIND TO MYSELF"
"I RESPECT MYSELF"
"I AM ENOUGH"
"I MATTER"

2. A visualization that I like to use with any self-love magic is to imagine that I am walking down a street and see an open door. I walk into the house, which is filled with versions of me at different ages and even a future version of myself. I hang out with them and tell them all of the loving and nurturing things that each version of me needs to hear. I spend time giving each advice, love, and attention. This can often stir up loving emotions, and if it brings tears, add them to your potion too.

FULL MOON ENERGY

||||||||||||||||||||||||||||||

This is a powerful potion to connect to the full moon energy. Use this for healing, manifestation, clarity, spiritual growth, or protection. This is especially great when calling in assistance with completing cycles, which could be in your work or relationships, or to illuminate the unseen.

You will need

* ✳ **VESSEL WITH A LID TO HOLD YOUR POTION**

* ✳ **100 ML (¹/₂ CUP) OF CHARGED FULL MOON WATER (SEE P.129)**

* ✳ **10 DROPS OF SANDALWOOD ESSENTIAL OIL**

* ✳ **5 DROPS OF LEMON ESSENTIAL OIL**

* ✳ **5 DROPS OF FRANKINCENSE ESSENTIAL OIL**

* ✳ **A FEW DROPS OF WITCH HAZEL, A PINCH OF SALT, OR A FEW DROPS OF UNSCENTED ALCOHOL**

1. Add the essential oils to your moon water. Because you will be mixing water and oil, add a pinch of salt or a few drops of unscented alcohol or witch hazel to help the oil and water blend.

2. Shake the potion before you use it to activate its magic. Splash or spritz this scented moon water when needing to call in full moon power. You might spray it around your body, your altar, or any area that you wish to bless with this energy.

3. Store your moon water in a cool, dark place to preserve its energy. If you plan to drink it or use it on your skin, keep it in the fridge and use within 2 weeks.

ENCHANTED INGREDIENTS

This is your guide to the magical properties of some of the most potent specimens in the plant kingdom, inviting you to forge a deeper connection with the Earth. You will notice that many of these ingredients feature in spells throughout this book, and this will offer a basic understanding of what they all mean.

Exploring the wisdom and magic of plants allows you to foster respect and harmony with nature. Each of the listed ingredients includes ideas for incorporating them into spells, rituals, potions, and everyday magic, with notes on toxicity to ensure your magical practice is safe and effective.

Each charmed plant is also aligned with a planetary power (see pp.240–261), to reflect their energetic, symbolic, and physical characteristics, as well as an element (Earth, Fire, Air, or Water, see pp.114–115). You can use these associations to guide your choices and elevate your spellwork. Herbs, plants, and oils don't always have to exactly match a planet's traditional correspondences because their role is more about channelling and enhancing the energy of that planet rather than strictly aligning with it. Magic works through resonance and symbolism, and plants hold qualities that evoke the power of a planet's energy, even if they aren't directly ruled by it. The key is choosing plants that tap into the magic of that planetary force, rather than sticking rigidly to astrological rulerships.

If you see that an ingredient is needed but you have a bad association with it, then don't use it. And if you gather your own herbs and flowers, do so respectfully, treading lightly in nature and ensuring that you don't take more than the plant can recover from, and never collect anything that is an endangered species (check online for what these are in your locale).

SAFE PRACTICE

The ingredients listed here can reasonably be used in the ways that are indicated. But, when working with any natural ingredients, always ensure that you do so safely. Check that no one is allergic to any of the ingredients, make sure that herbs and resins are safe before you ingest them or apply them to your skin, and if in any doubt, do not use. When burning incense, do so safely (see p.123).

ALLSPICE

PLANET: Mars

ELEMENT: Fire

MAGICAL USES: Allspice brings fiery and vibrant energy for abundance and luck magic. It's great for money-drawing spells and bringing success. You can add it to charm bags, sprinkle it in your wallet, or burn it for good fortune in business ventures.

ANGELICA ROOT

PLANET: Sun

ELEMENT: Fire

MAGICAL USES: Known as the "Root of the Holy Ghost", this is powerful for protection and purification. It wards off evil, boosts courage, and can be used in healing rituals. Carry it for personal safety or burn it to cleanse your home.

ALOESWOOD (AGARWOOD)

PLANET: Venus

ELEMENT: Water

MAGICAL USES: Aloeswood adds energy to spells. It removes negativity and can connect you to higher realms. Perfect for use in incense to create sacred spaces, especially for ancestral work or introspection. Wear as an oil to bring personal power.

BAY LEAVES (BAY LAUREL)

PLANET: Sun

ELEMENT: Fire

MAGICAL USES: Bay leaves are iconic in wish magic. Write your desire, sigil, or symbol on a leaf and burn it. They also protect against negative energy, attract success, and aid in psychic work. Particularly good for cleansing your tarot cards with their smoke.

BENZOIN

IIIIIIIIIIIIIIIIIIIIIIIIIIIIIIIIII

PLANET: Sun

ELEMENT: Air

MAGICAL USES: When it is burnt, Benzoin resin creates an uplifting energy and raises vibrations. Burn it to banish negativity, strengthen spells, or improve focus during rituals. Use in incense for money and prosperity work.

BERGAMOT

IIIIIIIIIIIIIIIIIIIIIIIIIIIIIIIIIIIIII

PLANET: Mercury

ELEMENT: Air

MAGICAL USES: Bergamot awakens personal confidence. Use it in money-drawing spells and when you need to uplift your energy. Its scent can assist with breaking through blocks, enhancing communication, and attracting luck. Use the oil in spells or wear it to boost your confidence.

BUCKTHORN

IIIIIIIIIIIIIIIIIIIIIIIIIIIIIIIIIIIIIIIIII

PLANET: Saturn

ELEMENT: Water

MAGICAL USES: Buckthorn is a transformer of energy and is super strong in banishing and protection magic. Use it for removing bad luck and shielding against negativity. Sprinkle it in doorways or add it to cleansing spells to keep your energy clear and safe.

BURDOCK

IIIIIIIIIIIIIIIIIIIIIIIIIIIIIIIIIII

PLANET: Venus

ELEMENT: Water

MAGICAL USES: Burdock is renowned for its protective and purifying qualities. It's often used to ward off negativity and cleanse spaces of unwanted energies. Use burdock in protective charm bags or strain a handful and use it in floor washes to create a harmonious environment.

CALENDULA (MARIGOLD)

PLANET: Sun

ELEMENT: Fire

MAGICAL USES: Calendula is associated with success, prosperity, healing, and positive energy. Use in spells to bring joy, protection, and to help in legal matters. Create an oil blend with the petals and anoint legal documents to work in your favour, scatter calendula petals around your home to invite happiness, or use them in bath rituals for cleansing.

CAMPHOR

PLANET: Moon

ELEMENT: Water

MAGICAL USES: Camphor has strong purifying properties. Use to cleanse spaces, banish negativity, and enhance divination practices. Burn camphor to purify your space and magical tools and herbs, and use in rituals to sharpen your psychic abilities.

CARAWAY

PLANET: Mercury

ELEMENT: Air

MAGICAL USES: Caraway seeds are traditionally used to protect against theft and to keep a relationship faithful. Carry them in a pouch with black tourmaline for protection.

CARDAMOM

PLANET: Venus

ELEMENT: Water

MAGICAL USES: Cardamom is used in love spells and to enhance focus. It is said that the spirits enjoy its aroma, and its scent can bring clarity in tricky situations. Use it in spells for renewal, love, and abundance.

CATNIP

||||||||||||||||||||||||||||

PLANET: Venus

ELEMENT: Water

MAGICAL USES: Catnip is used to increase love and happiness, and believed to attract good spirits and positive energies. Use in a charm bag to attract love, or burn as an incense to create a happy atmosphere.

CHAMOMILE

||||||||||||||||||||||||||||||||||||||||

PLANET: Sun

ELEMENT: Water

MAGICAL USES: Chamomile is known for its calming effects and is used in spells for peace and prosperity. Add to charms to keep under your pillow to ward off nightmares. Use in money-drawing rituals, adding it to charm bags or placing a few drops of essential oil around your front door to welcome money in.

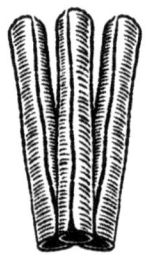

CINNAMON

||||||||||||||||||||||||||||||||||||||

PLANET: Sun

ELEMENT: Fire

MAGICAL USES: Cinnamon is a versatile herb used for protection, prosperity, to awaken spiritual vibrations, and to bring blessings to your home. Burn as incense to raise spiritual vibrations before spellwork, bless your petitions with its smoke, or include it in money-attracting spells.

CLOVES

||||||||||||||||||||||||||||

PLANET: Jupiter

ELEMENT: Fire

MAGICAL USES: Cloves are used for luck, courage, and to inspire passion. Add them to charm bags and poppets to bring confidence and inspiration. They can also be used in protection magic, their strong aroma creating a protective barrier to keep any negative energy at bay.

COMFREY

PLANET: Saturn

ELEMENT: Water

MAGICAL USES: Comfrey is associated with healing and with safety during travel. Create a charm bag with comfrey and black tourmaline crystals and place in your suitcase to keep your baggage safe when you are travelling.

COPAL

PLANET: Sun

ELEMENT: Fire

MAGICAL USES: Copal resin is burnt for purification and to raise spiritual vibrations. It's excellent for cleansing spaces and for meditation when wanting to connect with higher realms.

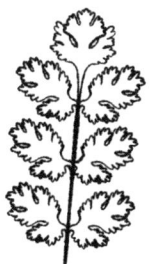

CORIANDER

PLANET: Mars

ELEMENT: Fire

MAGICAL USES: Coriander seeds are used in love spells and to help with fertility. A pinch of ground coriander seeds added to any spell can enhance and give extra power to the spell.

CUMIN

PLANET: Mars

ELEMENT: Fire

MAGICAL USES: Cumin is used for protection. Blend it with salt and sprinkle around your home to keep negative vibes at bay. Crush up cumin seeds and drink it with a lover when making a commitment to each other.

DAMIANA

PLANET: Venus

ELEMENT: Fire

MAGICAL USES: This South American shrub is known for its aromatic leaves. Damiana is used to enhance love and passion and to encourage prophetic visions. Use it in love-inciting incense or teas to bring vivid dreams and visions.

DILL

PLANET: Mercury

ELEMENT: Fire

MAGICAL USES: Dill is used for protection and represents renewal and new beginnings. Hang it in doorways to repel negative entities or carry it to bring good fortune.

DRAGON'S BLOOD

PLANET: Mars

ELEMENT: Fire

MAGICAL USES: This sticky red resin is powerful for protection, banishing, and amplifying spellwork. Add it to incense blends to boost their potency, or add to a carrier oil and use to anoint magical tools or charms.

EUCALYPTUS

PLANET: Moon

ELEMENT: Air

MAGICAL USES: Eucalyptus is useful for healing, to clear energy blockages, reduce psychic stress, and promote emotional wellbeing. Use its oil or burn its leaves to cleanse and purify spaces, the invigorating scent creating a barrier against negative energy.

FENNEL

|||||||||||||||||||||||||||||

PLANET: Mercury

ELEMENT: Air

MAGICAL USES: Fennel is known to ward off negative energies and evil spirits. It's also associated with purification and healing. Use in spells to call in courage, for personal growth, and new beginnings.

FRANKINCENSE

|||||||||||||||||||||||||||||||||||||||||

PLANET: Sun

ELEMENT: Fire

MAGICAL USES: Frankincense is revered for its powerful purification and spiritual properties. Burn its resin to raise spiritual vibrations, ideal for meditation, connecting to psychic energy, and connecting to the spirit realm. Can be used in all spellwork.

GINGER

|||||||||||||||||||||||||||||

PLANET: Mars

ELEMENT: Fire

MAGICAL USES: Ginger brings fire energy and fuel to magic, speeding up the effects of spells and adding extra power. It's associated with passion, prosperity, and success. Consuming ginger or using it in spells can ignite personal power and attract love or money.

GUM MASTIC

|||||||||||||||||||||||||||||||||

PLANET: Sun

ELEMENT: Air

MAGICAL USES: This resin in renowned for its ability to cleanse both physical and spiritual spaces. Gum mastic can be used to bring about change. Burn it as incense to purify spaces and drive away negativity, and use in spells to manifest desires and strengthen psychic abilities.

HIBISCUS
||||||||||||||||||||||||||||||||

PLANET: Venus

ELEMENT: Water

MAGICAL USES: Hibiscus flowers are linked to love, lust, and divination. Use in love spells to attract or enhance romantic relationships, or make into a tea to connect you to goddess energy and heighten your divination practice.

HIGH JOHN THE CONQUEROR
||||||||||||||||||||||||||||||||||||||||||

PLANET: Mars

ELEMENT: Fire

MAGICAL USES: High John root is a staple in Hoodoo and folk magic, symbolizing strength, luck, and overcoming obstacles. Carry in a charm bag or add to a poppet to attract prosperity and success, and to ward off negative energy.

HYSSOP
||||||||||||||||||||||||||||

PLANET: Jupiter

ELEMENT: Fire

MAGICAL USES: This aromatic herb is mostly renowned for its purifying properties. Use in cleansing rituals to remove negativity: sprinkle on objects and around your doorway, or carry in a charm bag for cleansing and protection.

JASMINE
||||||||||||||||||||||||||||

PLANET: Moon

ELEMENT: Water

MAGICAL USES: Jasmine flowers are associated with love, prophetic dreams, clarity, and lunar magic. Its scent can guide you to gain clarity through meditation. Place jasmine flowers under your pillow to encourage peaceful sleep and insightful dreams.

JUNIPER

PLANET: Sun

ELEMENT: Fire

MAGICAL USES: Juniper berries and branches are used for protection, purification, and health. Burning juniper cleanses spaces of negativity. Hang a bunch above your front door to provide protection against negative energy entering your home.

LAVENDER

PLANET: Mercury

ELEMENT: Air

MAGICAL USES: The scent of lavender calms the nervous system and purifies. Use it in spells for love, relaxation, and peace. Place lavender under your pillow to aid restful sleep and ward off nightmares.

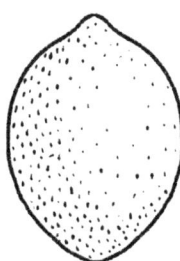

LEMON

PLANET: Moon

ELEMENT: Water

MAGICAL USES: Lemon is associated with new beginnings and fresh starts. It is a powerful energy cleanser, and slices of lemon covered in salt can absorb negative energy. Add to your cleaning products to clear out negative vibrations.

LEMONGRASS

PLANET: Mercury

ELEMENT: Air

MAGICAL USES: The scent of lemongrass, aka "spiritual speed", in potions will motivate and sharpen the mind. Burn in an incense to clear energy blocks and any obstacles that are in your path.

MARJORAM

PLANET: Mercury

ELEMENT: Air

MAGICAL USES: Marjoram is associated with happiness, protection, healing, love, and money. Create a blend with frankincense and lavender to offer healing in grief, or add to food to strengthen love and relationships.

MINT

PLANET: Mercury

ELEMENT: Air

MAGICAL USES: Mint is a multipurpose addition to most spells, and used in rituals it can promote healing and attract prosperity. Mint is also believed to stimulate mental clarity and assist with communication. Use it to bring green light energy to spells calling in new beginnings.

MUGWORT

PLANET: Venus

ELEMENT: Earth

MAGICAL USES: Mugwort is renowned for its connection to dreams and divination, and is used to enhance psychic abilities and for protection during astral travel. Drink it in a tea or place it under your pillow to bring vivid dreams.

MYRRH

PLANET: Moon

ELEMENT: Water

MAGICAL USES: Myrrh has deep healing and spiritual properties. Burn it as incense to elevate vibrations and purify spaces, use in healing rituals, and to consecrate sacred objects and magical tools.

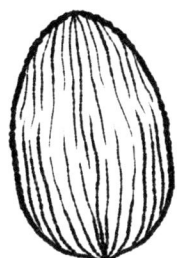

NUTMEG

||||||||||||||||||||||||||||||

PLANET: Jupiter

ELEMENT: Fire

MAGICAL USES: Nutmeg is associated with luck, money, and health. Carry a whole nutmeg seed to attract good luck, or anoint a green candle with nutmeg for a powerful prosperity spell.

ORANGE

||||||||||||||||||||||||||||||

PLANET: Sun

ELEMENT: Fire

MAGICAL USES: Orange is linked to joy, divination, and love. Use its peel and flowers in rituals to attract abundance, love, and happiness.

ORRIS ROOT

||||||||||||||||||||||||||||||||||||||||

PLANET: Venus

ELEMENT: Water

MAGICAL USES: Orris root is believed to strengthen psychic ability and so is often used in divination practices. A pinch of orris root added to incense spells can speed your magic up. Use this in spells to clear blocks and in love-drawing spells and rituals. You can also add its powder to charm bags to attract romance.

PATCHOULI

||||||||||||||||||||||||||||||||||||||||

PLANET: Saturn

ELEMENT: Earth

MAGICAL USES: Patchouli is renowned for its grounding and magnetic attracting properties. Its rich, earthy scent is associated with love and passion, making it a common ingredient in aphrodisiac blends. It is powerful for spells calling in abundance, and love and prosperity spells. If you do not like its very distinctive smell, do not use it in spellwork as it will work against you and not for you.

PINE

|||||||||||||||||||

PLANET: Jupiter

ELEMENT: Air

MAGICAL USES: Pine is associated with cleansing, protection, and prosperity. Burn pine needles or use its essential oil to purify spaces and ward away negativity, and use it in money-attracting spells and to promote healing.

POKE ROOT

||||||||||||||||||||||||||||||||

PLANET: Mars

ELEMENT: Fire

MAGICAL USES: Traditionally used in rituals for removing negative influences. Create a brew to use in floor washes to cleanse spaces of unwanted energies (unless you have pets, as they could be harmed. Do not drink or apply to your skin as it is toxic). Powerful for banishing ex-lovers from your energy field and helping you to move on from them: write your ex's name on paper and burn with the root, disposing of the ashes where nothing grows.

ROSE

|||||||||||||||||||

PLANET: Venus

ELEMENT: Water

MAGICAL USES: Roses are synonymous with love and beauty. Use in spells to attract love, enhance beauty, and promote harmony. Use its scent to bring healing, awaken self-love, and attract romance.

ROSEMARY

||||||||||||||||||||||||||||

PLANET: Sun

ELEMENT: Fire

MAGICAL USES: Rosemary is a versatile herb used for protection, purification, psychic work, and stimulating memory. Burn to cleanse spaces and use in healing rituals. A drop of diluted essential oil on your third eye can awaken your intuition in an instant.

RUE

PLANET: Mars

ELEMENT: Fire

MAGICAL USES: Rue is known for its strong protective and cleansing properties, and is used to ward off the evil eye. Open all of the windows in your home and let the smoke of rue drive out negative energy. This is a good one to burn after being unwell as an energetic reset.

SAGE

PLANET: Jupiter

ELEMENT: Air

MAGICAL USES: Sage is known for purification and protective energy. Burn sage to cleanse spaces of negative energies, and use in healing rituals, and to promote wisdom.

SANDALWOOD

PLANET: Moon

ELEMENT: Air

MAGICAL USES: Sandalwood is valued for its spiritual and protective qualities. Burn in incense to elevate spiritual vibrations. It is a powerful component when performing moon magic, especially when manifesting your desires during a new moon and waxing moon.

STAR ANISE

PLANET: Jupiter

ELEMENT: Air

MAGICAL USES: Star anise is associated with psychic awareness and protection. It's used in divination practices to enhance clairvoyance. Carry star anise to ward off the evil eye and attract good luck, and sleep with it under your pillow for guidance in your dreams.

SUNFLOWER

PLANET: Sun

ELEMENT: Fire

MAGICAL USES: Sunflowers symbolize happiness, vitality, and fertility. Use sunflower seeds in rituals to attract success and joy. Plant intentions with these seeds to bring abundance into your life.

THYME

PLANET: Venus

ELEMENT: Water

MAGICAL USES: Thyme is used for purification, courage, and mental clarity. Use thyme in spells when connecting to your inner voice for guidance and awaking your psychic powers.

VANILLA

PLANET: Venus

ELEMENT: Water

MAGICAL USES: Vanilla has a comforting and alluring aroma, making it a popular choice in love and attraction spells. Its scent is believed to enhance seduction. Use in spells when wanting to add sweetness to your life, relationships, or particular situations.

VETIVER

PLANET: Venus

ELEMENT: Earth

MAGICAL USES: Vetiver is known for its grounding and protective properties and is used in rituals to repel negativity. Anoint yourself with it to promote love and lustful energy, and use in money drawing spells or to enhance concentration.

VIOLET

PLANET: Venus

ELEMENT: Water

MAGICAL USES: Violets are linked to love, healing, and peace, and can be used in spells to shift energy after a run of bad luck. Carry violet flowers to attract luck, especially in matters of the heart. You can also use them in healing rituals to soothe emotions after experiencing heartache.

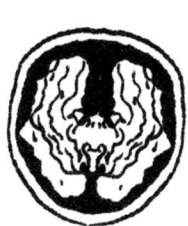

WALNUT

PLANET: Sun

ELEMENT: Fire

MAGICAL USES: Walnuts are associated with wisdom, strength, and abundance. Their appearance is similar to brains, and they connect to divine wisdom and help transform unhelpful beliefs. Use walnuts in spells when needing to enhance knowledge, for learning and gaining clarity.

YARROW

PLANET: Venus

ELEMENT: Water

MAGICAL USES: Yarrow can be used in spells when calling in courage, and can draw helpful people and energy into your life. Add to a charm bag to bring protection, use it in potions, and anoint yourself when wanting to attract courage and dispel fear.

CHAPTER SIX

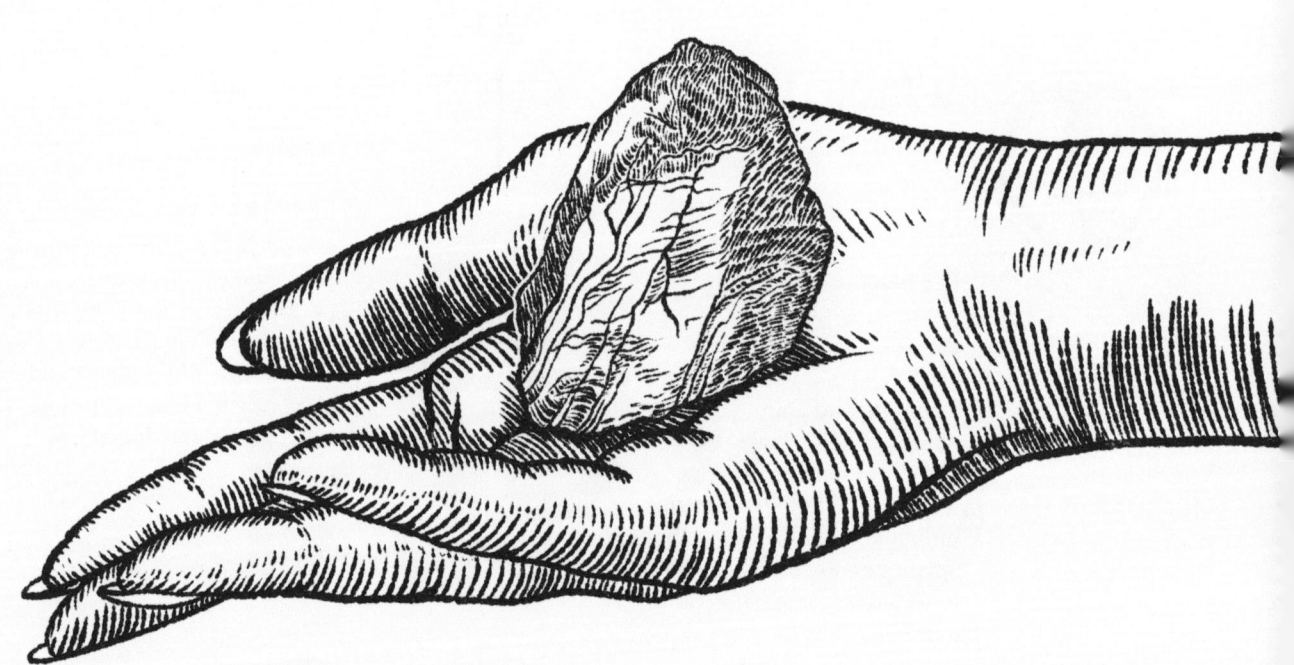

CRYSTAL
MAGIC

MYSTICAL STONES

Crystals are treasures from deep within the Earth, with many forming over thousands, sometimes millions, of years. Not only are they beautiful to look at, but each crystal also holds its own vibrational frequency that can support us in life and in our magical practices.

These natural minerals are formed beneath the Earth's surface and are infused with the magical properties and elements that come from our planet's core. Incorporating them into witchcraft channels these energies, increasing the power of spells.

Crystal magic has roots in ancient Egyptian, Indian, and Native American traditions, and crystals are used by modern witches as tools to enhance focus, for energy work, and in rituals. Once you have chosen your crystals, there are many ways in which they can be incorporated into your life and spellwork. They can work their magic instantly or be part of a more detailed ritual.

✳ CARRY THEM IN YOUR POCKET OR WEAR IN JEWELLERY AS CHARMS OR TALISMANS TO ATTRACT GOOD FORTUNE AND PARTICULAR OUTCOMES, OR TO KEEP YOU SAFE

✳ USE THEM AROUND YOUR HOME TO CLEANSE AND PROTECT YOUR ENVIRONMENT

✳ PLACE CRYSTALS ON YOUR ALTAR TO REPRESENT THE ELEMENTS, YOUR INTENTIONS, OR DEITIES YOU WISH TO INVOKE

✳ PUT CORRESPONDING CRYSTALS ON OR AROUND YOUR BODY TO HELP HEAL EMOTIONAL OR PHYSICAL AILMENTS, UNBLOCK ENERGY, AND FOSTER SPIRITUAL GROWTH

✳ USE WITH CANDLES, HERBS, OR OTHER MAGICAL TOOLS DURING SPELLWORK TO FOCUS YOUR INTENTIONS

START HERE

When you bring a new crystal into your life, first cleanse it to purify its energy (see p.23). You should also cleanse your crystals after you've used them in spells by placing them under the light of a full moon. Remember to bring them inside before the sun rises, as exposure to sunlight can fade and ruin some crystals.

CREATING A CRYSTAL GRID

A crystal grid is a powerful way to call in on the energy of a combination of crystals at the same time. When crystals are placed together it can really amplify their energy to a whole new level. Try creating a crystal grid and placing it on your altar or in a safe nook where you know it won't be disturbed.

As with all components of a magic spell, it's essential to cleanse and bless crystals with your intentions before using them. This clears away any lingering energy that the crystal may have picked up, ensuring it's a pure vessel for your magic. You might start by cleansing it with the purifying smoke from sage, rosemary, or camphor (see p.23). Alternatively, you could place it under the light of a full moon to bathe it in lunar energy.

Once cleansed, take each crystal in your hands and connect with it. Speak to it directly, telling it how you would like it to support you and the energy you wish it to bring into your spell. This moment of intention sets the tone for the magic to come and will create a connection between you and the crystal that strengthens the energy of your spellwork.

ENERGIZING

Before you get started, set your intention. It is important to be clear about what energy you want this crystal grid to bring you. Is it for love, protection, abundance, or clarity? Write it down or speak it aloud to add your energy into the process.

CHOOSE
YOUR CRYSTALS

Select a central stone (the "master" crystal) that aligns with your intention. For example, you might use an emerald for love or citrine for abundance (see pp.159–165). Surround it with supporting stones that enhance or complement that energy. Clear quartz is always a great addition because it amplifies everything.

CREATE
YOUR GRID

You don't have to be a geometry expert, and can simply place your crystals in a symmetrical and intentional way. However, sacred geometry patterns can help direct energy flow.

FLOWER OF LIFE
General manifestation and balance

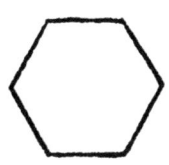

HEXAGON (HONEYCOMB)
Strength and unity

SPIRAL Growth and transformation

TRIANGLE Power and manifestation

STONE SELECTOR

Crystals come in a wide spectrum of colours, shapes, and structures, but remember that you don't need to have every crystal in existence. You should only use crystals that resonate with you and what you need for your practice.

SOURCING

As much as I adore crystals, it's important to acknowledge that there is a shadow side to the industry. The growing demand for these magical stones has sometimes led to unethical mining practices and exploitation of workers, which doesn't feel very magical at all. It's so important to be mindful of where you get yours from. Research sellers, ask questions, and ensure your crystals are sourced in an ethical way.

You might set out to buy a crystal for a specific spell or intention, but sometimes it's best to simply let your intuition guide you. You may find yourself inexplicably drawn to a particular crystal, and when you look up its meaning find that it totally aligns with what you need. Trust that attraction, because sometimes crystals choose us rather than the other way around. I have a few that have been with me for years and feel like old friends that I have a deep connection with. We can get attached to our crystals, but if they break or we lose them, it often means that their work has been done.

On the following pages I will outline the main types of crystals, the powerful types of energy they submit, and suggest simple ways you can use them in your magic. Each one also corresponds to a planet (pp.240–261), an astrological sign (pp.268–271), and an element (pp.114–115), bringing those corresponding energies when you use them. There are no hard and fast rules; different traditions might have their own takes, but the metaphysical associations listed here are among the most widely accepted. Remember to always trust your intuition and go with what resonates for you.

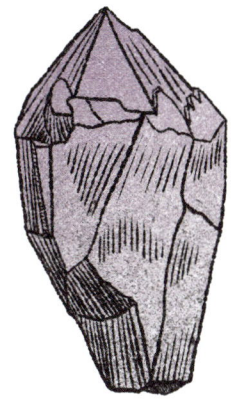

AMETHYST

||||||||||||||||||||||||||||||||||

ENERGY: Spiritual, healing (emotional and physical), heightens intuition, protection, meditation, calming

PLANET: Jupiter, Neptune

ZODIAC: Aquarius, Pisces

ELEMENT: Air, Water

MAGIC: Carry an amethyst crystal in a purple pouch with 3 star anise for psychic guidance.

APACHE TEAR

|||||||||||||||||||||||||||||||||||||

ENERGY: Gentle energy, protection, healing (especially grief)

PLANET: Mars, Pluto

ZODIAC: Aries, Capricorn

ELEMENT: Earth, Fire

MAGIC: Healing for grief, especially for animals that are grieving: put in a white pouch and leave in your pet's basket.

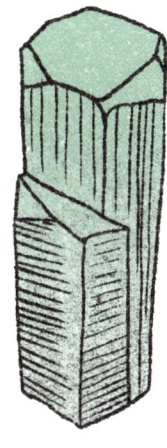

AQUAMARINE

||||||||||||||||||||||||||||||||||||||||||||

ENERGY: Calming, peace and harmony, clarity, meditation, communication

PLANET: Neptune, Uranus

ZODIAC: Aquarius, Pisces

ELEMENT: Water

MAGIC: Hold this crystal and drink some peppermint tea when needing to have an honest, challenging conversation.

BLACK TOURMALINE

||||||||||||||||||||||||||||||||||||||||

ENERGY: Protection, grounding, repels negative energy, helps with stress and anxiety

PLANET: Saturn

ZODIAC: Capricorn, Libra

ELEMENT: Earth

MAGIC: This crystal is known as a spiritual security system. Place it in the corners of your home for protection and keep one in your car or handbag too. Cleanse it regularly.

CARNELIAN

||||||||||||||||||||||||||||||||||

ENERGY: Inspires creativity, awakens passion, motivating, brings vitality, sharpens the mind, brings courage and helps you find your voice

PLANET: Mars

ZODIAC: Aries, Leo, Virgo

ELEMENT: Fire

MAGIC: Place in a red pouch with 3 pinches of dried ginger to motivate. Add a drop of lemongrass essential oil for turbo motivation!

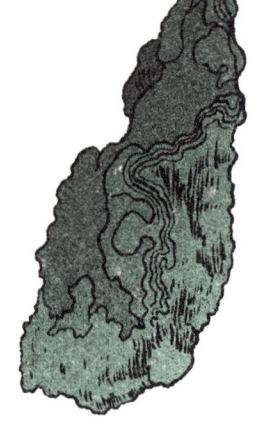

CHRYSOCOLLA

||||||||||||||||||||||||||||||||||||||||||

ENERGY: Calms your mind and nervous system, cleanses energies, encourages communication and self-expression

PLANET: Venus

ZODIAC: Taurus, Gemini, Virgo

ELEMENT: Water

MAGIC: Place a chrysocolla on your third eye and listen to a guided meditation.

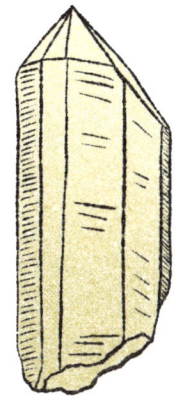

CITRINE

||||||||||||||||||||||||||||

ENERGY: Abundance, prosperity, creativity, self-confidence, transmutes negative energy into positive

PLANET: Sun, Mercury

ZODIAC: Gemini, Leo

ELEMENT: Fire

MAGIC: Place in a green pouch with 3 pinches of chamomile flowers. Add a money sigil (see p.183) for extra power.

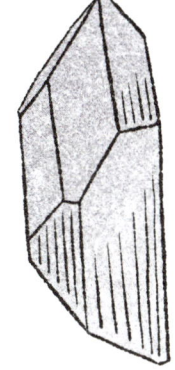

CLEAR QUARTZ

||||||||||||||||||||||||||||||||||||||||||||

ENERGY: A universal crystal that can be used for most magical workings, healing, enhances clarity and focus, regulates your nervous system, raises vibrational frequencies, adds power to spellwork

PLANET: Sun

ZODIAC: All signs

ELEMENT: All elements

MAGIC: Use to amplify your magic and store with all of your crystals to recharge them. Can be used as a substitute for any crystal in your spellwork. Keep clear quartz in jars with all of your magical ingredients.

EMERALD

||||||||||||||||||||||||||||||||||

ENERGY: Love, rebirth, and fertility, finding a home, making wishes and enhancing your intuition

PLANET: Mercury

ZODIAC: Aries, Taurus, Gemini

ELEMENT: Earth

MAGIC: Write down your wishes and place the emerald in the centre of the paper. Anoint the edges of the paper with patchouli oil, and then fold it four times towards you.

FLUORITE

||||||||||||||||||||||||||||||

ENERGY: Assists with focus, clear decision-making, stabilizes negative energy, balance, helps to break habits

PLANET: Mercury, Neptune

ZODIAC: Pisces, Capricorn

ELEMENT: Air, Water

MAGIC: When feeling overwhelmed with a difficult decision, bathe this crystal in frankincense incense and hold it to your heart while practising slow, gentle deep breathing to bring clarity.

GARNET

||||||||||||||||||||||||||||

ENERGY: Passion, vitality, protection, grounding, courage, stimulates the mind

PLANET: Mars

ZODIAC: Aries, Leo, Capricorn

ELEMENT: Fire, Earth

MAGIC: Carry in an orange pouch with 3 pinches of thyme and 5 cloves whenever you need courage.

LABRADORITE

||||||||||||||||||||||||||||||||||||

ENERGY: Awakens psychic power, psychic protection, raises your consciousness, inspires imagination, alleviates fear, promotes transformations

PLANET: Uranus

ZODIAC: Leo, Scorpio, Sagittarius

ELEMENT: Water

MAGIC: Bathe this crystal in the smoke of dried bay leaf and keep it with you when offering tarot card readings.

LAPIS LAZULI

||||||||||||||||||||||||||||||||

ENERGY: Strengthens intuition and psychic powers, helps with communication, wisdom, truth, and confidence

PLANET: Jupiter, Venus

ZODIAC: Libra, Sagittarius

ELEMENT: Air

MAGIC: Place near your bedside to assist with remembering dreams and bring intuitive insights. Drink mugwort tea when working with this crystal for next-level psychic energy.

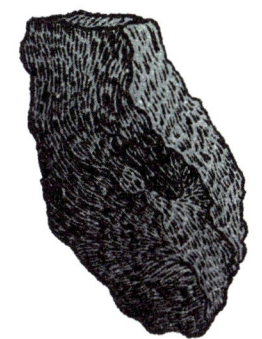

LODESTONE

||||||||||||||||||||||||||||||||

ENERGY: Attraction, draws energy, magnifying, grounding, and balance

PLANET: Venus

ZODIAC: Virgo

ELEMENT: Earth

MAGIC: Use in attraction spells. Place in the centre of your petitions, or add to a jar with herbs corresponding with what you are attracting.

MOLDAVITE

||||||||||||||||||||||||||||||||

ENERGY: Transformation and spiritual evolution, enhances communication with the higher realms

PLANET: Uranus

ZODIAC: All signs

ELEMENT: Storm (combination of all elements)

MAGIC: Use moldavite to shake up stagnant energy and create shifts. Bless the stone with an incense blend of dried rosemary and mint.

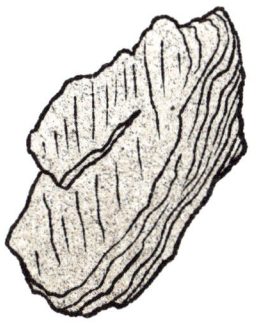

MOONSTONE

||||||||||||||||||||||||||||||||

ENERGY: Intuition, healing, dreams, new beginnings, promotes reflection and introspection, calms stress

PLANET: Moon

ZODIAC: Cancer, Libra, Scorpio

ELEMENT: Water

MAGIC: Use moonstone when journalling, and burn jasmine incense alongside for deep introspection.

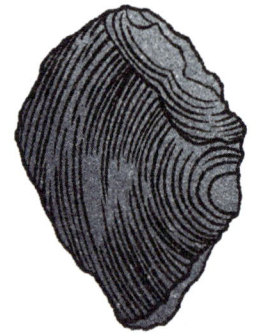

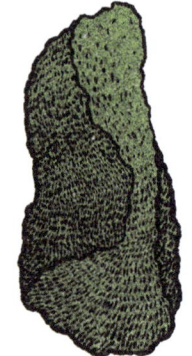

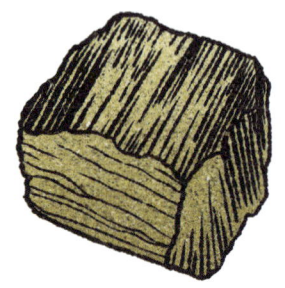

OBSIDIAN

ENERGY: Removes negative energy, protection in psychic work, disempowers negative spiritual energy, grounding, healing

PLANET: Pluto, Saturn

ZODIAC: Scorpio, Sagittarius

ELEMENT: Fire, Earth

MAGIC: Make a spell jar (see p.60) including an obsidian, 3 pinches of salt, 3 pinches of dried rosemary, and 3 pinches of dried sage, and sleep with it at the foot of your bed if feeling emotionally drained.

PERIDOT

ENERGY: Brings abundance and prosperity, protects against negative energy, and promotes healing

PLANET: Sun

ZODIAC: Leo, Virgo

ELEMENT: Earth

MAGIC: Draw money signs on 3 dried bay leaves and burn them to bless the peridot, then keep the crystal in your wallet.

PYRITE (FOOL'S GOLD)

ENERGY: Abundance, prosperity, protection

PLANET: Sun

ZODIAC: Leo

ELEMENT: Fire, Earth

MAGIC: Fill a bowl with money and place a pyrite on top. Store this by your front door to welcome in money.

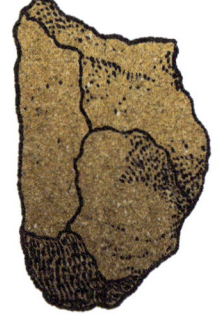

RED JASPER

ENERGY: Nurturing stone, provides stability and balance, stimulates sexual energy, brings courage, enhances vitality and endurance

PLANET: Mars

ZODIAC: Aries, Scorpio

ELEMENT: Earth

MAGIC: To awaken passion, anoint with rose essential oil and place under your pillow.

SELENITE

||||||||||||||||||||||||||||||||

ENERGY: Cleanses and charges other crystals, clarity, peace and harmony, neutralizes energy

PLANET: Moon

ZODIAC: Taurus, Cancer

ELEMENT: Air

MAGIC: Store on your altar to keep it energetically clean, or move it around your body to bring harmony.

SMOKY QUARTZ

||||||||||||||||||||||||||||||||||||||||||

ENERGY: Clears negative energy, raises vibrations, calms anxiety, emotional strength, grounding, healing, manifesting

PLANET: Saturn

ZODIAC: Capricorn, Scorpio, Sagittarius

ELEMENT: Earth

MAGIC: Clear blocks and whatever is holding you back. Write out what you need to clear and place a smoky quartz crystal in the centre of the petition. Blend some dried mint and pine and sprinkle in a circle around the crystal. Works best during a waning moon, and then burn the herbs and petition on a dark moon.

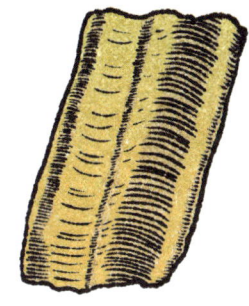

TIGER'S EYE

|||||||||||||||||||||||||||||||||||||

ENERGY: Courage, confidence, focus, inspires energy, clears creative blocks, quietens negative self-talk.

PLANET: Sun

ZODIAC: Leo, Capricorn

ELEMENT: Earth, Fire

MAGIC: Use to call in new opportunities around work. Make an anointing potion, blending 30 ml (2 tbsp) of carrier oil with 3 pinches of dried basil, 3 pinches of allspice, and 5 drops of bergamot essential oil. Anoint your intentions regarding career success with this potion.

CHAPTER SEVEN

SYMBOLS, RUNES, AND SIGILS

SYMBOLIC POWER

For thousands of years, symbols have been an important part of mystical and religious traditions around the world. They have been used for expressing beliefs, calling in protection, and communicating with the spirit realm. Just as the ancients used them in rituals, we can too.

Symbols come in many forms: they can be numbers, letters, images, shapes, runes, or sigils. Runes (see pp.177–181) are particularly powerful, as are sigils, which can be used to create personalized symbols (see pp.182–185). While developing your craft, symbols are accessible and simple tools, yet they're also potent ways to connect you with your intentions and channel energy. In this chapter, we'll explore what the most powerful symbols mean, and how you can tap into their energies to enhance your magic.

As with all magical practices, you should only work with symbols that you feel a connection with. Here are a few simple examples of how you can use symbols in your spellwork:

✳ **STIR SYMBOLS INTO DRINKS; A SPIRAL STIRRED CLOCKWISE INTO A CUP OF COFFEE CAN INVITE VISIONS AND NEW IDEAS**

✳ **DRAW HEARTS INTO FOOD YOU ARE PREPARING, TO SEND LOVE AND HEALING ENERGY TO EVERYONE WHO EATS IT**

✳ **PLACE A SIGIL OVER YOUR FRONT DOOR TO WARD OFF EVIL**

✳ **DRAW A SYMBOL IN THE AIR OVER YOUR ALTAR, OR IN ANY SITUATIONS WHERE YOU NEED PROTECTION**

✳ **WRITE SYMBOLS ON EXAM PAPERS FOR LUCK, OR ON THE INSIDE OF YOUR SHOES TO GUIDE YOU IN THE RIGHT DIRECTION**

✳ **DRAW RUNES ON PARCHMENT PAPER AND ADD TO POTIONS TO CHARGE THESE UP WITH THEIR ENERGY**

✳ **WRITE SYMBOLS OUT AND BURN THEM, SENDING THEIR VIBRATIONAL FREQUENCIES OUT INTO THE UNIVERSE**

START HERE

When using symbols, it's most important that they resonate with you. These might be images that you tend to gravitate towards in your everyday life – perhaps hearts, flowers or moons. Symbols might even show up in the form of doodles or dots. Keep this in mind as you begin to explore some of the most common and powerful symbols throughout this chapter. If they don't mean anything to you, let them go.

GALLERY OF SYMBOLS

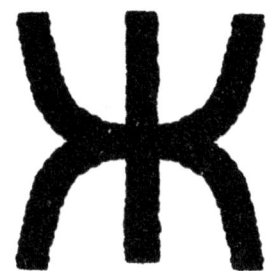

MONEY These symbols signify wealth, abundance, prosperity, and financial stability. Use them in spells and rituals to attract success, enhance luck, and to call in wealth and abundance. Common money symbols include coins, pentacles, and dollar signs, each amplifying intentions for growth, security, and resourcefulness.

PENTACLE/PENTAGRAM
The pentagram is an ancient symbol, the points of which represent Earth, Air, Fire, Water, and Spirit. Use it in elemental magic, protection spells, and to bring balance. You can draw this symbol in the air to connect you to yourself and bring safety: to do this, start from the top and move to the right.

HEARTS Represent love, passion, emotional depth, and spiritual energy. Hearts help to channel our feelings, connecting with themes of healing, compassion, and empathy. In spellwork they can strengthen bonds, enhance connections, and help to foster emotional clarity. Hearts can be used to great effect in love spells as well as spells to bring peace and harmony.

SPIRALS Represent cycles of creation, new beginnings, and visions. Often associated with nature, spirals embody rebirth, transformation, spiritual expansion, and the flow of energy. Use in rituals and spells for personal growth and for connecting with cosmic rhythms and universal forces. The triple spiral consists of three interlocking spirals and is an ancient Celtic symbol.

THE TRIPLE MOON This symbol shows a full moon with a waxing crescent moon on the left and a waning crescent moon on the right. It represents the different cycles of the moon, each symbolizing the phases of the goddess, maiden, mother, and crone archetypes. Use this symbol in magic when you need to summon nurturing peaceful energy or want to connect with the moon. It can be used when calling in your divine power and abundance.

ARROW An arrow represents movement, direction, and focus. This symbol is perfect for spells aimed at breaking through barriers or moving forwards with confidence. Draw an arrow pointing upwards on a red candle when you are setting intentions to call in action.

THE ANKH Also known as the "key of life", this is an ancient Egyptian symbol of eternal life. It resembles a cross with a loop at the top. In magical practice, it is often used as a talisman for protection, spiritual growth, and connection to divine forces. Use the ankh symbol in spells or rituals for protection, health, vitality, and immortality.

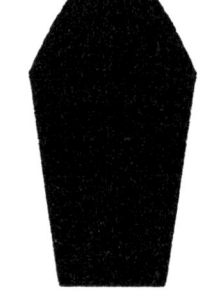

COFFIN This casket represents endings and the cycle of life and death. It signifies the conclusion of one phase, paving the way for rebirth or new beginnings. You might use this symbol in rituals that focus on personal growth, and in banishing spells: draw the outline of a coffin on a piece of paper, and inside this outline write out the worries you wish to banish, then burn it.

EYE This signifies heightened perception, protection, and inner wisdom. Often called the "all-seeing eye", it represents the ability to tap into hidden knowledge. This powerful emblem wards off negative influences and can connect you to divination and protection. For spiritual insights, carve an eye on a purple candle. You can also use the eye in protection spells to ward off negative energy.

EARTH Often depicted as a downward-pointing triangle with a horizontal line. Earth magic focuses on manifesting desires, nurturing expansion, and connecting with nature's energies to foster strength and endurance. Use the Earth symbol in spells for grounding, stability, and personal growth, and in fertility magic.

AIR Typically represented by an upwards-pointing triangle with a horizontal line, it signifies intellect, communication, and freedom. Air magic involves harnessing the energies of breath, thought, and inspiration. Use this symbol in clarity, wisdom, and communication spells, road opening spells, and for bringing in new energy.

FIRE Represents transformation, energy, and passion. Fire is a powerful tool for purification and manifestation, igniting the spirit and inspiring action. It is a catalyst for change and a source of strength. This symbol is great for summoning Fire energy when action is needed. Use it in transformation, purification, and banishing spells.

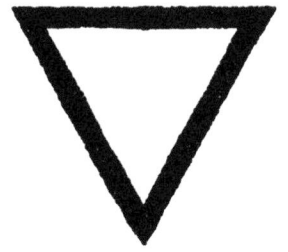

CELTIC KNOT The Celtic knot represents the four classical elements, and its endless loops signify interconnectedness, eternity, and the cycles of life. It can serve as a protective talisman, promoting harmony and balance. Use it in spells and rituals to ward off negative energy and bring protection.

CIRCLE Represents unity, completion, and protection, embodying the cyclical nature of life. The circle is often used to create a sacred space when performing rituals, creating boundaries that enhance focus and energy. Use the circle symbol for protection and manifesting spells.

WATER This symbol connects you to your intuition, fostering empathy and understanding while promoting tranquillity and spiritual growth. Use it for healing spells and whenever you want to tune in to your emotions; it is also great in cleansing rituals.

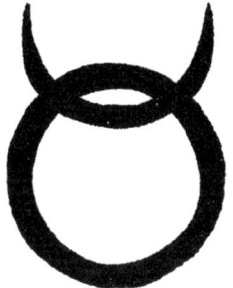

THE HORNED GOD This symbol is connected to Wiccan magic and represents the strength of masculine energy. It can be used together with a feminine symbol, such as the triple moon, to bring balance and harmony, and in spells to call in strength and vitality.

HEPTAGRAM This seven-pointed star connects to the planets and other powerful symbols of seven: seven days of the week, and the seven directions in Wicca (North, South, East, West, Above, Below, and Within). Use the heptagram to connect with the elements, bring power to your altar, and when wanting to connect to the spirit realm. It can also be used in spells for harmony and protection.

KEY Represents opening doors in magic, unlocking potential and inviting new opportunities. This is a great symbol to use in manifesting spells, to bless new beginnings and invite freedom for yourself. A key can also be used to signify endings, symbolizing closing a door and locking away what does not serve you.

RUNES

Runes are a type of symbol that originated in ancient Norse and Germanic traditions. Each carries distinct meanings and energetic vibrations. By using runes in our spells and rituals, we can tap into a powerful age-old system of protection, healing, and manifestation.

Runes are a primitive alphabet, with their name stemming from the old Norse word meaning "secret letter". Early societies didn't yet have writing systems, and so the act of writing was itself often viewed as a form of magic. The oldest runic alphabet is the Elder Futhark; its 24 symbols were used across Northern Europe from 200 to 800 CE. These runes were carved into wood, bone, and stone, and often represented farming, agriculture, and protection.

Each rune carries its own powerful energies, and they are a great tool for divination and protection. Their meanings can be used to bring specific power to spells and rituals – whether you seek guidance or balance. Runes also each have their own sound vibration, meaning you can recite their names as incantations in spells. Those who use runes believe they are particularly powerful because, as well as tapping into the spiritual meaning, you are also connecting with ancient wisdom.

✳ INCORPORATE RUNES INTO SPELLS BY WRITING THEM ON PAPER, ENGRAVING THEM ON CANDLES, VISUALIZING THEM OR SAYING THEIR NAMES ALOUD DURING RITUALS

✳ CHANNEL HEALING ENERGY USING RUNES ASSOCIATED WITH VITALITY, PLACING THEM ON YOUR BODY

✳ USE IN DIVINATION, CASTING RUNES TO SEEK INSIGHTS OR ANSWERS TO YOUR QUESTIONS

✳ COMBINE SEVERAL RUNES TO CREATE A SIGIL (SEE P.183)

✳ SELECT RUNES THAT HAVE PROTECTIVE QUALITIES AND USE AROUND YOUR HOME OR SACRED SPACE, OR PLACE THEM ON YOUR ALTAR

FEHU Represents wealth, abundance, and success. Can be used in road opening spells and when you are calling in new opportunities.

URUZ Use this vitality symbol for awakening your personal power, calling in courage, and overcoming obstacles.

THURISAZ This can be used to ward off evil; use in spells that call for protection and strength.

ANSUZ Represents wisdom, communication, inspiration, and insights. Can be used to connect to your spirit guides.

RAIDHO Excellent for use in spells related to travel or moving forwards, making progress, and achieving personal growth.

KENAZ Can be used to gain insight and clarity. Carve on a candle when studying and seeking inspiration.

GEBO Use in spells that need balance and harmony, especially those connected to partnerships and relationships.

WUNJO Brings happiness, harmony, and fulfilment. It's great for spells focused on joy, pleasure, and success.

HAGALAZ Use in spells when change is needed. This is a powerful rune of transformations (a bit like the Tower in tarot, see p.214).

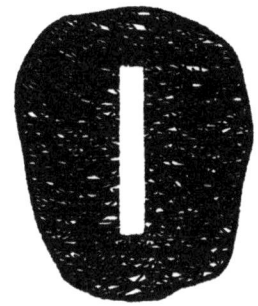

NAUTHIZ Use when resilience and endurance is needed. Great for summoning inner strength and willpower to see you through challenging times.

ISA Use when patience or stillness is required. This is a good one to meditate with when you are looking for clarity and need introspection.

JERA Represents the cycle of reaping and sowing, so connects well to spells involving long-term success. It can be good for spells around new beginnings and setting new intentions.

EIHWAZ Use in protection spells and when you are facing change. It can also represent death and new beginnings.

PERTHRO Use for divination spells, especially when you wish to uncover hidden truths. Can be used in luck spells, too.

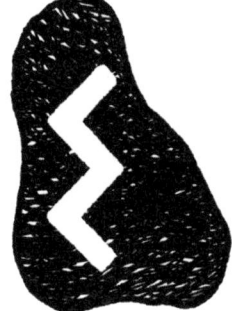

ALGIZ This is one of the most protective runes; use it to ward off evil and for personal safety.

SOWILO Connects to sun energy and represents success, health, and positive vibes. Use it in situations that need vitality and positive energy.

TIWAZ Connects to masculine energy and represents justice, authority, and leadership. This is a go-to when looking for assistance in legal matters.

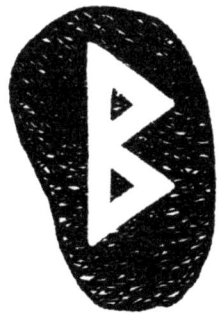

BERKANO Connects to feminine energy and represents new beginnings, fertility, healing, and rebirth. Great to use in healing spells.

EHWAZ Associated with partnerships, progress, and change. Use to enhance teamwork, focusing on mutual support and shared goals.

MANNAZ Helps to bring balance between yourself and others. Use it in spells regarding friendships, collaborations, and community.

LAGUZ Connected to the element of Water, representing intuition and emotions. Use in spells where you want to connect to psychic energy or awaken your imagination.

INGWAZ Connects to fertility and peace, so use in spells looking to create abundance, growth, and peace.

DAGAZ Meaning "dawn", this brings hope and promises transformations; use in spells for new beginnings and personal breakthroughs, where courage is required.

OTHALA Connects to the home, stability, and family heritage; use in spells when needing to feel safe and supported. This is also a good one when wanting to connect to your ancestors.

SIGILS

Sigils are symbols that carry a more personal energy or meaning, and this uniqueness means they can be potent ingredients in your spellwork, particularly for manifesting a desired outcome. They serve as visual representations of whatever you wish to manifest, and are tools for channelling your energy.

The word "sigil" originally comes from the Latin *sigillum*, translating as "seal" or "signet", which connects to "sign". These symbols were used during medieval times as a secret coded alphabet carrying symbolic meanings that represented spirits, angels, or even demonic energy that people wanted to summon. In the late 19th century, magical practitioners started to experiment and decode the symbols, creating various techniques to start using them.

Creating and working with sigils has evolved over time. While you might look up the meaning of an established sigil and choose to incorporate it into your spellwork, today's witches mostly focus on using sigils as self-created tools for channelling our personal energy. In modern witchcraft, sigils are a bridge between your subconscious inner world and the physical realm. Their energy can help us connect to our subconscious, with the belief that something that existed in our imagination can be made physical, reminding us that we have the power to transform our intentions into reality.

There are two schools of thought when it comes to using sigils: one is that you create it, burn it, and trust that it is out in the Universe; the other is that you connect to it, and it becomes a little magical friend that you can call in on at any time. There is no right or wrong, but I will give you some options for how you can use your sigils. Whatever approach you choose, the most important thing is that you must trust in your sigil in order for it to work.

MAKE YOUR OWN SIGIL

Sigils can be used as supercharging ingredients in spells, just like any other symbol we have looked at so far. However, they can also be powerful on their own. When you make a sigil, you turn the letters from a personal affirmation into a symbol, allowing you to bring something from your inner world into the physical realm. I'll now show you two different ways to create a personal sigil, and how you can help to bring their meaning into your life.

METHOD ONE

1. Think of the energy that you would like to call in.

2. Write out your mission statement or an affirmation. Write it in the past tense, as though you already have it, or it has already happened. For example: "I am focused."

3. Keep it simple – there is no need to overcomplicate your statement or affirmation, as you want it to be as clear as possible. Always focus on a single affirmation for each sigil that you make.

4. After writing your affirmation, remove the vowels, then remove any repeat letters.

5. Now place the remaining letters on the page and start getting creative with them. You may turn the letters upside down or sideways, or combine letters, lose curves, or add dots. You can also add any other shapes or simple drawings that resonate and connect to your intention.

6. As you continue to arrange these letters, repeat the affirmation in your head or say it out loud. Visualize it coming to fruition and feel the energy guide your hand.

7. Once you are happy with your sigil, spend some time connecting to it. You may want to leave it for just 10 minutes, or leave it overnight and come back to it.

8. When you look at your sigil, check in with yourself and see if it awakens the energy of your affirmation. Does it make you feel excited about the outcome?

I AM FOCUSED

I AM FOCUSED

M F C S D

METHOD TWO

|||||||||||||||||||||||||||||||||||||||||||||||||||||

1. Repeat steps 1–4 as indicated on the previous page.

2. Create a chart and give each of your letters a number.

3. Place the numbers in a circle. To choose in which order to place the numbers, try closing your eyes and connect to your higher self, then write the numbers down in the order they come to you; or you might already have a particular order that you connect to in mind.

4. When you've placed them in a circle, draw lines to connect the numbers sequentially in order to create your sigil.

I AM FOCUSED

I ~~A~~M F~~O~~C~~U~~S~~E~~D

M F C S D

1	2	3	4	5	6	7	8	9
A	B	C	D	E	F	G	H	I
J	K	L	M	N	O	P	Q	R
S	T	U	V	W	X	Y	Z	

M F C S D
4 6 3 1 4

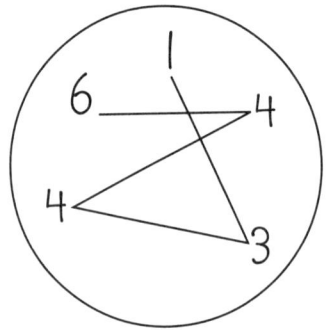
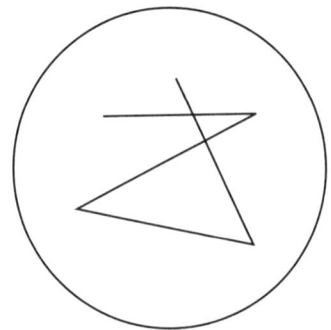

RELEASING YOUR SIGIL

When you feel a connection with the symbol that you have created, you will be ready for the next phase – releasing it into the Universe. There is no right or wrong way to do this, the most important thing is to do what feels right for you.

IMMEDIATE RELEASE

This way involves releasing your sigil into the world immediately, and you don't need to spend any time connecting to it first. Simply draw it on a piece of paper and burn it.

For an extra layer of magic, use a coloured paper that corresponds with your intention, or write it with coloured ink that aligns with your desired outcome (see p.111–113). Instead of burning it on paper, you may want to write your sigil on a bay leaf and burn it. You might choose to burn your sigil in the direction that connects to your intention (see p.31).

FORMING A PHYSICAL CONNECTION

You may choose this method if you have created a sigil that you wish to use regularly, or if you want to carve this sigil into a candle. There are many ways to connect physically with your sigil, but the key is to get yourself into an altered state of consciousness. This could be through methods like meditation, deep breathing, emotional release techniques, or summoning sexual energy.

Take the time to focus on the sigil and what it means to you, draw it on a bay leaf, and then choose how you wish to move into an altered state. When you have reached this point, anoint your sigil with your bodily fluids to bless it: this might be saliva, tears, or sweat. Once the sigil is anointed, burn it to release its energy into the Universe. In doing so, you can manifest the affirmation you created and bring it into your life.

CHAPTER
EIGHT

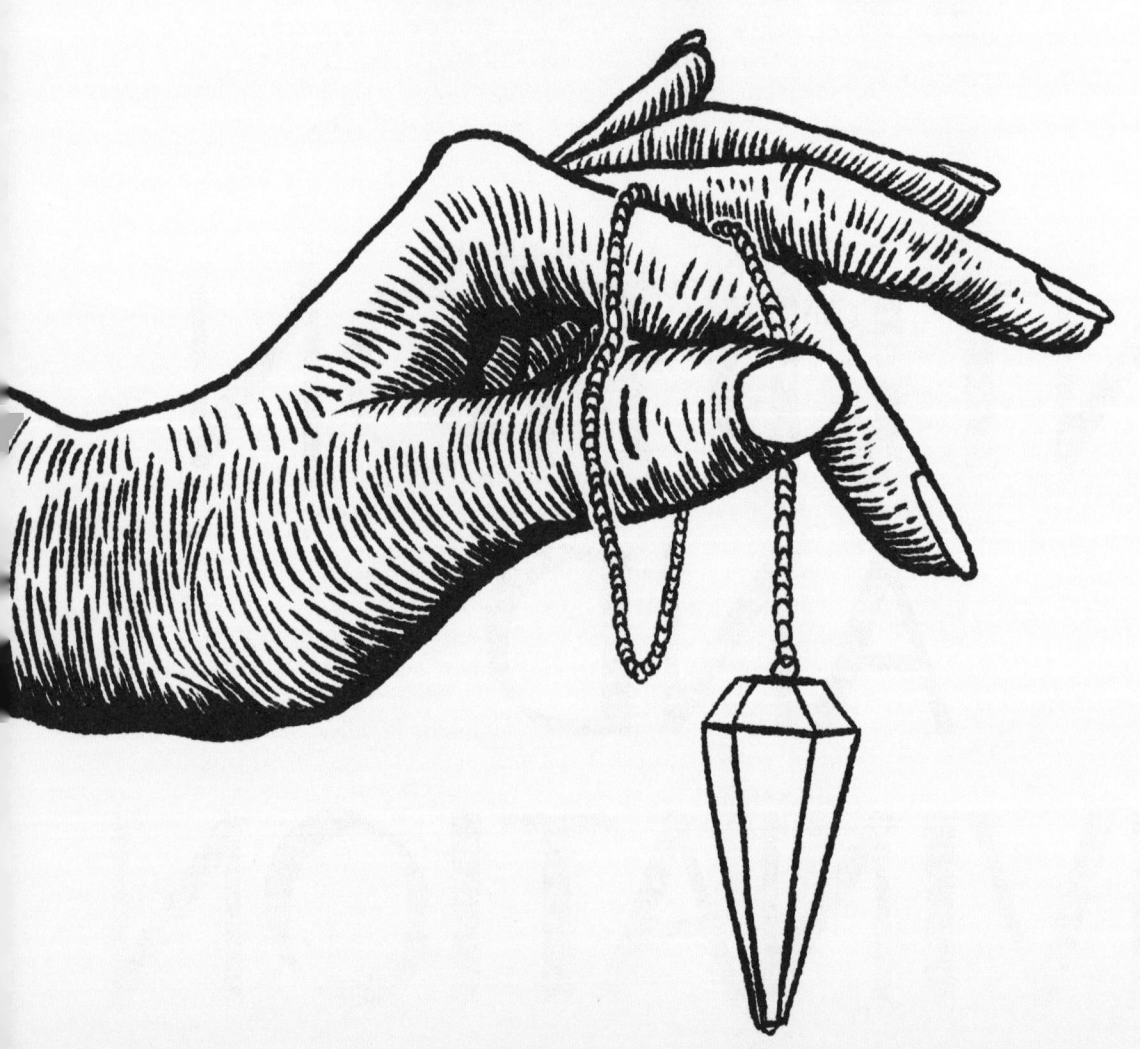

INTUITION
AND
DIVINATION

A WITCH'S INTUITION

Intuition is our sixth sense; it exists within each of us, a deep, innate way to connect with energies and insights that are beyond ordinary perception. Like divination (see p.200), it can guide our decision making, but uniquely intuition draws on cues we find within ourselves, without the use of additional objects. I like to think of intuition as "insourcing" and divination as "outsourcing".

We often experience our intuition as a gut feeling that appears out of nowhere: a mental image, a voice, a physical sensation, or a sudden knowing. They are messages that visit us from within the mind, glimmers from our subconscious – our own energy's response to the energy that is around us.

Learning to trust your intuition takes practice, but every one of us has access to it. This is a skill that witches can develop and work with; by incorporating our third eye into our craft, we can unlock our higher consciousness and develop a stronger connection between head and heart.

The more you practise intuition, the easier it will become to decode the messages and signs and get to know the difference between a genuine intuitive feeling and reactions that may be rooted in fear or self-limiting beliefs.

This is why it is important to feel calm and grounded when seeking intuitive guidance; if you are busy in your thoughts or are feeling stressed, your intuition can play tricks on you. When your nervous system is relaxed and your mind is clear, you can trust that your intuitive thoughts are not being influenced by anxiety or fear. Before embarking on any intuition magic, ground yourself with a breathwork exercise.

START HERE

Before you embark on any form of intuition or divination, take a moment to relax your nervous system using breathwork. Gently breathe all the way in through your nose and then purse your lips and slowly release the breath out of your mouth. Repeat this a minimum of five times to get you in the zone, ready to read the energy you are receiving.

TUNING IN TO YOURSELF

Intuition is, at its heart, the act of trusting yourself: of asking yourself a question and really listening to the answer, without being swayed by any ingrained, conditioned beliefs that may be blocking you or concerns that your intuitive interpretations are being influenced by desired outcomes.

To avoid confusion, remind yourself that your intuitive voice is your higher self. Trust that your higher self would never operate from a place of ego; higher-self energy would only ever guide you towards what is best for you. This higher self might also be a future version of your current self, but older and wiser.

While there are tools that you can use (see pp.191–193) and actions you can take (see pp.194–199) to strengthen your intuition, the most basic intuitive act is to be self-aware. I recommend keeping a record of times when you trusted your intuition and were glad you did, as well as moments when you ignored a gut feeling or turned a blind eye to a red flag and then regretted it. When you find yourself struggling to trust your intuition, re-read and reflect on past experiences where your intuition guided you and connect with that inner sense of knowing.

It really is a super power to be able to tune in and trust your intuition in witchcraft. You can use intuition to:

✳ **SELECT THE RIGHT SPELL TO USE, OR TAILOR SPELLS TO SUIT YOUR PERSONAL NEEDS OR CURRENT ENERGY**

✳ **GUIDE YOU TO SELECT INGREDIENTS THAT RESONATE MOST WITH YOUR ENERGY OR INTENTION**

✳ **DETERMINE WHEN THE TIME IS RIGHT TO DO SOMETHING**

✳ **ASSIST IN INTERPRETING MESSAGES IN READINGS, SUCH AS WHEN USING TAROT CARDS**

✳ **CONNECT WITH SPIRITS, DEITIES, OR ELEMENTAL FORCES**

✳ **RECOGNIZE AND UNDERSTAND SIGNS FROM THE UNIVERSE**

The more you practise working with your intuition, the deeper and stronger your connection will become. On the following pages you will find ways to hone your intuitive skills and, in doing so, elevate your magical practice.

BUILD YOUR PRACTICE

No matter what kind of witch you are or want to be, intuition is a key skill that is worth developing at every stage of your practice. How you engage with intuition is up to you:

Use intuitive tools to amplify your magic (see p.191)

Strengthen your intuition with an emotional connection (see p.194–195)

Access your intuition through bodily actions (see p.196–199)

INTUITIVE TOOLS

Amplify your intuitive magic by using one of these tools to heighten your psychic abilities and encourage deeper meditative states. They can also aid divination (see pp.200–203).

THIRD EYE OIL

|||||||||||||||||||||||||||||||||||||||||||||||||

The "third eye" is located in the centre of the forehead just above the space between the eyebrows. It's believed to be the seat of intuition and spiritual awareness. To help you attune to high levels of perception, anoint your third eye with this potion before any ritual calling for insight or clarity.

You will need

* ✳ **30 ML (2 TBSP) ALMOND OIL (OR A CARRIER OIL OF YOUR CHOICE)**
* ✳ **ESSENTIAL OILS: 5 DROPS EACH OF ROSE, JASMINE, AND SANDALWOOD**

1. Prepare your mix by blending the oils together. Find a quiet space where you won't be disturbed.

2. Before applying the oil, first set your intention by speaking aloud:

> ### "I ALIGN MYSELF WITH CLARITY AND INTUITION"

3. Gently apply the oil directly over the third eye area. Use a circular motion to massage it in lightly, focusing on the sensation and feeling the energy flowing into the area.

INTUITION INCENSE

||||||||||||||||||||||||||||||

Burn this incense to help awaken your inner sight and tap into inner wisdom, clearing the way to accessing intuitive insights.

You will need

* ✳ **4 BAY LEAVES**
* ✳ **PEN**
* ✳ **2 PINCHES OF SAGE**
* ✳ **PESTLE AND MORTAR**
* ✳ **CHARCOAL DISC AND HEAT-PROOF DISH**

1. Draw an eye on each of the bay leaves; bay leaves are associated with psychic abilities and the eye represents greater awareness and protection.

2. Blend the leaves and sage and burn on a charcoal disc (see p.123).

3. As the incense burns, close your eyes and breathe deeply. Focusing on the scent can help calm your mind, enabling deeper meditation.

VISIONS TEA

|||||||||||||

Drink this tea before bed and ask for messages in your dreams, or before undertaking any intuitive spellwork. Drink it with intention, and be ready to trust the visions that come.

You will need

✳ **2 TBSP OF FRESH MINT**

✳ **1 SPRIG OF ROSEMARY**

✳ **2 TBSP OF MUGWORT**

✳ **PESTLE AND MORTAR**

✳ **JAR TO STORE YOUR TEA**

1. Blend the herbs together in the pestle and mortar. Mugwort is associated with heightened perception and vivid dreams, with mint and rosemary bringing mental clarity (see pp.146 and 148).

2. Add a heaped teaspoon to a cup of boiled water and allow it to infuse for 5–10 minutes.

3. Sip the tea in a quiet, calm place. As you drink it, keep in mind the specific guidance that you are seeking.

STRENGTHENING YOUR INTUITION

Intuition can be likened to a muscle, needing regular use in order to develop it fully. The techniques here will allow you to strengthen your connection with your own intuition.

When you find the noise of your analytical mind a little too loud to think clearly or trust your intuitive messages, you can tap into the wisdom of your body. When you learn to listen, you may notice physical reactions: you might feel an instant calm or have a gut feeling, experience a tightening of the chest, a headache, or even – in extreme cases – break out in hives.

EMOTIONAL MESSAGING

||||||||||||||||||||||||||||||||||||||||||||||

This is a great exercise for learning how to connect to your intuition by allowing your feelings to subconsciously guide your actions. You will write out emotive statements and then practise connecting to their energy by seeing if you can identify them without looking.

1. Write out on five separate pieces of paper:

* **ONE THING THAT YOU ARE PROUD OF**

* **SOMETHING IN YOUR LIFE THAT YOU WANT TO BANISH OR RELEASE**

* **SOMETHING THAT YOU LOVE UNCONDITIONALLY**

* **A TIME IN YOUR LIFE WHEN YOU FELT PURE JOY**

* **SOMETHING THAT NEEDS HEALING**

2. Take some time to connect to each of the feelings you've written on the cards. You can do this by holding the paper either close to your heart, up to your third eye, in your hands, or all three – each time connecting to the energy of what is written.

3. Now place all of the pieces of paper face down. Close your eyes and move them around so that you don't know which ones are which.

4. Again with your eyes closed, hover your hands over the pieces of paper. Concentrate on one of the messages that you have written and allow yourself to tune in to the energy of that message.

5. Allow your hands to move around without consciously directing them. When it feels right to stop, open your eyes and turn over the piece of paper beneath them to see if you have been drawn to the correct energy.

THE O METHOD

||||||||||||||||||||||||||||||||||

This technique enables you to use your body's instinctive reactions to give you intuitive answers to any questions you my have. These might be big things you're looking for guidance on – for example, is it the right time to relocate to a new city – or small things, like whether to accept an invitation to go on a date.

1. Create an O shape with your fingers. To do this, touch the tip of your thumb with the tip of your index finger.

2. Place the index finger from your other hand inside the O shape.

3. Ask a question that has a firm "yes" answer, and as you do this try to break the O shape with your index finger.

4. For "yes" you will find that the circle will not break, and your fingers will remain tightly pressed together.

5. For "no" answers the O shape should break, and your index finger will break the circle.

6. Again, practise by asking yes-or-no questions that you are certain of first to get familiar with the method.

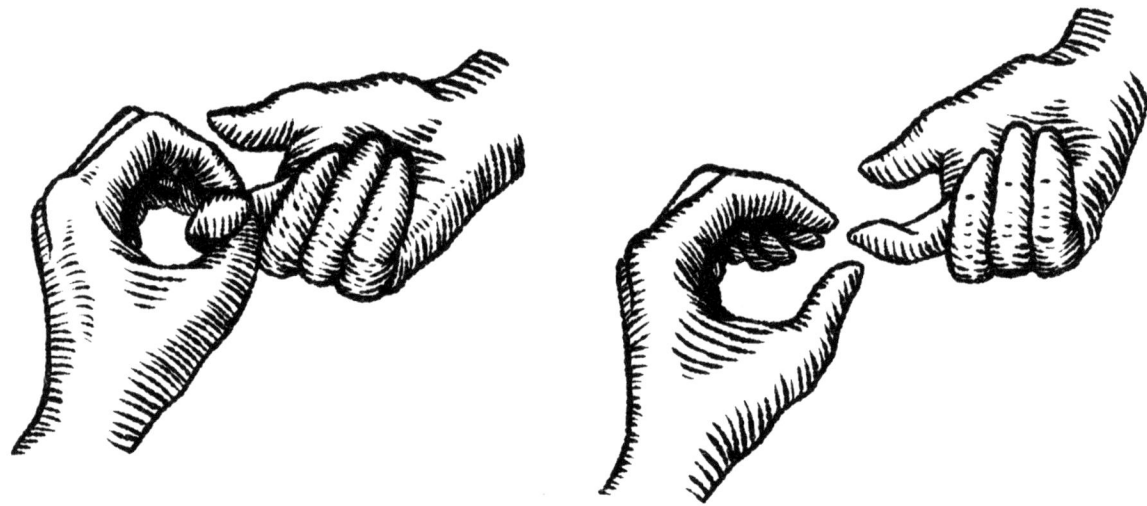

THE SWAY METHOD

||||||||||||||||||||||||||||||||||

This is a way to tune in to your intuition by turning yourself into a human pendulum, as you ask your body to respond to yes-or-no questions.

1. Start by taking some slow, deep breaths. Stand with your feet firmly on the ground, hip-width apart, your knees bent, and your arms relaxed by your sides.

2. Close your eyes. Take another couple of deep breaths.

3. Start by asking a question that you know the answer to, such as: "Is my name [...]?"

4. Pay attention to how your body naturally sways. Usually, for a "yes" answer your body will sway forwards, and for a "no" answer your body will sway backwards.

5. Ask a few more questions that you know the answers to, to check that you are in tune with your body.

6. Now, ask any questions that you want to know the answers to and see how your body responds.

7. Remember to stay relaxed through this process, and be sure that the swaying is happening naturally. If you find your body moving from side to side instead of back and forth, this can indicate that your body is unsure or that the answer to your question is neutral.

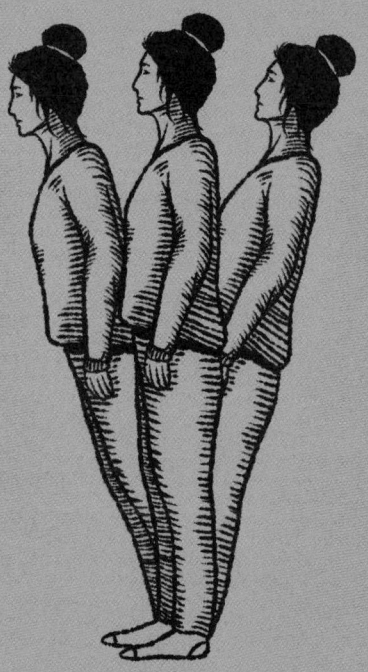

THE FULL BODY "YES"

|||||||||||||||||||||||||||||||||||||||||

When you are insourcing and you are unsure over a decision that needs to be made, try using the following technique.

1. Begin by taking slow and gentle deep breaths.

2. Think of the decision or choice you're considering. Phrase it as a yes-or-no question: for example:

"IS THIS CAREER MOVE RIGHT FOR ME?" "SHOULD I GO TO THIS EVENT?"

3. Place both hands on your stomach; notice the feeling; then place both hands on your heart and notice the feeling; and then on your third eye, again noticing the feeling.

4. We will often feel a sense of calm, openness, and lightness if our body is telling us yes, this is the right thing to do or course of action to pursue; our body can respond with total resistance if this is something that is wrong for us, with feelings of tension, heaviness, and dread.

WRITING WITH YOUR NON-DOMINANT HAND

This can be a powerful way to connect to your subconscious and intuition because it requires extra focus and bypasses the usual automatic patterns of your dominant hand. Using this practice can help to calm down and quiet the analytical mind, allowing for intuitive thoughts and answers that might not come through when you are writing with your dominant hand.

1. Begin by taking slow and gentle deep breaths.

2. Take the pen in your non-dominant hand and begin to write intuitively; try not to look down at the paper, and just let the writing flow.

3. If words don't come, think of a question or think about the situation you are seeking intuitive answers on and just allow yourself to draw, doodle, and make shapes.

4. When you have finished, look at what you have written or the shapes you have drawn from different angles and see if any of the words or images resonate.

DIVINATION

While intuition is a deeply personal experience where we connect to our inner guidance, divination involves working with physical tools to gain insights. If you have an intuitive insight that feels confusing, divination can help bring clarity, calling in signs from the Universe to confirm your sense of the message.

The practice of divination dates back thousands of years across many ancient civilizations. The Mesopotamians, Egyptians, and Chinese used it to seek guidance from gods and spirits when making important decisions, and in medieval Europe witches continued this tradition, invoking assistance from the mystical realms.

The word "divination" suggests communication with the divine; although it doesn't require a particular spiritual belief or especially heightened intuitive skills, you will have a better connection with divination tools if you have a good intuition (see p.188). We can "outsource" using various tools, including pendulums and scrying (pp.202–203), as well as tarot cards (Chapter 9), runes (pp.176–181), and numerology (pp.96–109). These can all connect you to energies beyond yourself, allowing you to access insights from surrounding energies and the spirit realms.

In witchcraft, divination is not about predicting the future with absolute certainty; it's about exploring possible outcomes, gaining clarity, and providing guidance in your spellwork. It is based on the principle that everything is connected, and that by reading meaning into symbols and patterns we can gain insights into deeper truths.

Divination can assist you in your magical practice in many ways: for example, when using tarot cards, don't just pick a card and immediately look up its meaning. Instead, observe the imagery of the card, feel the energy of the card, and notice any intuitive thoughts that pop into your head; journal how the card makes you feel and the instant message you divined when you looked at it.

CLEAR THE ENERGY

It is important to begin with a clean slate and clear away any lingering or distracting energy. You can do this with smoke cleansing (see p.23), or sound cleansing by ringing a bell or clapping your hands. You may want to use candles, incense, or crystals to enhance energy, and always cleanse your tools with smoke before using them in any ritual.

DIVINING TECHNIQUES

Before embarking on any form of divination, first set your intention: are you looking for guidance, clarity, or self-reflection? Clearly define what you seek to understand, and ensure that you are in a place that feels calm, focused, and protected.

USING A PENDULUM

Pendulums are great for magic on the move as they are small and can easily fit in your pocket or bag. They help you make decisions, reading energy and guiding your intuitive thoughts. You can buy elaborate pendulums, but all you really need is a simple weighted string. Tools like these act as shortcuts to your intuition; if they give a response that doesn't sit right, then that can reveal what it is you truly want. It's similar to flipping a coin and realizing your decision is already made while the coin is still in the air.

You will need

✳ **CHAIN OR STRING WITH A SMALL WEIGHT ATTACHED (SEE BELOW)**

1. Start by holding the chain or string between your thumb and forefinger, allowing the weight at the end to hang down freely.

2. To initially connect to your pendulum, ask it questions that have firm yes-or-no answers, so that you can understand its specific movements.

3. Now breathe deeply to calm yourself, then ask the pendulum a simple question (which demands a yes-or-no answer) that you want guidance with. Observe how it swings – often a back-and-forth motion indicates "no", while a circular movement may mean "yes".

SCRYING

Scrying involves gazing into a reflective surface such as a crystal ball, mirror, or the ultimate scrying tool, water. Your mind is allowed to relax and symbols, messages, and impressions can arise and pop into your subconscious. These can be interpreted based on personal or traditional symbolism. If you don't happen to have a crystal ball or a peaceful lake to hand, don't worry! Scrying with candlewax formations is a powerful way to tune in to scrying energy for intuitive guidance.

You will need

* **1 PILLAR CANDLE (BLACK OR WHITE WORK BEST)**
* **A BOWL OF COLD WATER**

1. Hold the candle in your hands and think of a specific question that you want guidance with.

2. Light the candle and hold it over the water; focus on the flame and continue to ask the candle your question.

3. When you feel the time is right, start to tip the melted wax from the candle into the water. You may choose to drip a few drops or to let it flow until it feels right.

4. Spend some time watching the patterns of the wax form in the water.

5. Gaze at the wax patterns and allow yourself to get lost in them; note down whatever comes to mind. Maybe you can see specific messages or symbols (see pp.170–175).

6. Allow yourself to tune into what these images mean to you personally. Remember to remain open-minded and allow your subconscious to guide your interpretations – never force meanings.

CHAPTER NINE

THE
TAROT

USING THE TAROT

The mystical guidance of the Tarot has been called upon for centuries. The symbolism and imagery of the cards offer opportunity for self-reflection, advice on how to navigate challenges, insights into personal growth, and clarity through confusing times.

Beyond readings that can provide powerful guidance, tarot cards can also be used as potent energetic tools in spellwork and rituals. As with plants and crystals, each card possesses its own unique magical frequency. As witches, we can use the cards in rituals to represent ourselves, or channel their energies to enhance our magical practice.

Tarot is essential learning for new witches, because working with tarot cards will strengthen your intuition, allowing you to trust in your inner voice, and deepen your spiritual skills. What's special about tarot cards is that you can use them on your own, or you can use them to strengthen bonds and build connections with others. They can be both personal and communal. As well as offering profound insights, they can also ignite powerful discussions. No witch's toolkit is complete without a beautiful deck of tarot cards.

The tarot deck contains 78 cards, each with its own unique symbolism, representing different aspects of life, archetypes, and spiritual journeys. The cards are split into two sections: the major arcana and the minor arcana. Each of the cards holds its own energy, and the magic comes from the fact that you are picking random cards from the deck, but there is a synchronicity that will draw you to choose cards related to the answers you are seeking. Before we get into how tarot cards can be used in readings and spellcraft, we're going to take a look at the cards themselves and unlock some of their hidden symbolic meanings.

START HERE

If you haven't already, I recommend starting your journey in tarot by visiting an experienced practitioner for a reading. This will help you understand how it works in practice. It will also, hopefully, spark an interest in the majestic cards, and allow you to see how you can use their wisdom in your own life.

THE DECK

THE MAJOR ARCANA

The 22 cards of the major arcana represent important life events and lessons, spiritual growth, and can also impart specific messages (see pp.208–215):

✳ **THE FOOL**
✳ **THE MAGICIAN**
✳ **THE HIGH PRIESTESS**
✳ **THE EMPRESS**
✳ **THE EMPEROR**
✳ **THE HIEROPHANT**
✳ **THE LOVERS**
✳ **THE CHARIOT**
✳ **STRENGTH**
✳ **THE HERMIT**
✳ **WHEEL OF FORTUNE**
✳ **JUSTICE**
✳ **THE HANGED MAN**
✳ **DEATH**
✳ **TEMPERANCE**
✳ **THE DEVIL**
✳ **THE TOWER**
✳ **THE STAR**
✳ **THE MOON**
✳ **THE SUN**
✳ **JUDGEMENT**
✳ **THE WORLD**

SUITS OF THE MINOR ARCANA

The 56 cards comprising the minor arcana are organized into four suits. They reflect daily experiences and emotions. As well as each card having its own meaning, the suits all carry their own powers collectively, too (see pp.216–223).

✳ **WANDS**
✳ **PENTACLES**
✳ **CUPS**
✳ **SWORDS**

Each of these suits comprises 14 cards – a run of cards from ace to ten followed by four court cards: Page, Knight, Queen, and King.

COURT CARDS

The court cards are found in each suit of the minor arcana. In a reading, they can represent people, personality traits, or energies, as follows:

✳ **PAGES:** younger people; students; new beginnings; learning and exploration; creativity; opportunity; growth mindset.

✳ **KNIGHTS:** dynamic; adventurous; romantic; youthful energy; courage; adventure; impulsiveness; curiosity; determination.

✳ **QUEENS:** nurturing energy; inner strength; fertility; empathy; supportive; truthful; concerned with balance and harmony.

✳ **KINGS:** authority figures; trusted leaders; wisdom, responsibility; active, outwards-directed energy; safeguarding; integrity.

TAROT MEANINGS

Now, let's explore what each individual card means. Alongside your own intuition, learning how to interpret tarot cards will allow you to perform insightful readings for yourself and others. Of course, there's a lot to learn, and you can refer back to these pages whenever you need to. The more you use your tarot cards, the more their unique, powerful meanings will sink in.

While tarot cards are connected with mysticism these days, it wasn't always this way. They were first used as playing cards in 15th-century Italy, but in the 18th century, European mystics began interpreting the cards as symbolic representations of universal truths, and by the 19th century, secret societies who were experimenting with the occult and ritual magic turned to tarot cards for guidance and self-reflection.

Every card in the tarot deck is rich in symbolic meanings and is connected to one of the four classical elements: Earth, Air, Fire, and Water. Each element holds a specific type of energy:

* **EARTH REPRESENTS PROTECTION; IT'S STABLE, MATERIAL, AND PHYSICAL**

* **AIR REPRESENTS BALANCE; IT'S THOUGHTFUL, COMMUNICATIVE, AND INTELLIGENT**

* **FIRE REPRESENTS STRENGTH; IT'S PASSIONATE, ACTIVE, AND ALL CONSUMING**

* **WATER REPRESENTS HARMONY; IT'S DEEP, FLOWING, AND HAS REFLECTIVE QUALITIES**

Understanding these elemental correspondences (see pp.114–115) can deepen your connection to the cards and the energy that they hold, allowing you to interpret them with greater intuition.

THE MAJOR ARCANA

THE FOOL

|||||||||||||||||||||||||||||||||||||

ELEMENT: Air

New beginnings, representing innocence, spontaneity, and freedom. Use in spellwork to inspire fresh starts and provide courage to take a leap of faith.

THE MAGICIAN

|||||||||||||||||||||||||||||||||||||

ELEMENT: Air

Represents manifestation and resourcefulness. Use in spells when calling in your personal power. Can also be used for manifesting all that you desire.

HIGH PRIESTESS

|||||||||||||||||||||||||||||||||||||

ELEMENT: Water

Can guide you to connect to your inner wisdom and awaken intuition. In a spell, it can enhance your psychic abilities and guide you to the truth.

THE EMPRESS

|||||||||||||||||||||||||||||||||||||

ELEMENT: Earth

Fertility and abundance. Use in spells to attract prosperity and nurture growth. An Empress spell might involve a ceremony to enhance creativity and manifest abundance in all areas of your life.

THE EMPEROR

|||||||||||||||||||||||||||||||||

ELEMENT: Fire

Signifies authority and stability in your life. It might refer to a person in your life, like a boss or father figure, or it could signify that you need to step into a leadership role yourself. Call in the energy of this card to create order, be assertive and decisive, or summon personal power.

THE HIEROPHANT

|||||||||||||||||||||||||||||||||||||||

ELEMENT: Earth

Offers spiritual guidance and can provide a deeper understanding of your spiritual journey. In a spell, you can use the Hierophant to connect to wisdom within and seek spiritual support.

THE LOVERS

|||||||||||||||||||||||||||||||||

ELEMENT: Air

The energetic vibrations of this card offer love and harmony. Use the Lovers card in a spell to strengthen your romantic relationships, deepen loving connections, and awaken desire.

THE CHARIOT

||||||||||||||||||||||||||||||||||||||||||

ELEMENT: Water

Represents determination and victory, and used in a spell it can summon the willpower to succeed. Use the Chariot card to help you focus and break through obstacles and anything that might be blocking your path to success.

STRENGTH

||||||||||||||||||||||||||||||||||||||||||

ELEMENT: Fire

This card signifies courage and resilience. It is associated with mastering inner challenges and emotions with the strength of willpower, patience, and self-control. Use in a spell to call in strength and bravery and to overcome self-doubt.

THE HERMIT

||||||||||||||||||||||||||||||||||||||||||

ELEMENT: Earth

Represents the need for solitude, and to recharge and go deep within for self-discovery. Use this card when soul searching or seeking the truth. Use in spells when you are seeking clarity and a deeper understanding of your purpose and path in life.

WHEEL OF FORTUNE

|||||||||||||||||||||||||||||||||||

ELEMENT: Fire

Represents the cyclical nature of life, destiny, and change, bringing positive changes and luck. Use in spellwork when you wish to enter a new cycle and invite positive changes into your life.

JUSTICE

|||||||||||||||||||||||||

ELEMENT: Air

Denotes fairness, truth, and the consequences of your actions. The energy of this card can be called upon to bring balance and resolve disputes. Use when creating spells around calling in fairness or seeking positive outcomes in legal cases.

THE HANGED MAN

||||||||||||||||||||||||||||||||||||||

ELEMENT: Water

A deeply introspective card that represents surrender, new perspectives, and spiritual transformation. In spellwork it can encourage letting go and allowing you to see things differently. You might use this card in a ritual to release control and gain insights.

DEATH
||||||||||||||||||||||

ELEMENT: Water

Conversely, this is not a doom-laden card, but represents transformations, endings, and new beginnings. In a spell, it can be used to bring changes and inspire a rebirth. Create banishing spells with this card or spells to release the old and welcome in the new.

TEMPERANCE
||||||||||||||||||||||||||||||||||||

ELEMENT: Fire

Temperance invites balance, harmony, and moderation. It often signifies the need to find the middle ground to achieve a state of equilibrium. Its vibration in your magical practice can bring peace to relationship spells and assist with healing and meditation.

THE DEVIL
||||||||||||||||||||||||||||||||

ELEMENT: Earth

Represents temptation or harmful behaviour. Use the energy of this card to help you reclaim your power and break free of whatever is not serving you, such as addictions or any other unhealthy attachments.

THE TOWER

ǀǀǀǀǀǀǀǀǀǀǀǀǀǀǀǀǀǀǀǀǀǀǀǀǀǀǀǀǀǀǀǀǀ

ELEMENT: Fire

One of the most powerful cards, this represents upheaval, revelations, and the breaking down of established structures. You can embrace the energy of this card to call in changes and release what no longer serves you, and to give stagnant energy a really good shake-up.

THE STAR

ǀǀǀǀǀǀǀǀǀǀǀǀǀǀǀǀǀǀǀǀǀǀǀǀǀǀǀǀǀǀǀǀǀ

ELEMENT: Air

A deeply positive card bringing inspiration, spiritual guidance, hope, and healing. In readings, it often appears after a period of turmoil. Use the magic of this card to tune in to dreams, find inspiration, and connect to your spirituality.

THE MOON

ǀǀǀǀǀǀǀǀǀǀǀǀǀǀǀǀǀǀǀǀǀǀǀǀǀǀǀǀǀǀǀǀǀ

ELEMENT: Water

Associated with mystery and the subconscious. It can indicate confusion or uncertainty, and may be directing you to confront aspects of yourself, offering a chance to unveil hidden truths. Use this card in your spellwork to connect to the subconscious and your intuition.

THE SUN
||||||||||||||||||||||||

JUDGEMENT
||||||||||||||||||||||||||||||||||||

THE WORLD
||||||||||||||||||||||||||||||||||||||||

ELEMENT: Fire

An uplifting card that radiates positivity and represents the triumph of light over darkness. Signifies success, abundance, and vitality. In a spell, it can attract happiness and good fortune. Use this card in your spellwork to call in gratitude, celebrate achievements, and radiate positive vibrations.

ELEMENT: Fire

This card is all about reflection and rebirth. It might represent a pivotal moment – a period of awakening and insight, or a time of reckoning, where you are being called upon to face your past and decide how to move forward. Use it in spells to assist with important decisions and in road opening spells.

ELEMENT: Earth

The final card in the major arcana represents completion, fulfilment, and achieving goals. Use it in a ritual to celebrate accomplishments, such as a ceremony to honour the end of a journey and welcome in expansive new beginnings.

CARDS IN THE MINOR ARCANA

We're now going to dive in to the cards in the rest of the tarot deck. As we discovered on p.207, the minor arcana is divided into four different suits: wands, pentacles, cups, and swords.

Each suit follows a similar structure to traditional sets of playing cards (hearts, spades, clubs, and diamonds), complete with an ace and court cards. Each suit also corresponds to an element, along with the astrological signs for that element: these connections can add extra nuance and depth to your readings. Here's a breakdown for each suit, and the cards that exist within them.

WANDS

||||||||||||||||||||||||||||||||

ELEMENT: Fire

ASTROLOGICAL SIGNS:
Aries, Leo, Sagittarius

MAGIC AND SPELLWORK:
Motivation, action, passion, excitement, raising energy, inspiration, goals

ACE Brings new beginnings and creative energy, igniting inspiration and motivation. Use this card in a ritual to spark ideas for a new project or new creative endeavours.

TWO Represents planning and making decisions, useful for invoking direction and clarity for future ventures and ideas. Use in spellwork to call in luck when taking a chance, for road opening spells, and intentions for exploring new opportunities.

THREE Associated with growth, exploration, and spreading your wings. This card is good for promotion at work spells, or to call in energy for taking on a new venture.

FOUR Celebrates harmony and can enhance joy and stability in the home. Use this card when you wish to create peace or need the support of others, and in spells to bless a new home or celebrate a milestone.

FIVE Represents conflict and competition. In a spell, it can help resolve disputes and find solutions. Use this card to bring clarity and resolution to any challenging situation.

SIX Signifies victory and recognition. Use this card in a spell to boost your confidence and self-assurance and in rituals to attract success and encourage self-belief.

SEVEN Represents awaking your inner personal power. Use in spells to create boundaries, for protection, or to invoke feelings of determination.

EIGHT Helps speed up progress and assists with communication. Use it to help with taking action, to bring momentum to life events, or to add a little bit of speed to spells. This card is helpful during Mercury retrogrades (see p.272).

NINE Represents resilience and stamina. In a spell, it can boost endurance and perseverance. Use when needing to call in strength through challenging periods and situations.

TEN Signifies burdens and responsibilities. In a spell, it can help manage and lighten loads. Use in spellwork and rituals to release stress, assist with closure, or bring energy for completion and acceptance.

PAGE Represents free-spirit vibes. Use when you need to summon enthusiasm or to inspire curiosity and adventure when feeling a little lacklustre.

KNIGHT Signifies passion and action. It can be used to call in courage to complete goals, help with procrastination, or discover new and uncharted territory.

QUEEN Represents confidence and independence. Use in a spell to boost self-esteem and to awaken your personal power.

KING All about leadership and vision and can be used to enhance authority and ambition. Use in spells to take charge when you are seeking your visions and goals.

PENTACLES

ㅤㅤㅤㅤㅤㅤ

ELEMENT: Earth

ASTROLOGICAL SIGNS:
Taurus, Virgo, Capricorn

MAGIC AND SPELLWORK:
Abundance, stability, health, manifestation, practical matters, financial prosperity, grounding energy, opportunities

ACE Symbolizes new financial opportunities and abundance. In a spell, it can attract wealth and stability. Use it to set intentions for new projects, when venturing into business opportunities, and for fresh starts.

TWO Represents balance and adaptability. Used in spells to manage responsibilities and find harmony around obligations, or when welcoming changes into your life.

THREE Signifies collaboration and skill and can be used to help with building team morale or to call for your hard work to be recognized. Use in rituals to improve cooperative projects and enhance teamwork.

FOUR Represents security and control. This card's energy can be used to call in financial stability and protect your personal prosperity. Used in spells it can support you through hard financial times and assist with calling in opportunities and stability.

FIVE Signifies hardship and recovery and can bring a healing energy to recover from financial or material loss. Use this card in a ritual to help with financial worries.

SIX Is all about energy exchange and balance, and can be used to promote giving and receiving. Use in gratitude magic or spells that call for support from others. It's also a great card to use if you are about to start a cooperative business venture, to bless the endeavour with fairness.

SEVEN Denotes patience in assessing situations and can aid in long-term planning and evaluation. Use in a spell if you are weighing up your options regarding a confusing situation.

EIGHT Signifies personal discipline and can be of assistance when working towards a goal. Use in spellwork when you are studying or need to boost your productivity.

NINE Represents awakening your confidence and is a reminder that you can be totally self-sufficient. Use in spells to manifest luxury items and success, and to call in financial independence.

TEN Calls for you to celebrate your abundance. Use this card in spells to help attract prosperity from both expected and unexpected places.

PAGE Suggests ambition and opportunity, bringing fresh energy and courage to create new ventures. Use in spells when starting a new project or setting out educational or career goals.

KNIGHT Denotes responsibility and perseverance, so has a steady, patient, and practical energy. Use this card in spells to inspire dedication and to assist you when working with long-term goals.

QUEEN Signifies nurturing and resourcefulness. Can enhance domestic harmony and financial acumen. Use in rituals to foster abundance and call in care for loved ones.

KING Symbolizes prosperity and feeling grounded in all that you do. Use this card in spells to call for stability in your work and in career-related spells.

CUPS

||||||||||||||||||||

ELEMENT: Water

ASTROLOGICAL SIGNS:
Cancer, Scorpio, Pisces

MAGIC AND SPELLWORK:
Emotions, intuition, love, healing, relationships, inner peace, spirituality

ACE Indicates fresh starts and new beginnings concerning matters of the heart; can assist with healing a broken heart or be used to open your heart to welcome love.

TWO Represents partnerships, harmony, and positive outcomes. It can also denote the healing power of love or friendship, suggesting connection, mutual respect, and deep bonds. Use in love spells or rituals aimed at creating a stronger bond.

THREE A joyful card that celebrates friendship and inspires collaborations, encouraging you to embrace positive interactions with others. Use to manifest social connections and bring together communities in gatherings, parties, or events.

FOUR Represents contemplation and re-evaluation. Use in a spell to gain clarity and psychic insights when calling in new perspectives around confusing situations.

FIVE Signifies loss and grief. Its energy can assist with healing, emotional release, and moving forwards from situations that no longer serve you.

SIX Brings nostalgic energy, evoking feelings of longing for a simpler time or suggesting that the past may be influencing the present in some way. It may indicate the need to heal from old wounds and find closure. Use to reconnect with happy memories and past influences that have had a positive effect on your life.

SEVEN This card awakens your imagination to show you choices and options. Use in spells to inspire dreams and open the road ahead.

EIGHT Represents a shift in perspective and can help with change and transitions. Use in spells when you are about to embark on a new path or leave behind what no longer serves.

NINE Assists with wishes and can attract happiness. It can signal that things are falling into place for you, and you are on the path to emotional and personal satisfaction. It also encourages you to show gratitude for the abundance already in your life. Use in manifesting spells when calling in your heart's desires.

TEN This card is about bringing harmony, and signifies comfort and acceptance. Use to bring peace and blessings to all relationships in your life.

PAGE Can inspire creativity and imagination. It may suggest that you should listen to your intuition, and could indicate that now is a good time to explore creative pursuits. Use to open yourself up to new experiences and inspire creative expression.

KNIGHT Excites passions. It represents someone who is driven by their heart, emotions, and intuition, and is in touch with their feelings and guided by their dreams and desires. Use in your spellwork to call in passion and open yourself up to romance.

QUEEN Carries the energy of compassion and intuitive wisdom. A figure of nurturing, compassion, and emotional balance, use in healing spells connected to matters of the heart, to connect to your inner wisdom, and to call in empathy and compassion.

KING Is all about emotional stability and diplomacy. This archetype embodies mastery over your emotions and calm understanding. Use if you are seeking harmonious energy and balance within a relationship.

SWORDS

ELEMENT: Air

ASTROLOGICAL SIGNS:
Gemini, Libra, Aquarius

MAGIC AND SPELLWORK:
Clarity, communication, truth,
decision-making, resolutions,
focus, learning, healing

ACE Signifies truth and justice
and can reveal powerful
insights. Use in spells to bring
mental clarity and assist when
making informed decisions.
It can also be used to remove
negative energy blocks.

TWO Represents decisions and
can help when making choices
and finding peace. In spellwork
it can assist with resolving inner
conflicts, when seeking extra
clarity for problem-solving, and
for calling in balance.

THREE Indicates loss and
sorrow. This could be the
emotional pain caused by a
romantic breakup, betrayal,
painful truth, or bereavement.
Use in spellwork for finding
peace, emotional healing, and to
help with heartache and grief.

FOUR Is all about rest and
recovery and can help you to
recharge your energy and find
peace. Use it in spellwork
involving meditation and
self-care, and when taking a
break (or calling in a holiday).

FIVE Symbolizes conflict and
tension. It may suggest an
ongoing argument or situation
where someone feels they have
been badly treated. In a spell,
it can help to resolve disputes
and promote compassion and
understanding.

SIX Represents transition and
moving past obstacles. In spells
it can help when you are moving
on from past situations, during
transitions, and for calling in a
clear mind for new beginnings.

SEVEN Signifies strategic
actions. It can indicate deception
around you, and the need for
caution and consideration. Use
in spells to enhance protection
against betrayal and call in
direction when moving through
confusing situations.

EIGHT Represents restriction and limitation, feelings of being trapped in a situation or stuck in an emotional struggle. In spells it can help you to gain clarity from brain fog, and its energy can brings freedom and the power to liberate yourself from limited beliefs.

NINE Is linked with anxiety and nightmares. Use this card for casting protection spells to banish negative thoughts and fears, and for protection against negative energy.

TEN Relates to past trauma and can mean endings and release, and can help to transform your pain into wisdom. Use in spells to release painful situations and embrace new beginnings.

PAGE Inspires curiosity and truth-seeking. Can represent the start of a new project or intellectual pursuit, and indicate a good time to pursue further education or learn something new. Use this card in spells to improve communication and to seek knowledge when you are concerned about dishonesty.

KNIGHT Awakens assertiveness and can help summon courage and assist with making quick decisions. In spellwork it can be used to encourage rational thinking and banish indecision.

QUEEN Can enhance insights and wisdom. The queen of the element of Air is skilled in analysing situations, making decisions, and using logic and reason to cut through confusion or deceitful behaviour. In a spell, this card can be used to summon clear thinking, inspire personal independence, and strengthen boundaries.

KING Represents authority and wisdom, and the highest level of understanding, objectivity, and critical thinking. In a spell, this card can invoke leadership skills, assist with decision-making based on facts rather than emotions, and boost strategic thinking.

CONDUCTING A READING

Tarot cards can be used as divination tools, allowing you to tune in to their meanings in order to search for guidance, get new perspectives, and gain clarity. Anyone can conduct a tarot reading; you don't have to be psychic, but the cards can help you to develop your powers of intuition.

Begin by shuffling the cards, and as you do this think of a question; then draw your cards. You might pick just one card, and then follow by choosing another for clarity, or you may want to do a spread (which is where you lay the cards out in a sequence). When you pick a card or conduct a reading, try to refrain from instantly checking what it means; instead spend some time looking at the card and see what you notice in the image, the first thoughts that pop into your mind, and any feelings the card triggers. Although cards do have specific meanings (see pp.209–223), they are open to interpretation and no two tarot readers will give an identical reading. Lean into that intuition, and trust yourself.

You might select a single card and use it to develop your intention, noticing whether it brings a positive or negative feeling around hopes and dreams, reminds you of a past experience, or brings awareness to an area of your life that needs your attention.

When it comes to tarot spreads, you can choose to follow one of the classic framework spreads, or you can simply allow your intuition to guide you when creating a spread. The most important thing is that you trust your connection to the spread that you are creating.

CONNECT TO THE DECK

Before you begin a reading, it's important to establish some kind of intuitive connection with the deck that you are using. To connect your energy to the cards, hold them in your less-dominant hand and knock on the deck three times with your dominant hand.

COMMON CARD LAYOUTS

|||||||||||||||||||||||||||||||||||||||||||||||

✳ **ONE-CARD SPREAD**
Ideal for daily guidance
or a quick answer. Draw one
card to focus on a particular
question or the energy
of the day.

✳ **THREE-CARD SPREAD**
Good for quick readings on
specific questions, situations,
or guidance on the past,
present, and future. Draw
three cards and lay them out
left to right, reading them in
that order.

✳ **SEVEN-CARD HORSESHOE
SPREAD** Useful for more
detailed insight on a situation
or problem. Seven cards are
laid out in a horseshoe
pattern and denote (reading
from top left): past, present,
hidden influence, obstacles,
external influences, advice,
and outcome.

✳ **CELTIC CROSS SPREAD**
One of the most used
spreads for in-depth analysis
of complex situations. It
utilizes 10 cards laid out in a
cross-and-line pattern, with
each card representing
different elements. Over the
page we will show how to
conduct a detailed reading
using this.

ONE-CARD SPREAD

THREE-CARD SPREAD

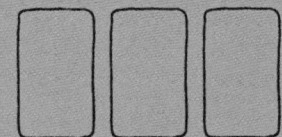

SEVEN-CARD SPREAD

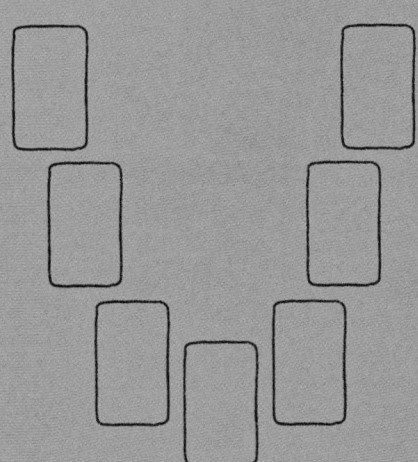

THE CELTIC CROSS SPREAD

The Celtic Cross is a classic tarot layout, often seen as a symbol of life's renewal and used to gain personal insights. Each card's position will guide you to create a story that looks at past influences and present challenges, offering up advice on potential future outcomes. Place each card in this formation as it is drawn randomly from the deck after shuffling.

As you lay out the cards, look for connections between them, such as repeating numbers, suits, or themes. Pay attention to major arcana cards, which indicate significant life events or lessons, and notice elemental interactions (lots of Cups, for example, might suggest emotional upheaval). Trust your intuition!

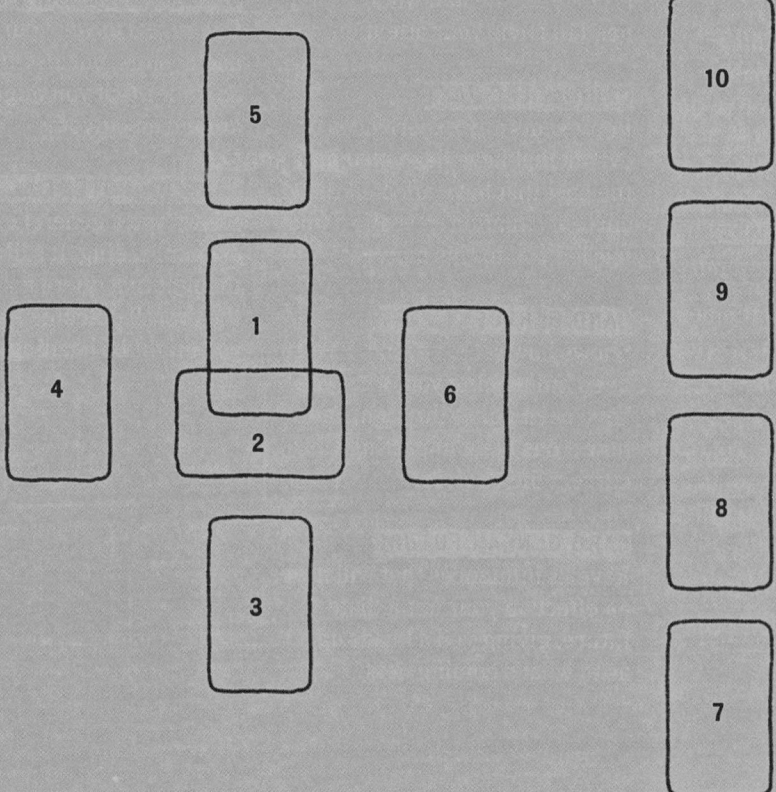

READING THE CARDS

||||||||||||||||||||||||||||||||||||||

1. Before shuffling, take a moment to set your intention. Focus on your question and the energy of the reading. You can ask questions like "What do I need to know about my career?", or ask for more general guidance.

2. Shuffle the deck in a way that feels natural, and draw the number of cards needed for your spread.

3. Place them all face down and then turn over one by one as you interpret them.

4. Each card has a meaning based on: its traditional symbolism; its position in the spread; the surrounding cards (they have an influence on each other); your intuition – what feelings or images immediately come to mind?

5. Look at patterns and themes to identify the message: what advice or insight is the reading offering?

6. Close the reading, thanking the cards for their guidance, and spend time reflecting. You might want to keep a tarot journal to record your readings and help with interpretation.

CARD 1: THE CURRENT SITUATION
Represents where you currently stand and shows you the main issue or focus of the reading.

CARD 2: THE CHALLENGE
This card is crossed over the first card; it reveals any obstacles or challenges that are affecting the current situation.

CARD 3: FOCUS
Shows the underlying basis of the situation, where your head is currently at, and where you need to focus your attention.

CARD 4: THE PAST
Represents any experiences or events that have happened in the past that have affected the current situation, revealing what has led you to this moment.

CARD 5: RECENT PAST
Shows how recent events have been influencing you, what you have been going through, and how it has been impacting your current life choices.

CARD 6: NEAR FUTURE
Reveals influences that will have an effect on your immediate future, giving you a heads up as to what's coming next.

CARD 7: ADVICE
Guides you to reflect on how you see yourself; it shows you how to view the question that you have asked.

CARD 8: EXTERNAL INFLUENCES
Represents the environment around you, what situations you are in, who is in your life, and what energy may be having an impact upon your current circumstances.

CARD 9: HOPES AND FEARS
Can reveal to you your hopes and desires, but also the anxieties that you might have around an outcome.

CARD 10: POTENTIAL OUTCOME
Shows you a general overview of your reading. It's like a final thought that offers insight into the overall outcome and where you might be heading.

TAROT SPELLCRAFT

Using tarot cards in witchcraft adds layers of symbolism, intention, and focus, enhancing the power and effectiveness of spells. The following pages offer ideas for incorporating the cards into your magical practice, and you will encounter a number of spells that feature tarot magic.

Due to the vast symbolism and strong mystical vibrations that tarot cards hold, choosing which cards to use for a spell can be intensely personal. You may connect to them via the meaning, element, astrological sign, the image, or simply because of the way the card makes you feel when you hold it. You might sometimes find that there is a spell you connect with, but the cards may not resonate for you. If this is the case, go through your deck and tune in to what feels right, or adapt and create your own tarot spells.

As with all the most potent spells, their success comes down to your personal connections, so always check in with how the cards' energies make you feel. When you are fully comfortable within a ritual, you are at your most powerful.

SET YOUR INTENTION

Before casting a tarot spell, ensure that you are clear on your goal: what do you want to manifest? Each tarot card carries its own energy, so be sure to select a card (or cards) that aligns with your intention.

USING THE CARDS IN SPELLWORK

You can incorporate tarot cards into your spellwork, rituals, and magical practice in a variety of ways:

✳ **PLACE A CARD ON YOUR ALTAR, USING IT AS A FOCAL POINT DURING MEDITATION**

✳ **CARRY A CARD WITH YOU AS A TALISMAN, FOR PROTECTION OR LUCK**

✳ **YOU MAY WANT TO ANOINT YOUR CHOSEN CARD WITH ESSENTIAL OILS OR A POTION TO INCREASE ITS POTENCY**

✳ **BURN SOME INCENSE AND BATHE A CARD TOGETHER WITH A LIST OF INTENTIONS IN THE SMOKE**

✳ **YOU MAY CHOOSE TO DO A SIMPLE ONE-CARD SPELL, OR PERHAPS CREATE A MORE ELABORATE RITUAL**

✳ **CONSULT A CERTAIN NUMBER OF CARDS CONNECTED TO THEIR MEANING IN NUMEROLOGY (SEE PP.96–100)**

If you are placing a particular card on an altar, you might light some candles and sit at the altar in meditation as the candles continue to burn. You can do this in one sitting or continue to relight them and burn them over a few nights. You can also choose the number of nights to correspond with the numerology of the spell you are calling in. Remember, everything can have a meaning in a magic spell.

Once a spell is complete, remember to thank the card and any other energies, spirit guides, or deities you invoked during your ritual. Cleanse the card or cards used with the smoke of some sage, rosemary, or camphor before returning them to the deck. Safely store the cards and any other tools you used and ground yourself to return to everyday consciousness (see p.37).

Now, I'll give some more detailed instructions for specific spells, to help get you started.

A ONE-CARD SPELL

IIIIIIIIIIIIIIIIIII

Think of your intention for the spell, the energy that you wish to summon, and the ideal outcome you hope to bring about. Spend some time on this, using whatever method works best for you: you could visualize it or journal about it until you settle upon a clear image in your mind of what you wish to evoke. Next, choose a card with the corresponding meaning and energy for the spell that you want to create.

You will need

From your tarot deck, select just one of the following cards:

* ❋ **A SUIT CARD THAT REPRESENTS YOURSELF OR AN ENERGY THAT YOU WOULD LIKE TO CONNECT WITH**

* ❋ **A COURT CARD THAT CONNECTS WITH THE ENERGY YOU WANT TO BRING TO THE SPELL**

* ❋ **A CARD FROM THE MAJOR ARCANA THAT HOLDS THE POWER OF THE OUTCOME THAT YOU WANT THE SPELL TO BRING**

Remember, this is just a guide. You are welcome to pick any other cards that you connect with and feel will add power to your spell and bring the energy that you want to your ritual.

See pp.208–223 for the meanings of each of the cards.

1. Invoke the energy of your chosen card: hold it with both hands in a prayer position, hold it to your heart, in front of your third eye, or place it before you and gaze at it. You can even speak to it and ask it to bring you the energy that it holds. Do whatever feels right for you in order to feel connected to the card.

2. While doing this, spend some time noticing the card's vibration; note how its energy makes you feel. Is this the right card for you? If not, it is perfectly okay to swap it for another or try a few cards and choose the one you feel most connected to.

3. Now that you have chosen your card, it is time to set the scene. Create a playlist with music that will inspire your magic, and gather the herbs, oils, candles, sigils, or crystals – or whatever else you wish to use to enhance your card's energy (refer to the relevant chapters).

4. Set out all of the magical tools that you have collected and create your altar (see pp.24–27).

5. Place the card centre-stage on your altar and begin visualizing. If you can't see a clear picture, don't worry; just focus on the energy that you wish to step into.

6. Think about how this card is going to assist you; what do you need it to do, and what energy does it need to bring?

As you do this, begin to feel the card's energy merging with your own.

7. Write out the energy you want the card to bring and read it aloud in a powerful voice. You may wish to leave your altar set up, and place what you have written beneath the card.

ELEMENTAL SPELL

||||||||||||||||||

When working with the elements in any spell, select tarot cards that align with the specific energies of Earth (for protection), Air (for balance), Fire (for strength), and Water (for harmony). This spell is a good idea if you require each one of the powers of the different elements – for example, during a major life transition.

You will need

✳ **EARTH (FOR PROTECTION): ACE OF PENTACLES**

✳ **AIR (FOR BALANCE): ACE OF SWORDS**

✳ **FIRE (FOR STRENGTH): ACE OF WANDS**

✳ **WATER (FOR HARMONY): ACE OF CUPS**

✳ **COMPASS**

Remember, this is just a guide. You are welcome to pick any other cards that you feel will add power to your spell and the energy that you wish to bring to your ritual.

1. Place the cards based on the directions that are linked to each element.

✳ North for Earth

✳ East for Air

✳ South for Fire

✳ West for Water

2. You can choose to sit in the centre of these cards as you create your spell, or arrange them on your altar. The energy that they attract will bring a balance of harmony and power to your spellwork.

3. Call upon the elements (see pp.34–35) and focus on your intention. Visualize your desired outcome.

4. Close the spell by expressing gratitude to the elements, and leave the cards on your altar, or carry them with you for continued energy.

See pp.209–223 for the elemental associations of each of the cards.

HEALING SPELL

〰〰〰〰〰〰〰〰

This ritual taps into the nurturing energy of the Queen of Cups to honour your feelings and create a healing space for your heart. It's beneficial for when you have experienced heartbreak or loss. This card represents intuition and emotional balance, and can help you align with love and compassionate understanding.

You will need

* ✳ **SMALL BLUE CANDLE**
* ✳ **CARVING TOOL SUCH AS A TOOTHPICK OR CRAFT KNIFE**
* ✳ **DILUTED LAVENDER ESSENTIAL OIL (TO DILUTE, ADD 2 DROPS OF LAVENDER ESSENTIAL OIL TO 15 ML [1 TBSP] OF CARRIER OIL)**
* ✳ **YOUR TEARS (OPTIONAL)**
* ✳ **QUEEN OF CUPS**

1. Carve a water symbol on the candle (see p.115) and light it.

2. Anoint your temples and heart with the lavender oil (and your tears, if you wish).

3. Rub your hands together and take a big, deep breath of the lavender oil.

4. Hold the Queen of Cups to your heart and take deep, slow, and gentle breaths.

5. Connect to the energy of the card; visualize the Queen standing in front of you and feel her presence. Tune in to the nurturing messages that she is sending you.

6. Ask her for guidance on your healing journey and allow yourself to receive her loving energy and support.

7. Seal the spell by expressing gratitude to the Queen as you snuff out the candle.

MANIFEST A POSITIVE OUTCOME

||||||||||||||||||||||||||||||||||

Use this spell to help bring your intentions into reality and manifest whatever it is that you desire, such as a new job opportunity or a favourable outcome. You can also use it generally to help to shift Cosmic energies in your favour.

You will need

* ✳ **THE MAGICIAN**
* ✳ **THE STAR**
* ✳ **THE EMPRESS**
* ✳ **SMALL YELLOW CANDLE**
* ✳ **CARVING TOOL SUCH AS A TOOTHPICK OR CRAFT KNIFE**

1. Lay the cards out side by side.

2. Carve an infinity symbol (∞) in the candle with your initials on either side (carve it horizontally).

3. Light the candle.

4. Hold your hands over the cards and summon the energy that each card will bring you; tune in to any messages that the cards might have, and to your desired outcome.

5. While the candle continues to burn, connect to your dreams and visualize how you would like everything to work out.

6. Write down your manifestations as you imagine your perfect outcome being enacted.

7. Pay attention to any ideas or thoughts that pop into your mind; be open to messages that might help you bring a positive outcome to fruition and write them down.

8. Sit with the candle until it has completely burnt down.

9. Leave the tarot cards out, or place them on your altar so their energy can continue to remind you to visualize the outcome you desire.

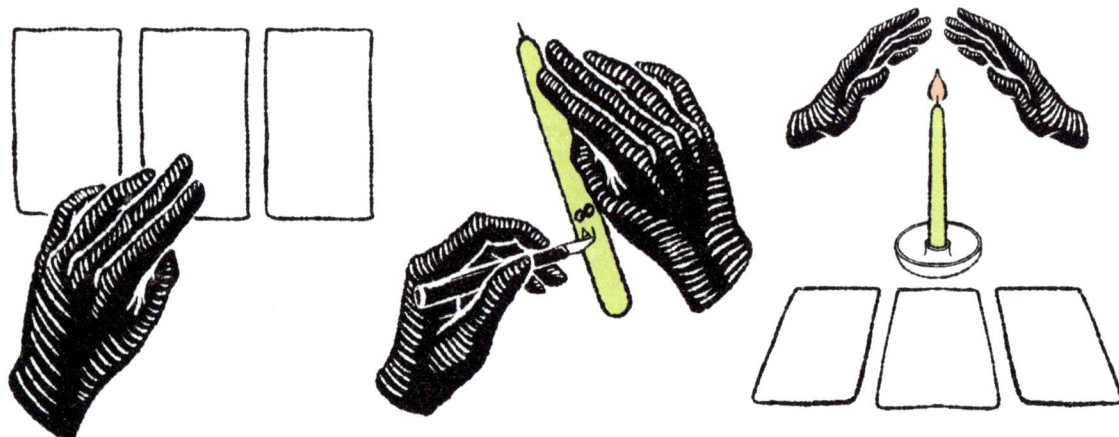

ENERGY RENEWAL

||||||||||||||||||||||||||||||

This is a ritual for releasing negative energy. It can work as a reset or to clear whatever you wish to banish from your life. It can help for something specific – like letting go of a toxic ex-partner – or it can be used to herald in a new era, for example at the beginning of a new year or month.

You will need

* ❋ **WHITE CANDLE**
* ❋ **DEATH**
* ❋ **THE FOOL**
* ❋ **HANDFUL OF SALT**
* ❋ **SAGE, ROSEMARY, OR A CLEANSING HERB OF YOUR CHOICE**

1. Light the candle so that it is sitting directly in from of you.

2. With your palms facing up, place the Death card in your left hand and the Fool in your right hand.

3. Hold your palms up, with each hand on either side of the candle.

4. Think of all that you wish to banish, or what it is that you wish to move away from; get a feel for this energy and direct it towards your left arm, sending it to your hand so that Death can soak it up.

5. As you do this, your left hand will start to feel a little heavy: allow it to drop.

6. Once this happens, imagine a bright white healing light, filled with fresh energy; feel it travelling down through your head and to the Fool card in your right hand.

7. As this happens, you might notice your right hand moving upwards, or it might feel tingly.

8. When you feel this connection, call in this energy; invite it to travel around your body and feel it surround you.

9. When you have a good sense of this feeling, open your eyes and blow out the candle.

10. Throw three handfuls of salt over the candle to signify completion of the spell.

11. Cleanse the Death card with some sage or cleansing herb of your choice to remove any negative energy it absorbed.

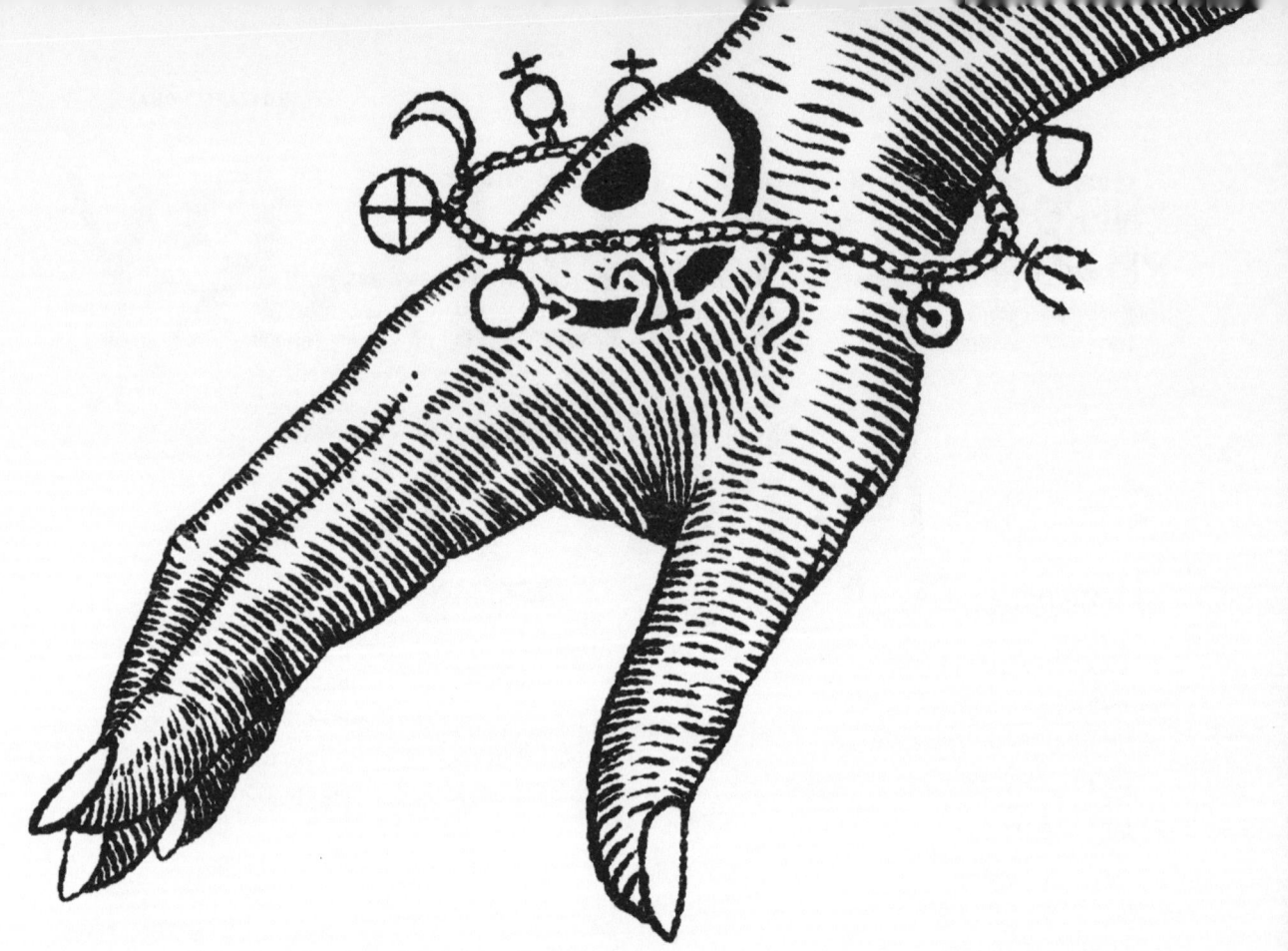

CHAPTER
TEN

PLANETARY MAGIC

The planets have been hanging out above us since the dawn of time, quietly (and sometimes not so quietly) influencing our lives, moods, and magic. Planets carry their own unique powers, and we can tap into these celestial energies to deepen our magical connection with the Universe, align with natural cycles, and intensify our spellwork.

One of the most powerful ways to work with planetary magic is through astrological timing. Each planet rules particular hours and days during which its energy is strongest, and when you choose these moments you can add some serious oomph to your rituals and spells. Working with planetary days is a way to utilize planetary timing, whether or not you also wish to dive into more complex astrology charts (see pp.263–271). For example, if you're working with Venus to enhance love or beauty, you might choose to perform your ritual on a Friday (the day ruled by Venus).

The planets are constantly moving in their orbits around the sun, and the speed at which they move determines when you can tune in to their energy. The planets' orbits also vary in length, so their energy is available at different times. When planning a spell or ritual, check where the relevant planet is in the sky. The easiest way to know what sign a planet is in is to consult an astrology app or website, as these tools will tell you exactly where each planet is at any given moment.

Before we can discover our place beneath the celestial sky (see pp.263–267), we first must understand the energies of individual planets and the principles of planetary magic.

START HERE

How deeply you wish to go to connect with planetary magic as part of your witchcraft practice is up to you: you can burn a corresponding herb or bring their colours, correspondences, and symbols into your spellwork, or conduct a full reading of your birth chart to see how the planets' energies affect you. But why not begin by simply star bathing: gaze up at the night sky and experience how the beauty and energy of the stars influence your mind, body, and soul.

⊙

THE SUN

ELEMENT: Fire

ENERGY: Vitality, self-expression,
creativity, personal power, activation,
healing, growth, success

DAY: Sunday

COLOURS: Gold, orange, yellow

PLANTS, HERBS, AND SCENTS:
Sunflowers, Angelica, bay, cinnamon,
juniper, orange, rosemary, copal

The sun represents vitality, confidence, and your personal power.
Work with sun energy when you are wanting to boost your creativity
or leadership skills. We can also tap into the energy of the sun's
stages throughout the day.

Cast spells at sunrise for new beginnings, fresh starts, and road
opening spells – sunrise is a great time to set intentions. Morning
sun can bring the energy of expansion and growth needed for
making plans. Noon is when the sun is at its strongest, so charge
your tools beneath it at this time, and harness its energy to create
courage spells or to add zest to your magic. Sunset energy is good
to tap into when seeking clarity or you want to meditate and reflect;
you may wish to create releasing spells as the sun is setting.

NOTE: In astrology, the sun
and moon are considered
to be planets.

SUN POWER SPELL

||||||||||||||||||||||||||||||||||||||||||||||||||||||||

Use this incense blend to connect to the sun's energy and bring its power to your magical workings.

You will need

* ❋ **PESTLE AND MORTAR**
* ❋ **3 PINCHES OF FRANKINCENSE**
* ❋ **PINCH OF CINNAMON**
* ❋ **PINCH OF DRIED GINGER**
* ❋ **CHARCOAL DISC**
* ❋ **CAULDRON OR HEAT-PROOF VESSEL**
* ❋ **PEN AND PAPER**

1. Blend the spices in a clockwise direction in a pestle and mortar to produce your incense blend.

2. Burn some of this incense on the charcoal disc (see p.123).

3. As the incense burns, bless your hands and pen in the smoke, then write a love letter to the sun, expressing your gratitude for everything it provides. List the things you love about it.

4. Ask for the sun's assistance in what you need, and state that you'd like to connect with its energy.

5. Bless your letter by passing it through the incense smoke.

6. Read the letter aloud, watching the smoke carry your words into the sunlight.

7. Finally, say:

"MAGIC SUN, I CALL IN YOUR POWER, BLESS MY PETITION THIS MAGICAL HOUR, AND SO IT IS."

☽

THE MOON

ELEMENT: Water

ENERGY: Intuition, rebirth, emotions,
psychic power, dreamwork, transformations

DAY: Monday

COLOURS: Silver, white, blue

PLANTS, HERBS, AND SCENTS: Camphor, jasmine,
lemon, mugwort, myrrh, sandalwood

ORBITAL PERIOD: 29.5 days, spending about
2.5 days in each sign

In mythology, the moon is linked to the Roman goddess Luna and the Greek goddesses Selene and Artemis, each symbolizing the moon's nurturing, protective, and transformative energies. These goddesses were considered to be the guardians of dreams and hidden knowledge.

The moon rules our emotions, intuition, and subconscious mind. As the celestial body closest to Earth, its power and influence is often strongly felt, which makes it a potent force in magic. It is a powerful planet to work with because it's visible to us and we can connect to the energy of its different phases. On pages 244–245, we will explore the different phases of the moon, and what they mean.

RELEASE AND BANISHING SPELL

This is best performed during a waning moon or a dark moon phase (see p.244). As the moon wanes, use this spell to banish and remove all that you want to release.

You will need

* JUICE OF HALF A LEMON
* 3 PINCHES OF SALT
* 3 PINCHES OF SAGE
* 1 BLACK CANDLE
* PEN AND PAPER
* 3 HANDFULS OF SALT

1. Roll the candle in the mixture so that it is covered in the lemon juice, salt, and sage.

2. Light the candle.

3. Write out all that you want to release, then draw a big cross over it and write "goodbye" three times.

4. Burn the paper over the black candle.

5. Blow the candle out and throw three handfuls of salt over it all.

6. Wrap it up and throw it away in someone else's bin (to show that it no longer belongs with you).

ABUNDANT MOON POTION

Use this during a waxing or full moon (see p.245). This is a personal power potion, to use whenever you want to connect to this expansive moon energy. You can anoint your body, put a few drops in a bath, or use it to bless your tools.

You will need

* 6 DROPS OF SANDALWOOD ESSENTIAL OIL
* 6 DROPS OF JASMINE ESSENTIAL OIL
* 20 ML (4 TSP) OF CARRIER OIL: IF YOU INTEND TO WEAR THIS POTION, USE ALMOND OIL
* BOWL (ANY COLOUR IS FINE, BUT SILVER IS PREFERRED)
* JAR OR BOTTLE TO STORE YOUR POTION IN

1. Blend the sandalwood and jasmine oils with the carrier oil and add to a bowl.

2. Go outside and hold the bowl up towards the moon, catching the moon's light in the oils.

3. As you are holding the bowl, acknowledge the moon's reflection and tune in to the connection you are making.

4. Feel the moon's energy charging up your potion and connect to its power.

5. When you feel like a connection has been made, pour the potion into a bottle or jar. Store it somewhere safe, away from sunlight, ready to use in your rituals when needed.

MOON PHASES

Each phase of the moon has its own transformative powers that can be harnessed: the new moon is ideal for setting intentions; waxing moon for growth; full moon for completion and psychic spells; waning moon for banishing spells; and dark moon for psychic spells. Beginning with the new moon, follow the cycle in an anticlockwise direction.

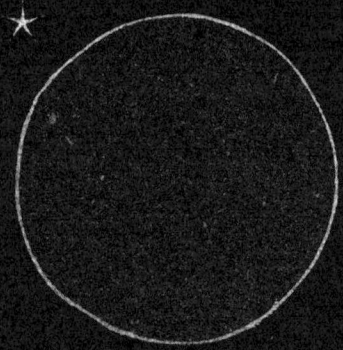

NEW MOON

The new moon is the beginning of the lunar cycle. This phase can be seen as a blank slate, and is a good time for new beginnings, starting a fresh project, and for planting seeds of intention.

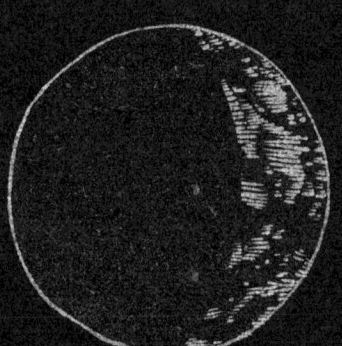

WAXING CRESCENT

This is a perfect time for spells related to growth and expansion. As you watch the moon grow, ask yourself what you would like to grow in your life and use this moon's energy to build momentum around your magic. If your magical workings feel a bit stagnant, connect to the waxing moon's energy and ask for guidance.

WAXING GIBBOUS

As the moon grows larger still, this is a time to amplify intentions and fine-tune your goals. This phase is ideal for working on abundance, confidence, and clarity. This energy supports perseverance, ensuring that intentions made during the new moon come closer to fruition.

DARK MOON

The last trace of the waning crescent, when the moon is invisible in the sky, is a time to banish whatever you don't want to bring in to the new moon cycle. When the sky is at its darkest, the veil between the physical and unseen worlds is thin, making it a potent time to connect to spirit guides.

WANING CRESCENT

The waning crescent moon symbolizes release, introspection, and closure. This is a good time to declutter your mind and your home. Perform releasing spells to help let go of the past and make room for new intentions and personal growth.

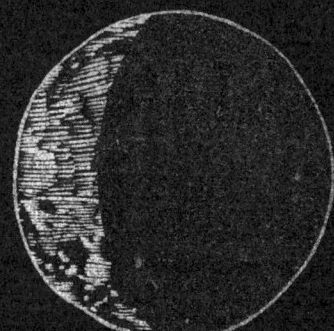

WANING GIBBOUS

After the full moon, the waning phase begins. As the moon starts to fade it is a time for introspection, and for considering what changes you wish to make in your life. Look at what is hindering your spellwork at this time, and allow the waning moon to guide you with adjustments that need to be made.

FULL MOON

When the moon is full it is at its peak power and can be used to amplify all magic. Use this moonlight to charge your magical tools beneath, practise psychic work, and ask for it to give you insights; in my experience it will always show you what needs to be seen.

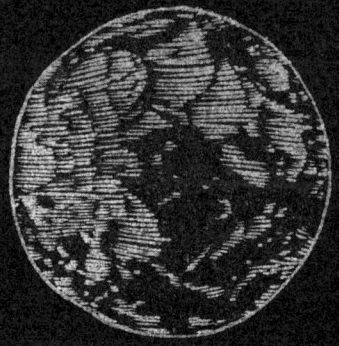

☿

MERCURY

ELEMENT: Air

ENERGY: Communication, intellect,
learning, travel, technology

DAY: Wednesday

COLOURS: Yellow, orange, silver, blue

PLANTS, HERBS, AND SCENTS: Benzoin, sage, dill, fennel,
lavender, mint, rosemary, thyme, lemongrass

ORBITAL PERIOD: Orbits around the sun in about 88 days, and
travels through each zodiac sign in about 3–4 weeks; goes
retrograde 3–4 times a year

Mercury rules all forms of communication, intellect, and technology, making it the perfect planet to call upon whenever you need help speaking your truth or expressing your feelings clearly. Its energy can assist in clearing mental blocks, gaining clarity, and even banishing brain fog.

Because Mercury is the fastest moving planet, you can tap into its energy when you need to speed things up. If you're seeking a quick answer, or if your spellwork is urgent, Mercury can help bring rapid results. It's also great for enhancing focus and concentration, so is particularly helpful for studying. Whether you're preparing for an exam, writing an essay, or tackling a challenging project, Mercury's energy will give you the boost you need.

Beyond communication and intellect, Mercury also rules short-distance travel, technology, and work-related interactions. You can use Mercury's energy for travel spells, spells that focus on negotiating deals, and even for resolving technological issues.

COMMUNICATION AND CLARITY POTION

Let this potion help you to release any misunderstandings, clearing the way so that you can communicate with clarity and authenticity. Do not perform this spell for communication when Mercury is in retrograde (see p.272), but it *can* be used to clear fog and stagnant energy during a Mercury retrograde.

You will need

* ⁕ **5 DROPS OF THYME ESSENTIAL OIL**
* ⁕ **5 DROPS OF MINT ESSENTIAL OIL**
* ⁕ **20 ML (4 TSP) OF CARRIER OIL (ALMOND OR JOJOBA)**
* ⁕ **1 BAY LEAF**

1. Blend the potion in a bowl.

2. Draw the symbol for Mercury on the bay leaf.

3. Burn the bay leaf over the potion, blessing it with its smoke and connecting it to Mercury's energy.

4. Ask out loud what you wish the spell to help you with.

5. Anoint your third eye and/or temples with the potion and meditate or journal any thoughts that come to mind.

6. Rub the potion on the centre of your throat to bring power to your voice when using it for communication.

♀

VENUS

ELEMENT: Earth and Water

ENERGY: Love, beauty, relationships, attraction,
fertility, harmony, pleasure

DAY: Friday

COLOURS: Pink, red, silver, green

PLANTS, HERBS, AND SCENTS: Rose, vanilla, cardamon,
violet, ylang ylang

ORBITAL PERIOD: Takes about 225 days to orbit the sun,
staying in each zodiac sign for 3–4 weeks

Venus is the planet of love, beauty, and harmony. It rules over
how we express ourselves in all matters of the heart, relationships,
desires, and everything that brings us fulfilment and joy. In Roman
mythology, the goddess Venus ruled pleasure and beauty, and it
is said that flowers grew wherever she walked.

Venus energy encourages us to seek pleasure, indulge in
sensuality, and maintain harmonious relationships. Harness this
energy in spellwork to bring romance into your life, to deepen
connections with a current lover, or to awaken self-love.

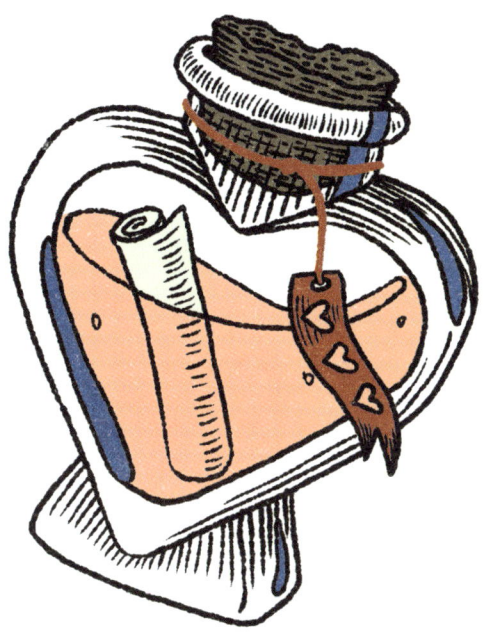

LOVE POTION

||||||||||||||||||||||||||||||||||||||||||||||||||

This is a potion to awaken your heart energy and inspire warm, loving energy in your life. You could perform this ritual during a waxing moon (see p.245), associated with growth, which is a good time to focus on drawing someone closer or increasing feelings of attraction.

You will need

* ✳ **6 DROPS OF ROSE ESSENTIAL OIL**
* ✳ **2 DROPS OF CARDAMOM ESSENTIAL OIL**
* ✳ **2 DROPS OF VANILLA ESSENTIAL OIL**
* ✳ **20 ML (4 TSP) OF CARRIER OIL (ALMOND OR JOJOBA IS BEST)**
* ✳ **PAPER**
* ✳ **PEN WITH PINK INK**
* ✳ **GLASS JAR OR BOTTLE**

1. Hold your hands on your heart and think of something or someone that makes your heart swell with love (this should be a person that you already have a connection with, not a stranger).

2. Feel this energy fill your whole body and then transmit to your hands.

3. When you feel you are fully in this energy, blend the potion ingredients together.

4. Draw the symbol of Venus on the paper and roll it up; add it to the mixture.

5. Label your jar or bottle with heart symbols.

6. Massage your body and heartspace with this potion when needing to amplify loving energy, and use it to anoint anything that requires your loving energy.

♂

MARS

ELEMENT: Fire

ENERGY: Passion, power,
determination, strength, action

DAY: Tuesday

COLOURS: Red, magenta, black

PLANTS, HERBS, AND SCENTS: Allspice, basil, black pepper,
cayenne, chilli, cinnamon, dragon's blood, ginger

ORBITAL PERIOD: Takes about 2 years to make a full orbit,
spending about 6–7 weeks in each sign

Mars represents action, courage, and drive. This fiery planet is
named after the Roman god of war, whose name means "bright" and
"burning one", symbolizing his role as a fierce warrior embodying
strength and tenacity. Mars can bring power to your decision-
making, inspire decisive action, and awaken your fire energy.

Mars energy is bold and forceful, which makes it a power player
when you need to summon strength or protection. Invoke Mars in
spells when you want to overcome your fears, fire up your passions,
or call in confidence. Additionally, Mars is perfect for motivation
spells when you need to break through procrastination or build
up the courage to take on a challenge.

FIRE AND POWER SPELL

||||||||||||||||||||||||||||||||||||||||||||

Connect to the power of Mars energy whenever you need to metaphorically breathe fire and create action. Perform this spell at Mars' hour (look this up on an astrology app) on a Tuesday for the most concentrated energy.

You will need

* ☀ 1 RED CANDLE
* ☀ CARVING TOOL SUCH AS A TOOTHPICK OR CRAFT KNIFE
* ☀ 1 PINCH OF DRIED GINGER
* ☀ 1 PINCH OF CINNAMON
* ☀ 1 PINCH OF CAYENNE PEPPER
* ☀ 40 ML (3 TBSP) OF OIL (EITHER CASTOR, OLIVE, OR ALMOND)
* ☀ PESTLE AND MORTAR
* ☀ PLATE
* ☀ RED PEN AND PAPER

1. Carve an arrow facing upwards on the candle.

2. Blend the spice mixture well using a pestle and mortar and then pour it out onto the plate.

3. Gently roll the candle in this blend so that it's completely covered.

4. Light the candle.

5. With the red pen, create a petition, writing down what in your life needs Mars' power, where action needs to be taken, and the energy that you wish to invoke.

6. Hold the petition in between your hands above the flame and say three times:

"I CALL IN THE POWER OF MARS TO GIVE ME THE STRENGTH TO TAKE ACTION."

Declare your petition aloud in a powerful voice and then burn it in the flame.

7. As it burns say,

"MAY THE ENERGY OF MARS MULTIPLY THE STRENGTH I SEEK."

8. When the petition is burned, blow the candle out and clap your hands three times over it and say,

"AND SO IT IS."

♃

JUPITER

ELEMENTS: Air and Fire

ENERGY: Luck, prosperity, growth, wisdom,
success, abundance

DAY: Thursday

COLOURS: Royal blue, purple, gold

PLANTS, HERBS, AND SCENTS: Oak, clove, nutmeg,
sage, dandelion, cedar, honeysuckle, hyssop

ORBITAL PERIOD: Takes about 12 years to complete its journey
around the sun, staying in each zodiac sign for about a year

Jupiter is the planet of expansion, luck, and abundance, known for its
ability to bring growth, wisdom, and opportunities. In mythology,
Jupiter was the Roman god of great fortune and the ruler of the
heavens, with the power to bestow wisdom, justice, and abundance
upon those under his protection.

Tune in to Jupiter's energy when you are seeking expansion in
your life. This might be through spiritual growth or education, or
wherever you are looking to broaden your horizons. Jupiter's energy
helps to manifest abundance and attract success, so is perfect for
spells related to luck, wealth, work, and long-term goals, helping
you set intentions for big-picture success and lasting abundance.

MONEY SPELL

||||||||||||||||||||||||||||||||||||||||||||||||

Connect to Jupiter's energy for financial prosperity, success, and good fortune. Perform this spell on Thursday, Jupiter's day, and for extra oomph, during a waxing or full moon to call in abundance.

You will need

* ✳ **8 CLOVES**
* ✳ **2 WHOLE NUTMEGS**
* ✳ **PESTLE AND MORTAR**
* ✳ **5 DROPS OF CINNAMON ESSENTIAL OIL**
* ✳ **50 ML (3¹⁄₂ TBSP) CARRIER OIL (ALMOND OR JOJOBA)**
* ✳ **GLASS JAR**
* ✳ **PEN AND PAPER**

1. Blend the cloves and nutmeg in a pestle and mortar.

2. Add this mixture to the jar with the carrier oil.

3. Write out the amount of money you would like to manifest and then draw the Jupiter symbol three times around the amount.

4. Roll it up and put it in the jar.

5. Keep the jar somewhere safe or on your altar, and for the next nine nights hold the jar and say the amount out loud nine times.

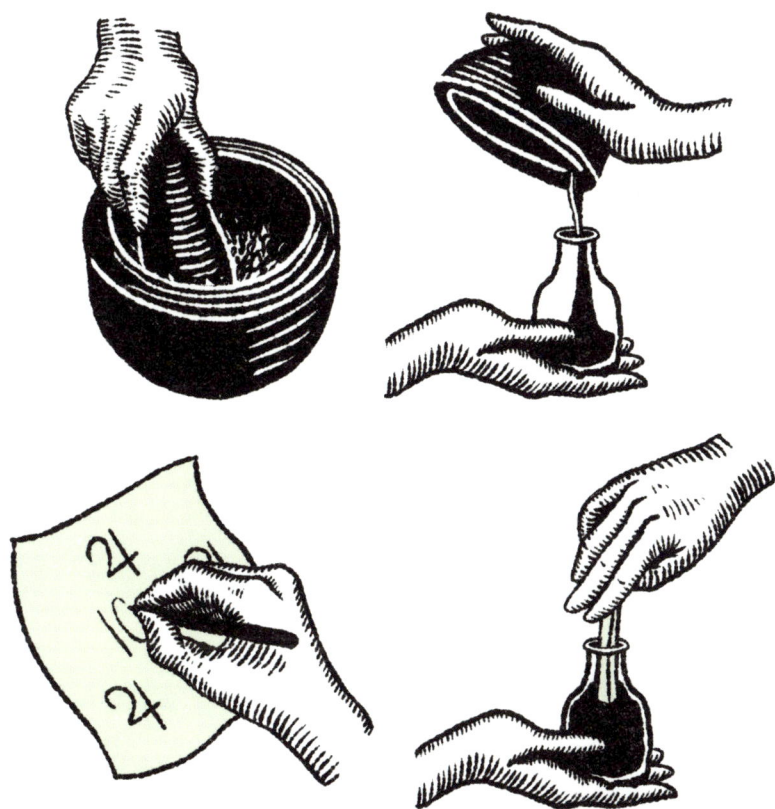

♄
SATURN

ELEMENT: Earth

ENERGY: Discipline, structure, protection,
boundaries, responsibility, karma

DAY: Saturday

COLOURS: Black, grey, dark blue

PLANTS, HERBS, AND SCENTS: Comfrey,
patchouli, myrrh, vetiver

ORBITAL PERIOD: Slow and steady, taking around
29 years to orbit the sun, and spending about
2.5 years in each sign

Saturn is the planet of structure, responsibility, and authority.
This planet's energy is serious and focused, helping you to manifest
long-term goals through hard work, patience, and persistence.
The planet is named after the Roman god Saturn, the god of time
and discipline, who ruled agriculture, wealth, and the cycles of life.

This kind of energy inspires you to concentrate on your long-
term goals and keep your eyes on the prize when manifesting.
Saturn's influence works well in spells involving strengthening
personal boundaries as well as protection magic. Its energy can be
harnessed for banishing spells and rituals to break old habits or
invoke self-discipline.

PERSONAL GROWTH SPELL

IIIIIIIIIIIIIIIIIIIIIIIIIIIIIIIIIIIIIIIIIIIIII

Saturn's energy encourages us to reflect around personal growth and change. As we grow, we must cut the cords from old versions of ourselves. Use this spell to sever ties with old energy or ways of being that you have evolved and moved on from.

You will need

✳ **1 BLACK CANDLE**

✳ **SOME STRING OR YARN (BLACK OR NEUTRAL)**

✳ **FEW DROPS OF MYRRH ESSENTIAL OIL**

1. Light the candle.

2. On one end of the thread, tie some knots while thinking about what you are moving on from, and at the other end tie knots focusing on what you are calling in or energies that you want to move into.

3. As you tie each knot, say what you are focusing on out loud.

4. Anoint the thread (see p.126) with the myrrh oil and then hold the thread over the flame and let it burn through the centre of the thread.

5. Sit with the candle for a while and focus on the flame, and journal any thoughts or epiphanies that come to mind at this time.

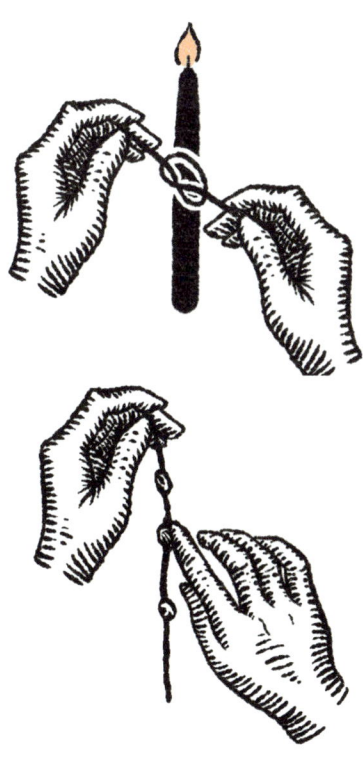

♅

URANUS

ELEMENT: Air

ENERGY: Freedom, innovation, change,
rebellion, originality, intuition

DAY: Wednesday (although because of its unpredictable
and rebellious nature, it can be connected to any day)

COLOURS: Electric blue, teal, silver

PLANTS, HERBS, AND SCENTS: Eucalyptus, peppermint,
star anise, lemon balm, cloves, lavender, pine

ORBITAL PERIOD: Takes about 84 years to orbit the sun,
spending roughly 7 years in each zodiac sign

Uranus is the planet of innovation and change. This planet can be
quite a rebel and the energy it carries can shake things up. In Greek
mythology, Uranus was the god of the sky and the heavens, known
for being forceful and rigid with his ruling of the cosmos. Uranus
brings lessons that in order to move forwards, destruction must
sometimes take place.

Uranus energy helps us to break free from unhelpful restrictive
structures. Call in Uranus when working with transformation magic,
calling for social change, or embracing new ideas and inviting
creative breakthroughs. This planet is about pushing the boundaries
of tradition and awakening your political activist energy.

PSYCHIC VISIONS

IIIIIIIIIIIIIIIIIIIIIIIIIIIIIIIIIIIIIIIIIIIIIIIIIIIIIIIIIIIII

Connect to Uranus to tune in to psychic downloads and messages from your subconscious, inviting flashes of inspiration and visionary thinking.

You will need

* **PURPLE CANDLE**

* **CARVING TOOL SUCH AS A TOOTHPICK OR CRAFT KNIFE**

* **4 DROPS OF PEPPERMINT ESSENTIAL OIL**

* **4 DROPS OF CLOVE ESSENTIAL OIL**

* **20 ML (4 TSP) OF CARRIER OIL (ALMOND OR JOJOBA)**

* **PEN AND PAPER**

1. Carve the symbol of Uranus into the candle.

2. Light the candle.

3. Blend the oils and anoint the edges of a piece of paper with the potion.

4. Turn all the lights out, so that the only light is from the candle.

5. Anoint your temples with the potion (see p.126).

6. Close your eyes and imagine your third eye blinking open.

7. Once you have connected with your third eye, see the piece of paper through it.

8. Write, scribble, or doodle on the paper with your non-dominant hand; as you do this, try to connect it to your third eye and allow the hand move on its own, as though it were being energetically guided.

9. When you are done, look at what is on the paper and search for hidden messages within your scribbles. Hold the paper at different angles, and allow it to blur to see what messages appear.

10. If you can't see anything, simply hold the paper in between your hands and feel its energy; take note of whatever comes to mind.

$$\Psi$$

NEPTUNE

ELEMENT: Water

ENERGY: Psychic abilities, dreams,
spirituality, intuition, creativity

DAY: Friday

COLOURS: Green, blue, violet

PLANTS, HERBS, AND SCENTS: Jasmine, lotus,
sandalwood, sage, yew, myrrh, lavender, star anise

ORBITAL PERIOD: Takes around 165 years to complete
its journey around the sun and spends about 14 years
in each zodiac sign

Neptune connects us to the realms of dreams, intuition, and
mysticism. In Roman mythology, Neptune is the god of the sea and
all bodies of water, symbolizing not only the vast depths of the ocean
but also the subconscious mind. In astrology, Neptune is aligned
with deep human emotions and uncovering hidden truths. Much like
the sea, this planet's energy can be both calm and chaotic, inspiring
us to dive in to the mysteries of the unseen in spellwork.

In magic, invoke Neptune's energy when seeking guidance
through divination tools like tarot cards (see Chapter 9), scrying
(see p.203), or astrology (see pp.263–273). Neptune is ideal for spells
that aim to uncover buried truths, inspire creativity, or delve into the
subconscious for hidden wisdom and spiritual insights.

DIVINATION INCENSE

||||||||||||||||||||||||||||||||||

This incense will enhance the atmosphere and energy in any ritual when attempting to gain insight and clarity. Perform this spell as Neptune rises (you can check this on an astrology tool website).

You will need

✳ **FEW PINCHES OF DRIED LAVENDER**

✳ **FEW PINCHES OF SANDALWOOD**

✳ **CHARCOAL DISC AND HEAT-PROOF VESSEL**

✳ **TAROT DECK**

1. Blend the sandalwood and lavender and place on the charcoal disc (see p.123).

2. Hold the cards over the smoke and call in on Neptune's intuitive guidance to bring you the answers that you seek.

3. Continue to burn the incense as you pull the cards.

4. As you draw each card, journal what it means to you and how it makes you feel.

5. Take note of the very first thought that comes to mind when you pick each card.

♇

PLUTO

ELEMENT: Water

ENERGY: Transformation, rebirth, power,
death, shadow work

DAY: Tuesday

COLOURS: Black, deep red, burgundy, dark purple

PLANTS, HERBS, AND SCENTS: Wormwood,
blackthorn, patchouli, cypress, dragon's
blood, mugwort

ORBITAL PERIOD: Takes 248 years to complete its
orbit around the sun and stays in each zodiac sign
for 12–31 years

Pluto is the planet of transformations, rebirth, and hidden powers. It aligns with the cycles of life, inviting us to explore what lurks in our shadows and guiding us to shed what doesn't serve us to create room for rebirths, personal evolutions, and life upgrades.

In Roman mythology, Pluto was the god of the underworld, ruling over the spirit realm and all that was unseen. He symbolized the duality of life and death, and the power of transformation. Pluto's energy works well for spells that call for change and clearing out old stagnant energy to make space for new beginnings.

ENERGY SHAKE-UP

|||||||||||||||||||||||||||||||||||

Connecting to Pluto can help shift stagnant energy, so is useful when feeling stuck or blocked. To connect to this energy, look up what time Pluto is coming into transit and work a little before this time (check this on an astrology app or website).

You will need

✳ **1 BAY LEAF**

✳ **PEN**

✳ **PINCH OF SANDALWOOD**

✳ **PINCH OF DRIED ROSEMARY**

✳ **3 PINCHES OF DRIED SAGE**

✳ **PESTLE AND MORTAR**

✳ **CHARCOAL DISC AND A HEAT-PROOF VESSEL**

1. Draw the symbol of Pluto on the bay leaf.

2. Blend the sandalwood, rosemary, and sage using a pestle and mortar.

3. Burn the bay leaf over the blend to activate the spell.

4. Burn the incense on the charcoal disc by your front door, welcoming energy shifts and transformations.

5. You can also write down the transformations you wish to move through, and bless what you have written in the smoke.

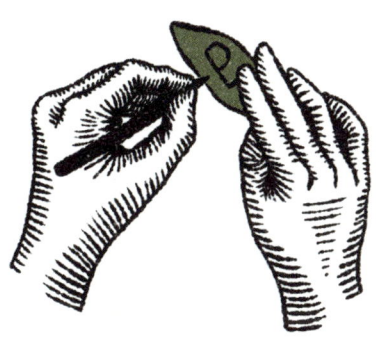

HOROSCOPIC ASTROLOGY

Now that we have uncovered the power of the planets we live beneath, it's time to take the next step: delving into the magic of astrology. Astrology explores the connection between the planets and events on Earth. This ancient understanding can be harnessed for self-awareness, decision-making, and predicting future outcomes.

Most of us know our zodiac signs, and even the least-spiritually minded love to read horoscopes (tailored guidance corresponding to our signs) – but astrology can allow us to go much deeper than that. The more you understand about your connection to the Cosmos, the more powerful your spells can become by allowing you to align your magical practice with your personal astrological energy.

It all begins with your birth chart. Each person has a unique relationship with the planets based on where these were positioned at the time of their birth. These planetary positions have a direct impact on our unique personality traits, tendencies, and paths in life. Understanding them can provide guidance on love and relationships, career, finances, and so much more.

To create your birth chart, you'll need to know the exact date, time, and location of when you entered the world. You can then add this information to an online tool (type "birth chart calculator" into a search engine and you will be spoilt for choice) to generate your chart. It is important that this information is correct, as the snapshot of the sky at your time of birth is taken every four minutes.

If you don't know your birth time or place, focus on your sun sign instead, or the position of those planets that can still be determined based on your birth date alone. If you do want a rough estimate of your chart, you can generate a "noon chart" by setting the time of birth to 12:00pm. This won't give you the rising sign or house placements (more on these on pp.266–267), but it's a good way to get a general feel for your planetary positions.

DEVELOPING YOUR PRACTICE

Before we get stuck in, it's important to note that we are only dipping our toes into this subject. There are so many elements and aspects to each sign, house, and planet that it's beyond the scope of this book to explore them all here. If this section whets your appetite and you would like to lean into the subject further, I recommend some good resources at the back of the book.

BIRTH CHARTS

When we explore our birth charts, we can gain a deeper understanding of ourselves by looking at planetary positions at our time of our birth; these reveal where our strengths and weaknesses lie and highlight how the movements of the planets affect us individually.

You can think of your birth chart as a planetary puzzle, with each piece representing an aspect of your personality or your life, and all of them fitting together to create the whole picture. Reading your chart is complex, but with practise you'll start seeing how these pieces work together to offer a more complete picture of who you are and your life path ahead. As you delve in, it is important to remember not to label or limit yourself, but to gain insight and use this to guide you.

The key pieces of this puzzle are your signs, houses, planets, aspects, angles, and elements.

SIGNS These represent your personality; each of the 12 zodiac signs has its own traits, qualities, strengths, and challenges (see pp.268–271).

HOUSES There are 12 houses, each representing a different area of your life, such as career, relationships, health, finances, and travel. Your birth chart shows you which planets and signs live within each house, highlighting where their energy is most active (see p.266).

PLANETS When a planet occupies a house, it brings focus and influence to that part of your life, while houses without planets may represent areas of your life where certain aspects feel more challenging. Planets represent our energy or actions,

so when a planet sits in a sign, it means that it is giving its energy to the personality of that sign (see p.265).

ASPECTS These reveal where the planets sit in relation to each other in our charts; when we look at these aspects they show how the energies of the planets interact with each other. Note that aspects and angles are complex, and are beyond the scope of this book – you would usually consult an astrologer to read these.

ANGLES These are measured in degrees on your chart and give a deeper insight into your birth chart. They show the dynamics between planetary placements and they can reveal areas of harmony and challenges.

ELEMENTS Each sign is connected to a classical element that influences its traits and characteristics. The elements can also show you where you are in balance or out of balance in your chart. For example, an alignment would be if your sun, moon, and rising signs are in compatible elements (like all Fire or all in Earth); here there tends to be a natural ease in self-expression. If your sun, moon, and rising signs are in different elements, you may feel personal conflicts and find yourself struggling for balance. We'll explore what sun, moon, and rising signs are on p.265.

READING YOUR CHART

To begin your reading, follow the circle in an anti-clockwise direction. You may notice that you have more signs in some of the houses, and this can mean that you feel more connected to whatever these houses represent. There might be houses that are empty, with no planets living in them, and when this happens it might be because you don't focus on those areas of your life, or they represent aspects that you have little interest in.

Outer circle represents the astrological signs

Each section represents a house

Houses show where the planetary energies in your chart are

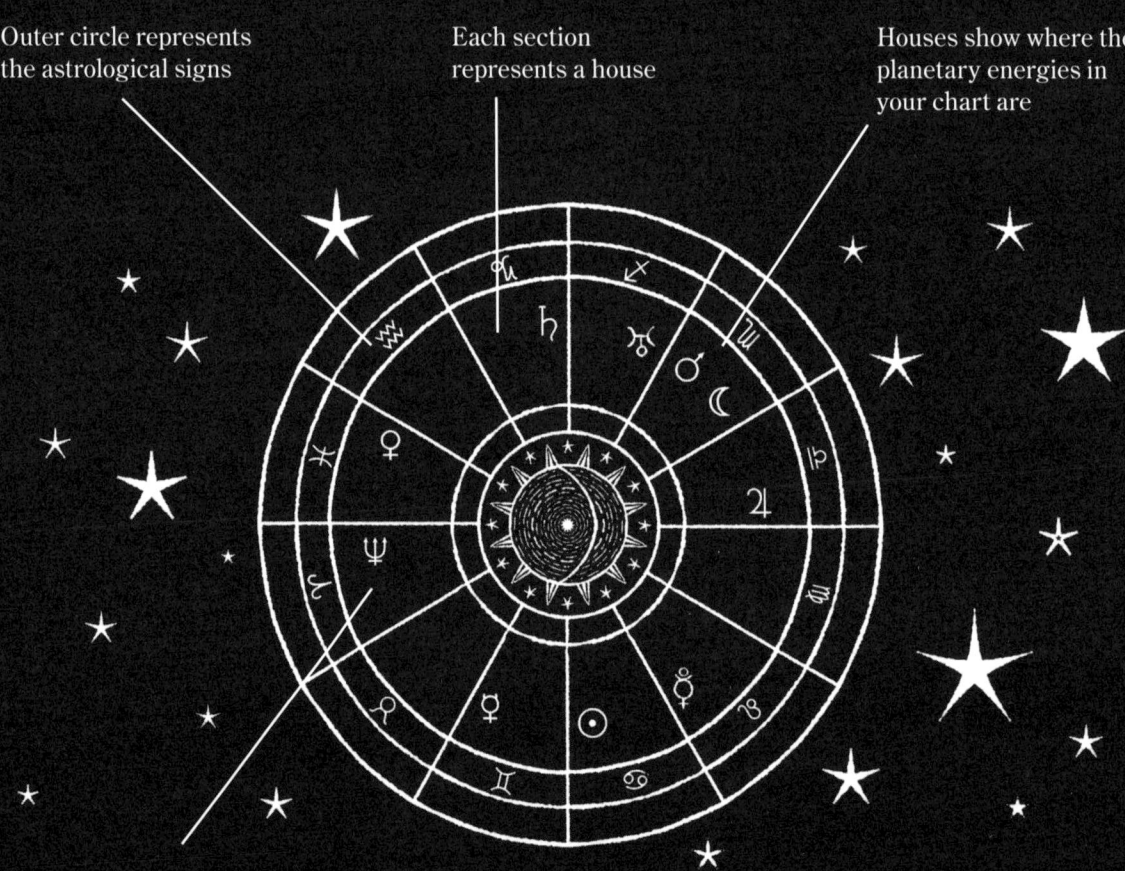

Neptune is the rising sign here

SUN, MOON, AND RISING

To start with, you might want to explore your "big three", aka sun, moon, and rising. These are the key elements of your birth chart.

SUN Represents the essence of who you are; it reflects your self-image, your ego, and how you show up in the world. This is your traditional zodiac sign, based on the date you were born. Your sun sign is often considered your "true self".

MOON Rules your emotional side and your subconscious. When you explore your moon sign, you will often find out what your deepest needs are. It reveals how you express feelings and how you connect with your emotions.

RISING Also known as the 'ascendant', this shows how you present yourself to the world, what people usually see, and the first impressions that you make.

THE PLANETS

In astrology, the planets each have their own specific types of energy (see pp.242–261 for more information about these). In a nutshell:

MERCURY Will show you how you communicate with others and how you process and analyse information.

VENUS The planet of love, romance, and relationships. Your sign in Venus will highlight what you find attractive and how you like to share your style and creativity.

MARS Reveals your ambition. It will show what drives you. This planet is connected to how you assert yourself, how you approach challenges, and your sexual energy.

JUPITER This is the planet of luck, growth, and expansion. Jupiter will often connect to your views on the meaning of life.

SATURN A teacher that brings life lessons through challenges and growth. A sign that sits in this planet will teach you about structure and self-discipline, and advise on how to handle your responsibilities.

URANUS Represents rebellion and how you connect with societal programming. Your placement here will show you where you wish to break free from traditions and cultural expectations.

NEPTUNE Your placement in Neptune represents your spirit and your soul. It connects to your spirituality and your mystical side.

PLUTO This is the planet that represents transformations, death, and rebirth. It influences you when seeking your destiny and purpose in the world.

HOUSES

Your birth chart has 12 houses, and each house represents an element of your life, such as your career, love life, or home life. When a planet is located in a house, it adds its own particular energy to that area of your life.

1ST HOUSE All about first impressions and your vibe. This represents your personality and how others perceive you. Your rising sign (ascendant) lives here, and it influences all of the houses.

2ND HOUSE Represents all that you value in life. This is your house of possessions and finances. It can show you how you earn and spend money, and what is of importance to you both physically and emotionally.

3RD HOUSE Rules learning, communication, and short trips. It also includes relationships with siblings and friends. This house shows how you think, speak, and interact with your surroundings.

4TH HOUSE Represents your home life, family values, and where you plant your roots in life. It reflects your upbringing, family relationships, and where you find comfort and feel safe.

5TH HOUSE All about creativity, hobbies, romance, and how you like to have fun. It's where you express your playful side, fall in love, and how you seek all of life's pleasures.

6TH HOUSE Connects to your work life, routines, and rituals. It can govern your productivity, as well as how you view health and wellness.

7TH HOUSE The house of close alliances, such as romantic relationships, friendships, and business partnerships. It shows how you relate to others and what you seek within close connections in your life.

8TH HOUSE Delves into your deepest desires and personal transformations. It also covers life's big transitions, such as birth and death, endings of all kinds, and rebirths.

9TH HOUSE Connected to higher learning, religious beliefs, philosophy, deep thinking, and truth seeking. It influences how you view the world.

10TH HOUSE Rules your career and work-related success. It can govern your established long-term goals, how you wish to represent yourself, and what you are known for.

11TH HOUSE Focuses on friendships and how you connect within your social network. It can influence your hopes, desires, and aspirations.

12TH HOUSE Connected to your inner world and parts of yourself that are hidden. It is a place for reflection and dreams. It can be connected to the darker shadow parts of yourself.

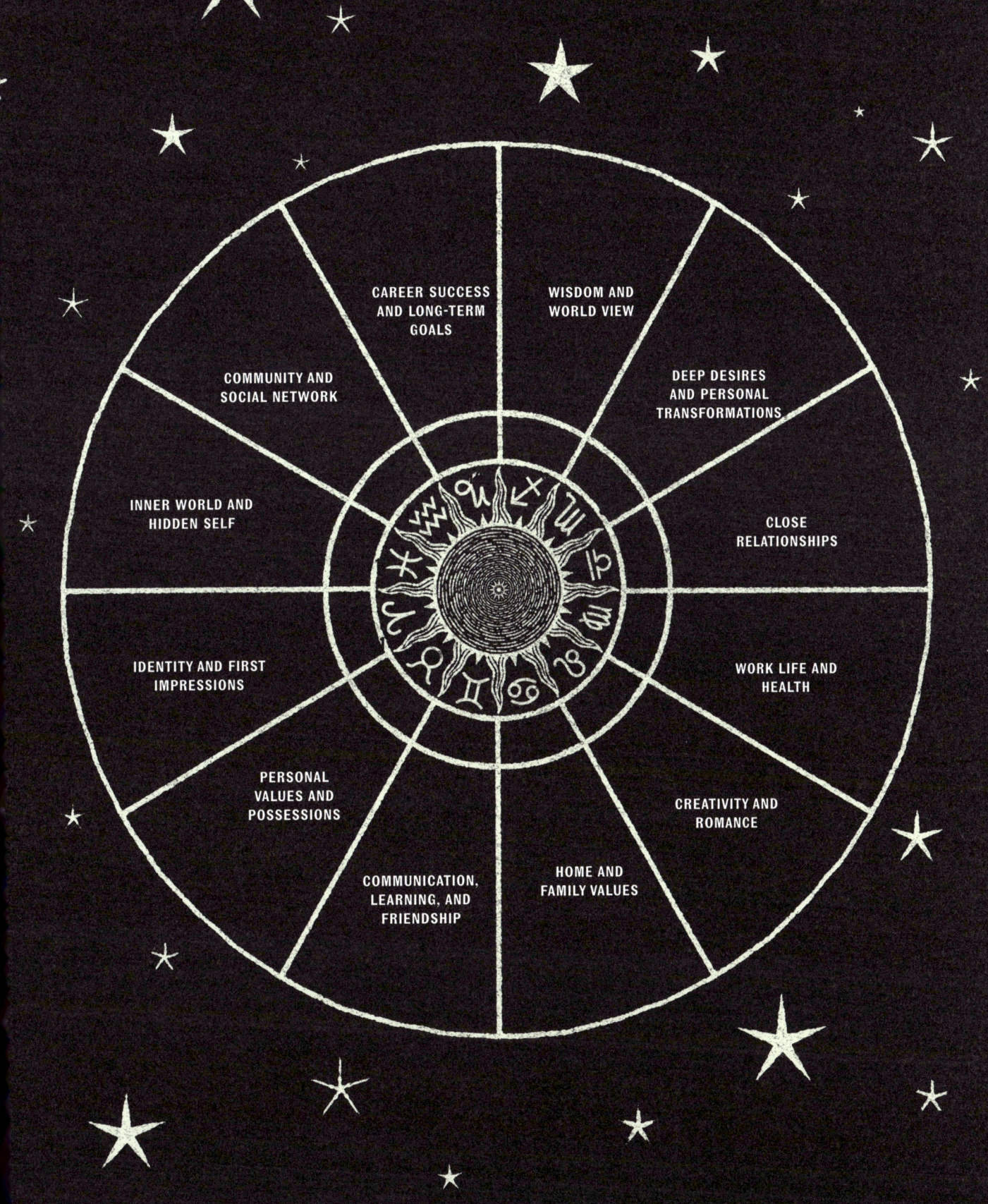

ZODIAC SIGNS

Your birth chart is divided into 12 sections, each representing a zodiac sign. Each sign is ruled by a specific planet, characteristics of which you may choose to harness in your spells. When a planet moves through one of the 12 signs it can amplify or shift that planet's energy; for instance, if a planet is travelling through a Fire sign, its energy might be feeling more powerful, action-orientated, and reactive, but if it was travelling through an Earth sign it might feel more grounded, less impulsive, and a bit more patient.

ARIES

||||||||||||||||||||

**SUN SIGN DATES:
21 MARCH–19 APRIL**

Energetic, bold, and pioneering. Aries energy drives action and independence, and brings new beginnings.

ELEMENT: Fire

PLANETARY ENERGY: Mars

MAGIC: courage and motivation spells.

TAURUS

||||||||||||||||||||||||||

**SUN SIGN DATES:
20 APRIL–20 MAY**

Stable and patient energy. This sign focuses on creature comforts and enjoying life's pleasures. Taurus energy is concerned with security and material wealth.

ELEMENT: Earth

PLANETARY ENERGY: Venus

MAGIC: wealth and stability spells, spells for a new home, or to bless your home.

GEMINI

||||||||||||||||||||||||

**SUN SIGN DATES:
21 MAY–20 JUNE**

Curious by nature, versatile, and communicative. Gemini energy encourages learning, flexibility, and quick thinking.

ELEMENT: Air

PLANETARY ENERGY: Mercury

MAGIC: communication and learning spells.

CANCER

LEO

VIRGO

SUN SIGN DATES:
21 JUNE–22 JULY

SUN SIGN DATES:
23 JULY–22 AUGUST

SUN SIGN DATES:
23 AUGUST–22 SEPTEMBER

Emotional, nurturing, and protective. Cancer energy is centred around home, family, and intuitive feelings.

Confident, creative, and charismatic. Leo energy emphasizes leadership, self-expression, and passion.

Practical, analytical, detail-oriented, and organized. Virgo energy is diligent, loyal, caring, and thoughtful,

ELEMENT: Water

ELEMENT: Fire

ELEMENT: Earth

PLANETARY ENERGY: Moon

PLANETARY ENERGY: Sun

PLANETARY ENERGY: Mercury

MAGIC: emotional healing and protection magic; self-care spells and self-devotion rituals.

MAGIC: self-confidence, courage, and creativity spells.

MAGIC: organization, getting everything in order, spells for productivity and to gain clarity.

LIBRA
||||||||||||||||||

SUN SIGN DATES:
23 SEPTEMBER–22 OCTOBER

Harmonious, diplomatic, and relationship-focused. Libra energy seeks balance, fairness, and beauty.

ELEMENT: Air

PLANETARY ENERGY: Venus

MAGIC: spells to bring equanimity, peace, and harmony; love spells.

SCORPIO
||||||||||||||||||||||

SUN SIGN DATES:
23 OCTOBER–21 NOVEMBER

Intense energy; life-changing, passionate, and loyal. Scorpio energy deals with power, deep emotions, and transformations.

ELEMENT: Water

PLANETARY ENERGY: Pluto

MAGIC: transformation spells for rebirths and magic to explore your shadow side for hidden truths.

SAGITTARIUS
||||||||||||||||||||||||||

SUN SIGN DATES:
22 NOVEMBER–21 DECEMBER

Sagittarius energy is optimistic and adventurous, and is all about exploration, learning, and expanding your horizons.

ELEMENT: Fire

PLANETARY ENERGY: Jupiter

MAGIC: creating opportunities, travel spells, and magic to create expansion in your life.

CAPRICORN

**SUN SIGN DATES:
22 DECEMBER–19 JANUARY**

Known to be disciplined, responsible, and ambitious. Capricorn energy is focused on long-term goals, success, and structure.

ELEMENT: Earth

PLANETARY ENERGY: Saturn

MAGIC: success and goal-setting spells, and for blessing your dreams and ambitions.

AQUARIUS

**SUN SIGN DATES:
20 JANUARY–18 FEBRUARY**

Forward-thinking and a bit of a rebel. Aquarius energy is all about individuality and innovative ideas.

ELEMENT: Air

PLANETARY ENERGY: Uranus

MAGIC: activism spells to open up the channels to new ideas, and blessing different ways of doing things; confidence spells to break traditions.

PISCES

**SUN SIGN DATES:
19 FEBRUARY–20 MARCH**

Associated with dreamwork, connecting to your intuition, and psychic energy. Pisces energy aligns with creativity, spirituality, and truly feeling your emotions.

ELEMENT: Water

PLANETARY ENERGY: Neptune

MAGIC: awaken and tap into your psychic abilities by tuning in to your intuition and dreams; emotional healing spells.

PLANETARY CYCLES AND TRANSITS

There are significant planetary cycles and transits that happen throughout our lifetime. Often these phases are a time for learning and evolution, when growth, change, and transformations happen. Retrogrades occur when a planet appears to move backwards in the sky, and during these periods the planet's energy can feel challenging or out of sync. Working with planets in retrograde can be a powerful time to use this reversed energy to reflect, revise, and reconsider.

MERCURY RETROGRADE This happens about three times a year when Mercury appears to move backwards in the sky. This impacts everyone at the same time, and can affect technology, travel, and communication. Its energy can bring misunderstandings, delays, and a need to revisit the past. Advice for this time is to slow down, review whatever is going on in your life more closely, and take time to release what is no longer serving you.

VENUS RETROGRADE This is another collective astrological phenomenon, which happens about once every 18 months, when Venus appears to move backwards in the sky. It can affect love, relationships, and personal values. This is a good time for reflection on past relationships or unresolved emotional pain, and for re-evaluating how you deal with love and finances. This is not the best time to start new relationships or make new financial investments.

MARS RETROGRADE This occurs roughly every two years, when Mars appears to move backwards. It affects energy, drive, and motivation, and you may feel frustrated, stuck, or less motivated to pursue goals. This is a good time to reassess your goals and visions.

LUNAR AND SOLAR ECLIPSES Eclipses happen in pairs, about twice a year, with a solar eclipse (new moon) and lunar eclipse (full moon). Solar eclipses will often signify powerful new beginnings, sudden shifts, and big changes. Lunar eclipses are about endings, revelations, and emotional breakthroughs. Eclipses often bring unexpected changes, forcing you to look at things differently.

SATURN RETURN This occurs around the ages of 29–30, 58–60, and 86–88, which is when Saturn returns to the position it was in at your birth – so its timing is specific to you. Often your Saturn return brings a major life shift and changes. This can feel really challenging, but trust that whatever comes after this storm will bring wisdom and lessons that will build a solid foundation for the next phase of your life.

JUPITER RETURN This happens every 12 years, when Jupiter returns to the position it was in at your birth. Jupiter returns can bring new opportunities, luck, expansion, and abundance, making it a powerful time for personal and spiritual development.

CHIRON RETURN Chiron return happens at around the age of 50, when Chiron returns to its original position in your birth chart. This is a time for deep healing, confronting any old wounds, and for embracing emotional growth. It can assist with awakening your wisdom and learning from past pain you have experienced.

NORTH NODE RETURN This happens around the ages of 18–19, 37–38, 56–57, and 75–76, when the North Node returns to its position at your birth. This highlights your life's purpose and destiny. It encourages you to connect with your soul's path and let go of old habits tied to your South Node.

PLUTO TRANSIT When Pluto makes transits through personal planets or certain points in your chart, it can lead to extreme transformations that can be connected to your emotions, personal power, or anything you have been struggling with. Because Pluto's transits are slow-moving, they can last for several years, bringing gradual but intense personal growth.

URANUS OPPOSITION This happens in your early 40s and it is linked to the "midlife crisis" stage. Uranus inspires you to break free from parts of your life that no longer serve you. It inspires radical change, finding independence, and exposing yourself to new experiences.

NEPTUNE SQUARE This happens around your early 40s, when Neptune makes a challenging aspect to its position in your birth chart, which can bring confusion. This occurs when Neptune forms a 90-degree angle to another planet: for example, Neptune square sun may challenge identity; Neptune square moon can heighten emotional sensitivity; Neptune square Mercury may cloud decision-making; and Neptune square Venus can cause confusion in relationships. It is a time for spiritual growth, but also inspires the need to confront areas in your life that you have been ignoring.

MARS RETURN This takes place approximately every two years, when Mars returns to its original position in your chart at the time of your birth. It brings with it Fire energy to inspire new beginnings and awaken motivation.

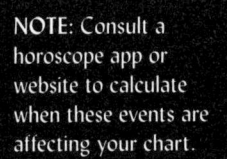

NOTE: Consult a horoscope app or website to calculate when these events are affecting your chart.

CHAPTER ELEVEN

WHEEL OF
THE YEAR

NATURE'S CYCLES

The Wheel of the Year is a symbolic calendar used in witchcraft to mark the changing seasons. It serves as a practical and spiritual roadmap, connecting us with ancient Pagan traditions, aligning us with nature and Mother Earth, and allowing for meaningful self-reflection and powerful rituals.

Each year, we travel through eight "sabbats", or celebration days. These sabbats follow the cycles of nature and mark the main turning points of the year. They include:

* **TWO SOLSTICES (FOR WINTER AND SUMMER): THESE MARK THE SHORTEST AND LONGEST DAYS OF THE YEAR**

* **TWO EQUINOXES (FOR SPRING AND AUTUMN): THESE OCCUR WHEN THE SUN IS DIRECTLY ABOVE THE EQUATOR, RESULTING IN ALMOST-EQUAL LENGTHS OF DAY AND NIGHT ACROSS THE GLOBE. THESE MOMENTS OF BALANCE HERALD IN NEW SEASONS**

* **FOUR "CROSS-QUARTER" DAYS: THESE REPRESENT THE MIDPOINTS BETWEEN THE EQUINOXES AND SOLSTICES. THESE INCLUDE UNIVERSALLY RECOGNIZED CELEBRATIONS SUCH AS MAY DAY AND HALLOWEEN**

Originally, these cycles were aligned with significant moments in the agricultural calendar, connected to planting and harvesting. Even though most of us today don't need to interact with the land in the same way our ancestors did, understanding the symbolism of the Wheel can be a reminder to connect with nature and reflect on our own journeys. When we align our energy with nature, we can bring ourselves into a state of flow and allow the transitions in the natural world to guide us through our own rituals, reflections, and rebirths.

START HERE

Consider the moments in your year that you already use as times for transformation and intention-setting. Perhaps you use the New Year at the start of January for goal-setting, and September – the start of the new school year – for realigning with your purpose. The events and rituals in the Wheel of the Year are not so different, and can be integrated alongside – or instead of – the seasonal shifts you already experience.

THE EIGHT SABBATS

Over the next few pages, we will explore the eight most celebratory, transformative occasions of the Wheel of the Year. As each sabbat is tied to the seasons, you'll notice that the dates differ depending on whether you're in the Northern Hemisphere or the Southern Hemisphere. For each sabbat, I have suggested rituals to help you welcome more meaning and magic during these sacred times.

By following the rhythms of the seasons, we can slow down and reflect. It is a powerful reminder that everything goes in cycles, and as nature around us is constantly in a state of change, so are we. When we recognize this energy, we can summon our own personal power to bring change to our lives to transform, shed, and grow.

Working through the Wheel of the Year is a personal journey, and the practices you choose, whether they be magical or non-magical, should feel powerful and meaningful to you.

Magic doesn't always have to be about candles and spells: sometimes it's in small, practical things, like cleaning your house or cooking a meal with intention. It can be as simple as taking yourself for a walk and connecting to seasonal nature, lighting a candle and journalling, reflecting on what was happening in your life during the previous sabbat.

Please remember that these everyday actions can hold just as much transformative energy as a ritual, especially when done mindfully. This is why I've included a mix of practical ideas alongside magical spells and rituals over the following pages. Choose what resonates or make up your own practices: when getting in flow with the seasons, you want to be in your own personal, authentic flow too.

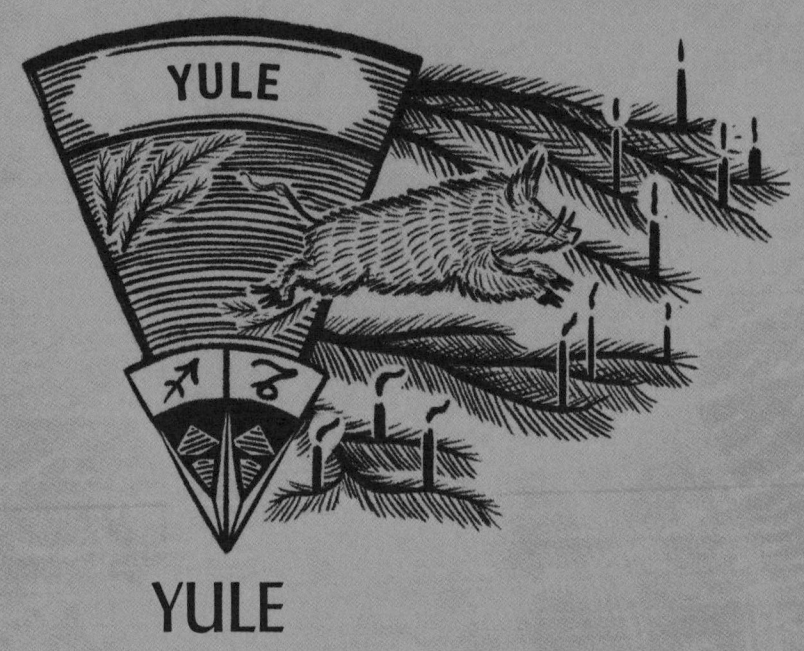

YULE

20–23 DECEMBER (Northern Hemisphere)
20–23 JUNE (Southern Hemisphere)

Yule is a festival often associated with the winter solstice, but it's important to note that the two are not identical. Yule has Pagan and Norse roots, celebrated around the same time as the winter solstice and later incorporated into Christmas traditions. The winter solstice marks the precise astronomical moment when the Earth's axial tilt is furthest from the sun, resulting in the shortest day and the longest night of the year. This moment occurs at opposite times in the hemispheres. From here the daylight starts to return, and we gain one extra minute of daylight each day.

Yule holds deep spiritual significance in many cultures, particularly in Norse, Celtic, and Roman traditions, and is often celebrated as a time of renewal and transformation. Yule tells the tale of the goddess who gives birth to a son, the Sun God, who brings the promise of longer, brighter days; winter will soon be over, and with spring will come an abundance of food and crops.

This period is traditionally a time of deep introspection. It invites us to reflect on the past to prepare for the future, cultivating self-love and healing. We can align our inner work with the return of the sun's light, connecting us to the cyclical nature of life: we are constantly transforming, moving from our own personal darkness to light.

Use this time to slow down and rest. Gather as many candles as you can and light your kitchen with them, play soothing music, and cook a healthy and hearty stew. Make sure it includes earthy, grounding ingredients such as carrots, potatoes, and bay leaves, and take your time.

WINTER SOLSTICE TRANSFORMATION

As you have turned inwards, use this ritual to honour and reflect on any transitions and lessons that have taken place. What have you worked through? What have you learnt about yourself? How have you evolved?

You will need

* ✳ PINCH OF DRIED LAVENDER
* ✳ 1 STICK OF CINNAMON
* ✳ CHARCOAL DISC*
* ✳ PESTLE AND MORTAR
* ✳ CAULDRON OR HEAT-PROOF VESSEL
* ✳ 1 RED CANDLE
* ✳ SOME EARTH FROM OUTSIDE (PREFERABLY FROM AN AREA IN NATURE THAT YOU LOVE)
* ✳ PEN AND 2 PIECES OF PAPER
* ✳ 3 HANDFULS OF SALT

*You can also use 2 parts lavender and 1 part cinnamon essential oils on a diffuser instead of burning them on charcoal

1. Blend the cinnamon and lavender in a pestle and mortar in a clockwise direction and sprinkle a little of this on the charcoal disc (or add a drop of lavender and cinnamon essential oils to a diffuser).

2. Bless the candle in the smoke, then light the candle.

3. Bless the earth in the smoke and sprinkle it around the base of the candle.

4. Gaze into the flame and think about any darkness that you have worked through; these can be self-realizations, shadow elements of yourself, areas of transformation, epiphanies, or maybe something you wish to leave behind. Write these down on the paper.

5. Burn this paper and, once it has turned to ash, throw three handfuls of salt on it, acknowledging that you are closing the door on it.

6. Write out on a separate piece of paper the intentions and hopes that you wish to call in for yourself as the sun returns.

7. Add more cinnamon and lavender to the charcoal disc and bless this paper in the smoke.

8. Keep this paper on your altar or somewhere safe. You can review it again on Imbolc.

Alternative ritual ideas:

* ✳ CREATE A VISION BOARD AT THIS TIME
* ✳ WATCH MOVIES OR DOCUMENTARIES THAT INSPIRE DEEP THINKING, INTROSPECTION, AND MEANINGFUL DISCUSSIONS WITH FRIENDS

IMBOLC

2 FEBRUARY (Northern Hemisphere)
2 AUGUST (Southern Hemisphere)

At Imbolc, we emerge from the darkness of winter and start to notice the first signs of spring; crocuses and snowdrops appear and bring with them feelings of inspiration. This time is all about the growth that is happening beneath the surface: seeds that are lying dormant, waiting for the right moment to emerge. This is considered to be one of the "cross-quarter days", seeing as it falls midway between the winter solstice (Yule) and the spring equinox (Ostara).

Imbolc is steeped in Gaelic traditions and is also linked to the goddess Brigid. In Celtic mythology, Brigid symbolizes new beginnings and fertility. Pagan communities honoured her through rituals for creativity, healing, and protection, lighting candles and bonfires to welcome her energy into homes and hearts.

This is a powerful time for calling in fresh perspectives and ways of being, to look back on insights we have gained over the winter months. Think back to late September (March in the Southern Hemisphere), as the days shortened and the autumn equinox arrived: what were you focusing on, and how did you show up in the world as the season shifted into colder, darker days?

This is also a good time to cleanse and purify your home. Open the windows and burn cleansing herbs such as sage or rosemary, use cleansing citrus essential oils in a diffuser, or burn resins like camphor or frankincense on a charcoal disc. With the windows open, work your way through your home, starting at the room furthest from the front door and ending at your front door, facing outwards, closing your front door when finished.

SEEDS OF CHANGE SPELL

As you create energetic space and welcome back the light, what new and revived energy would you like to invite? Remember: this is a novel and evolved energy, so the seeds you plant must be for something new, not something that you have manifested before.

You will need

* 5 WHITE CANDLES
* PLANT THAT IS FLOURISHING (THIS CAN BE A HOUSEPLANT OR OUTDOOR PLANT)
* SMALL HANDFUL OF POPPY SEEDS

1. Place the five candles around the plant.

2. Light each candle.

3. As you light the candles say:

"I CALL IN THE LIGHT, I CALL IN THE ENERGY OF THE GROWING SUN, I CALL IN THE POWER OF THE SUN. MAY THE SUN BLESS THESE SEEDS OF GROWTH."

4. Now hold the poppy seeds to your heart and think about what it is you wish to begin to grow at this time. Set an intention that you wish to be complete by spring equinox.

5. Sprinkle the seeds into your plant pot.

6. Allow the candles to continue to burn all the way down.

7. Keep the plant pot in a good spot where it gets the right amount of light and continue to nurture it; as you tend to it, remember the intentions you have set for Imbolc.

Alternative ritual ideas:

* DECLUTTER YOUR HOME OR WORKSPACE
* INVITE IN ANYTHING YOU'VE ALWAYS WANTED TO TRY, LIKE LEARNING A NEW SKILL OR EXPLORING A NEW HOBBY
* WRITE A LETTER TO YOURSELF AND STORE IT SOMEWHERE, AND THEN OPEN IT AT THE NEXT IMBOLC (THIS PRACTICE CAN BE DONE AT ANY OF THE SABBATS)

OSTARA

20—23 MARCH (Northern Hemisphere)
20—23 SEPTEMBER (Southern Hemisphere)

Also known as spring equinox, on this day of magical transition the Earth's axial tilt is neither leaning towards nor away from the sun, resulting in nearly equal lengths of both day and night.

Across different cultures, the spring equinox is celebrated with various rituals, festivals, and ceremonies that show gratitude for the Earth's abundance. Ostara (or "Eostre") is named for the Germanic goddess associated with fertility, birth, and the awakening of the Earth.

For me, the spring equinox represents more than just a change of season; it feels like the true beginning of a new cycle in the Wheel of the Year. I often find this time to be more potent for setting intentions and making resolutions than New Year. The new calendar year may offer a fresh start, but it's one manufactured by humans. Spring, on the other hand, is a new beginning birthed by nature itself. There's something incredibly powerful about aligning with that natural rhythm, as if the Universe is conspiring to help us grow.

Take a moment now to step outside and connect with nature. Don't just observe it, but feel it, paying attention to the life that flows through the trees, the soil, and the air. Spend some time walking outdoors and realize that you are not a witness to nature but an integral part of it. Recognizing this can put you in the most synchronized magical flow of abundance. Know that you are an important part of this cycle, and allow it to help you sync with the season's magic, inviting abundance, growth, and transformation.

ROAD OPENING SPELL

||||||||||||||||||||||||||||||||||||||||||||||

Call in on this spring energy to put a spring in your step. How can you take a leap of faith at this time? As spring is popping, how would you like your energy to align? What do you see in the open road ahead of you? What new beginnings do you wish to call in?

You will need

* ✳ **FLOWERS AND FOLIAGE THAT ARE NATURALLY FLOURISHING AT THIS TIME OF YEAR**
* ✳ **PINCH OF DRIED ROSEMARY**
* ✳ **PINCH OF DRIED DILL**
* ✳ **CARRIER OIL OF YOUR CHOICE**
* ✳ **PLATE**
* ✳ **1 YELLOW CANDLE (A SMALL YELLOW SPELL CANDLE WOULD BE BEST)**
* ✳ **PEN AND PAPER**

1. Wake up just before sunrise.

2. Create an altar of flowers facing east (or west in the Southern Hemisphere): ideally you should be facing the sunrise and looking at it through a window.

3. Mix the dill and rosemary with the carrier oil.

4. Tip this mixture onto a plate and roll the yellow candle in it so that it is covered in the blend.

5. Place the candle in the centre of your altar, and at the stroke of sunrise light the candle.

6. Sit with it, allowing yourself to visualize what you wish to manifest in this next cycle.

7. Try to work with new intentions: sometimes our old wishes can carry stagnant energy, and this is all about renewal.

8. Write your intentions and wishes down as though you already have them: for example, "I am so grateful for.........", or "I am so happy ....happened."

9. Read out what you have written to the candle flame.

10. Now take what you have written and bury it beneath a favourite tree. As you walk past the tree over the coming months, connect the growth of the tree to that of your intentions.

Alternative ritual ideas:

* ✳ **SPEND TIME GARDENING, PLANTING HERBS AND FLOWERS OR REPOTTING PLANTS INDOORS**

* ✳ **DO A PROPER SPRING CLEAN OF YOUR HOME, THROWING AWAY ITEMS THAT YOU DON'T NEED**

BELTANE

30 APRIL–1 MAY (Northern Hemisphere)
31 OCTOBER –1 NOVEMBER (Southern Hemisphere)

Beltane, also known as May Day, is a festival of fire, fertility, and passion, honouring the start of summer and the renewal of nature. It's a "cross-quarter day", given that it falls midway between the spring equinox (Ostara) and the summer solstice (Litha).

This is a time when a fruitful harvest would have been celebrated, and blessings given to the livestock. The Celtic festival was originally known as "La Bealtiane", which translates to "bright fire". And fire played a key role in Beltane traditions, with cattle often led between two large bonfires, the sacred smoke believed to protect the animals and ensure a prosperous season. Fire and its ashes were used in various rituals, continuing into today's Beltane celebrations.

In Pagan traditions, the union of the divine feminine and masculine is honoured at Beltane, the sacred marriage of goddess and god, symbolizing the fertility of the land. This is a good time to connect to the power of the sun and celebrate gratitude for the renewal of the Earth.

Beltane is also a time of joy and revelry. Dancing around the maypole, adorned with ribbons and flowers, is a well-known tradition, representing the interweaving of life's energies. You might decorate your altar with blossoms and symbols of fertility, such as eggs and seeds.

At this time of year, write a wish on a yellow ribbon and tie it on a hawthorn, ash, thorn, or sycamore tree. Tune in to Beltane energy to inspire action and confidence in your life. If you have access to an outside space, invite friends over and create a circle around a fire, sharing what you are grateful for with each other. This is a great time for a party!

A SPELL FOR PURE PLEASURE

As the sun is shining and the natural world is bursting forth in its most abundant flow, perform this spell to channel this bountiful energy into your own life.

You will need

* **PREPARED INDULGENCES**
* **1 ORANGE CANDLE**
* **ROSE PETALS**
* **PEN AND PIECES OF PAPER**
* **GLASS JAR**

1. Ahead of this ritual, create a list of ways in which you can indulge yourself: food, clothes, scent, music, treats – all of the ways you can romance yourself.

2. Plan an outfit that you feel amazing in for your ritual, and prepare a menu of all of the favourite foods that you will eat.

3. On Beltane, have everything ready to create your altar, adding the rose petals and lighting the candle in the centre.

4. Write down a list of what abundance means to you and note all the areas where it flourishes in your life. Now note down your intentions, listing your deepest desires on one piece of paper, and then on separate pieces of paper write out all that you are grateful for.

5. Add all of the pieces of paper to the glass jar along with your list of intentions.

6. Allow the energy of gratitude to charge up your intentions. Keep the jar in the sunlight for a few hours and continue to add to it as and when (this will continue to feed it with good energy).

Alternative ritual ideas:

* **PLAN A PICNIC IN THE SUN WITH FRIENDS AND INCLUDE DISHES THAT USE ONLY SEASONAL INGREDIENTS**

* **CREATE A SUMMER PLAYLIST AND DANCE AROUND YOUR HOME TO IT, OR LISTEN TO IT WHILE WANDERING AROUND IN NATURE**

MIDSUMMER, OR "LITHA"

20–23 JUNE (Northern Hemisphere)
20–23 DECEMBER (Southern Hemisphere)

Also known as the summer solstice, this is when the sun is at its strongest and nature is in full bloom. The Earth's axial tilt is closest to the sun, which results in the most daylight hours and the shortest night of the year. This can be a potent time to align yourself with the sun's energy.

Historically, Litha was a time of fire, fertility, and abundance. In many cultures, bonfires were lit to celebrate the sun's strength and vitality, with people dancing and leaping over the flames for blessings. In Pagan traditions, Litha represents the battle between light and dark. Celts and Druids celebrated it as a festival of fire and sun worship, with the sacred site of Stonehenge, in Wiltshire in the UK, thought to have been a focal point for solstice rituals.

Modern Pagans and witches often celebrate Litha with rituals and feasts, honouring the sun's warmth, prosperity, and the cycle of life. It is a time of joy, love, and spiritual reflection. Think about what areas of your life could benefit from some of this radiating solar power: ideas, creative projects, and business or personal desires can connect to this solstice sun to inspire growth and momentum.

The summer solstice is also a time to express gratitude, thanking Mother Earth for all the abundance that you have in your life. Allow the sun to shine its powerful light on your personal achievements. Think about everything that you have accomplished over the year and celebrate yourself and all that you have attained.

ACTIVATION AND AMPLIFICATION SPELL

||||||||||||||||||||||||||||||||||||||||||||||||||||||||||||||||||||||||||||

This is a great time to charge up your magical tools and ingredients with powerful sun energy. Think about all the light and energy the sun provides and tap into this power, using it to activate areas of growth that you wish to work with in your own life. What are you going through that could use some amplification? What do you wish to activate?

You will need

* PEN AND PAPER
* SUMMER FLOWERS OF YOUR CHOICE
* BOWL OF SUNFLOWER SEEDS
* BOWL OF MARIGOLD FLOWERS
* PICK 5 OF YOUR FAVOURITE (SUN-SAFE) SPELL INGREDIENTS TO BLESS WITH THE SOLSTICE RAYS
* BALL OF BRIGHT ORANGE OR GOLD THREAD

1. While the sun is at its peak power, call on its energy to bless some of your favourite spell ingredients that are in your toolkit.

2. Create an altar with summer flowers that resonate.

3. Write down your intentions on a piece of paper.

4. Leave the items you wish to bless, and the marigolds and sunflower seeds (for growth and vitality) beneath the solstice sun (from sunrise to midday is ideal).

5. Allow the sunlight to bless these items with its powerful energy. Imagine the energy of the seeds amplifying your intention, like the sun's rays help a plant grow. Visualize your intention blooming like a sunflower, growing and flourishing.

6. Wrap your list of intentions with the thread and store it on your altar.

Alternative ritual ideas:
* WAKE UP EARLY AND WATCH THE SUNRISE
* TAKE A PICNIC OUT WITH YOU, AND STAY OUT TO WATCH THE SUNSET

LAMMAS

1 AUGUST (Northern Hemisphere)
2 FEBRUARY (Southern Hemisphere)

Lammas, also known as "Lughnasadh" in Gaelic traditions, is a period for harvesting all that has grown over the summer months. It represents the midpoint between the summer solstice (Litha) and autumn equinox (Mabon). As summer ends, it is time to celebrate and give thanks for this bounty. This is an ideal moment to reflect on the hard work and patience that has brought the harvest to fruition.

Connect this moment to your own life cycle: how have you grown? What do you have gratitude for? What lessons have been learnt? Reflect on this as you prepare for the shift towards the darker half of the year. Acknowledge your own personal wins and the things that you are grateful for. What wishes have been granted? What spellwork has been completed?

Ask yourself what can you surrender to; remember that just as farmers must trust the cycle of the seasons after tending their crops, we too must recognize when to push forwards and when to let go. Not every seed planted will flourish and grow, and that's okay. Know that there is wisdom in knowing what to nurture and what to release. As you celebrate your successes, also acknowledge any setbacks or shifts in direction, understanding that they are part of the cycle. Use this point to set intentions for the months ahead, aligning with growth, harvest, and rest.

At this time, you may wish to collect bay, olive, and eucalyptus leaves and rosemary. Hang them to dry and then use string to suspend them from your altar, or blend them together and burn in a cleansing ritual.

CALLING IN ABUNDANCE

IIIIIIIIIIIIIIIIIIIIIIIIIIIIIIIIIIIIIIIII

Connecting to the energy of the harvest season turns up the power of your intentions, which makes it a very potent time for spellwork that calls in abundance.

You will need

* **SMALL HANDFUL OF GRAINS (BARLEY, WHEAT, OR OATS)**
* **SELECTION OF FRESH FRUIT OR VEGETABLES**
* **ANYTHING THAT HAS CONNECTIONS TO PROSPEROUS AND ABUNDANT ENERGY: THIS COULD BE PETALS, COINS, OR TAROT CARDS**
* **JEWELLERY**
* **1 GOLD CANDLE**
* **CARVING TOOL SUCH AS A TOOTHPICK OR CRAFT KNIFE**
* **PEN AND PAPER**

1. Create an altar using the ingredients you have gathered together.

2. Engrave your full name along the length of the candle, adding an infinity symbol (∞) at either side of your name.

3. Place the candle in the centre of the altar.

4. As you focus on the flame, think of all the abundance you already have in your life, then write down your intentions for what you wish to call in. Write out what has come to fruition on one side and what you wish to call in on the other.

5. Store the paper away safely.

6. This would be the perfect time to use a sigil (see p.183).

7. Speak the following aloud:

"ENERGY OF LAMMAS, I CALL ON THEE. I CALL OF ABUNDANCE AND PROSPERITY TO ALWAYS FIND ME. SO MOTE IT BE."

8. Seal the spell by carefully snuffing out the candle, or allow it to burn down as you meditate on your intention.

Alternative ritual ideas:
* **CALL OLD FRIENDS FOR A CATCH UP**
* **TAKE YOURSELF ON A SOLO DATE AND TREAT YOURSELF**

MABON

21–23 SEPTEMBER (Northern Hemisphere)
20–23 MARCH (Southern Hemisphere)

Mabon, also known as the autumn equinox, marks a period of balance, when day and night are equal. This is one of the most dramatic transitions within the Wheel of the Year, as we prepare for the journey inwards that the darker and colder part of the year will bring. This is a moment to slow down, take stock, and find harmony between light and shadow, both in nature and in ourselves.

Autumn is the perfect season to reflect on the abundance the previous months have brought us, whether it's harvests, personal achievements, or the wisdom gained from our experiences. As we enter this period of introspection, we're reminded of the cyclical nature of life: growth, decline, and rebirth. These cycles, which shape the Earth's journey, also happen in our own lives, reminding us that we are constantly evolving. This is the time to honour the fruits of our labour.

Use Mabon as an invitation to look inwards, to nurture yourself and embrace the slowing down of the seasons. Increase your self-care rituals: get cosy in your space, amd make hearty soups and comforting stews using grounding ingredients (remember to stir your intentions into them in a clockwise direction. See p.123).

Start a hobby that will carry you through the colder months. Treat yourself to new stationery and invite a journalling practice into your routine, allowing it to guide your reflections in the coming weeks. Wake up a little earlier, take a moment to sip something warm and soothing, and write by candlelight during those quiet, dark mornings. This is your time to reconnect with your inner self, honouring the balance between the external and internal worlds. Let Mabon be the beginning of your cosy, reflective season.

MABON RELEASING RITUAL

This season is all about letting go of anything you don't wish to carry through the winter months, or into the witches' New Year – Samhain, which is the last of the sabbats in the Wheel of the Year.

You will need

* 1 BLACK CANDLE
* AUTUMN LEAF THAT HAS FALLEN (IF YOU DON'T HAVE ONE TO HAND, YOU CAN DRAW THE SHAPE ON SOME PAPER)
* HEAT-PROOF BOWL
* HANDFUL OF AUTUMN EARTH (SALT CAN BE USED AS A SUBSTITUTE)
* BLACK PAPER
* 1 ORANGE CANDLE
* SANDALWOOD INCENSE TO BURN ON A CHARCOAL DISC, OR ESSENTIAL OIL IN A DIFFUSER
* DECK OF TAROT CARDS
* PEN AND PAPER

1. Light the black candle and write down on the leaf all that you don't want to carry through winter: habits you wish to change, relationships you want to release ties to, or obstacles in your life.

2. Set fire to the leaf in the flame of the black candle, then throw it in the bowl to burn.

3. As it burns, connect to the transformation of it turning to dust and feel a release.

4. Blow out the black candle and break it in half, then throw the three handfuls of earth or salt on to it. With each handful say aloud:

"I RELEASE, I RELEASE, I RELEASE."

5. Ensure the fire is out and wrap the candle and ashes in the black paper.

6. Once the banishing spell is completed, throw this away either where nothing grows or in someone else's bin (preferably on a route that you don't walk past often). This signifies that whatever you have released or banished is no longer your problem. Don't worry, the spell is finished, and you will not be transferring any energy to anyone else if disposing of it in this way.

7. Light the orange candle and begin to scent your ritual with the sandalwood.

8. Pull out three tarot cards. As you pick your cards ask them what you need to nurture your inner world.

9. Tune in to these cards and write down your instant thoughts as you pull them; they might not make sense in this moment but may later on.

10. Create a list of nurturing intentions and energies that you wish to bring into your life in the winter months.

11. Drip wax from the orange candle in a clockwise circle around this list. Keep the paper on your altar or somewhere safe.

Alternative ritual ideas:

* WORK THROUGH JULIA CAMERON'S BOOK *THE ARTIST'S WAY* CREATE A BOOK GROUP WITH FRIENDS AND MEET ONCE A WEEK TO DISCUSS YOUR PROGRESS

SAMHAIN

31 OCTOBER (Northern Hemisphere)
1 MAY (Southern Hemisphere)

Samhain, also known as Halloween or All Hallows' Eve, is the celebration of the witches' New Year, and not only is it the most popular mainstream celebration, but it is also the most sacred of all the sabbats. It occurs midway between the autumn equinox (Mabon) and winter solstice (Yule).

Samhain is a powerful marker of transition. It signifies the end of the harvest and represents the thinning of the veil between the physical and spiritual worlds, allowing us to communicate more easily with our ancestors and spirit guides.

As we celebrate the cycle of death and rebirth it is a time to acknowledge that in order for life to continue, there must be death. This sabbat encourages us to reflect on what must be released in order to make room for new beginnings. It is a time to set intentions, to decide on what wishes and energies you want to prepare and nurture over the winter months.

Think of the trees in winter: while they appear to be bare, beneath the surface they are quietly preparing for the seasons ahead. Their roots are absorbing nutrients and moisture from the soil, gathering what they need to sustain themselves through the cold winter. And, just like the trees, you should also rest and prepare for the summer months ahead.

While the boundary between the living and the dead is at its weakest, this is the time to reach out to those who have walked before us, seeking their wisdom and guidance. You may want to create an ancestor altar (see p.28). This is a powerful moment to ask for their support in your magical work, inviting their energy into your rituals. Whether it's a quiet moment of remembrance, a ritual, or to make a connection and ask for guidance, Samhain reminds us to connect to the past, the present, and the future.

ANCESTRAL CONNECTION SPELL

||||||||||||||||||||||||||||||||||||||||||||||||||||||

Create an ancestor altar (see p.28) including anything that connects you to them – photos, mementos, their favourite flowers or food. If you don't have a strong connection, research herbs they used or flowers that grew in their region to connect with their world.

You will need

* ❋ **4 WHITE CANDLES**
* ❋ **1 COLOURED CANDLE (CHOOSE A COLOUR THAT REPRESENTS YOU)**
* ❋ **HERBS AND FLOWERS**
* ❋ **DECK OF TAROT CARDS**
* ❋ **PENDULUM**
* ❋ **DROP OF ROSEMARY ESSENTIAL OIL**
* ❋ **5 ML (1 TSP) CARRIER OIL**
* ❋ **FRANKINCENSE RESIN**
* ❋ **CHARCOAL DISC AND HEAT-PROOF VESSEL**

1. Set the candles in a circle and surround them with the herbs and flowers.

2. Light the candles and say aloud:

"I WISH TO CONNECT WITH ANCESTORS KNOWN AND UNKNOWN."

3. Spread the cards out on the table, hold pendulum in your non-dominant hand, and say:

"ANCESTORS, I CALL ON YOU; WHAT IS THE MESSAGE FOR ME TO SEE?"

4. Allow the pendulum to land on a card. If you don't have a pendulum, say the chant as you shuffle the cards and see what card jumps out. Look at the card to see what message it holds (see pp.209–223).

5. Now rub the diluted rosemary essential oil on your third eye and burn the frankincense on a charcoal disc. Close your seeing eyes.

6. Focus your energy on seeing out of your third eye. Call the name of an ancestor that you wish to connect with. You can also ask if there is anyone who wishes to come through: this can be loved ones who have departed, and spirit guides often connect with us in this way too.

7. Once you have a clear view, ask a question. Remember older ancestors might not understand our modern lives, and may disapprove. Take time to explain things are different in your world.

8. If you don't feel comfortable with the energy of anyone who comes through, know that you are in control and can ask them to go away – visualize them disappearing.

9. Ask them to send you signs and tell them that you are open and ready to receive.

10. Be sure to look out for any signs after this ritual. These might include thoughts of them popping into your head, hearing a song they liked being played a lot, or become aware of their favourite colour being around you.

Alternative ritual ideas:

* ❋ **COLLECT HERBS THAT YOUR ANCESTORS WOULD HAVE HAD ACCESS TO IN ORDER TO CREATE A TEA**

* ❋ **LOOK THROUGH OLD PHOTOS OR WATCH A DOCUMENTARY CONNECTED TO YOUR LINEAGE**

RESOURCES

Here is a little directory of some of my favourite practitioners, shops, and resources. These are places and people that I trust to provide powerful, ethical, and high-quality offerings. Whether you're looking to expand your knowledge or find ethical and magical supplies, these recommendations will connect you with some of the best in the mystical world.

First, a little shoutout to my own magical business, **Mama Moon Candles**. I create handcrafted candles, potions, incense, and spell kits, all imbued with the potent magic of herbs, essential oils, and moon energy. Every product is designed to be an accessible tool to assist you with your magic and manifestations. I also offer oracle card readings infused with magic, helping you tap into divine guidance while adding spellwork and manifestation techniques to make the most of your readings.

MAMA MOON CANDLES
@mamamooncandles
mamamooncandles.com

BOOKSHOPS AND RETAILERS

UK

The Atlantis Bookshop, London
@theatlantisbookshop
theatlantisbookshop.com

Black Moon Botanica, Edinburgh
@blackmoonbotanica
blackmoonbotanica.co.uk

Cat & Cauldron, Glastonbury, Somerset
@catncauldron
witchcraftshop.co.uk

Courtyard Books, Glastonbury, Somerset
@courtyardbooks
courtyardbooksglastonbury.co.uk

Crooked Books, Hebden Bridge, Yorkshire
@crookedbookshb
uk.bookshop.org/shop/crookedbooks

The Haunted Bookshop, Bristol
@thehauntedbookshop_bristol
thehauntedbookshop.co.uk

Spooks of Haworth, Yorkshire
@spooksofhaworth
spooks.co.uk

Treadwell's, London
@treadwellsbooks
treadwells-london.com

Watkins Books, London
@watkinsbooks
watkinsbooks.com

The Wyrd Shop, Edinburgh
@wyrdshop.edinburgh
wyrdshop.com/home.htm

USA

Enchantments
@enchantmentsnyc
enchantments.nyc

Hauswitch
@hauswitch
hauswitchstore.com

House of Intuition
@houseofintuition
houseofintuitionla.com

Temple of Witchcraft
@temple_of_witchcraft
temple-of-witchcraft.square.site

HERBS AND OIL SPECIALISTS

G Baldwin & Co
London, UK
baldwins.co.uk

Forest Whole Foods
Dorset, UK
forestwholefoods.co.uk

Star Child
Somerset, UK
starchild.co.uk

Organic Matters
Vancouver, Canada
omfoods.com

CRYSTAL STOCKISTS

When buying any crystal, it is incredibly important to be aware of where they have been sourced from. As mentioned on p.158, there is nothing magical about crystals that have been unethically mined. For more information about ethical sourcing, head to Crystal Clear, a not-for-profit social enterprise that supports crystal miners around the world:
@crystal_clear_cic
crystalclear.life

Here are some trusted online sources:

UK

She's Lost Control
@slc_london
sheslostcontrol.co.uk

USA

Enchantments
@enchantmentsnyc
enchantments.nyc

Hauswitch
@hauswitch
hauswitchstore.com

House of Intuition
@houseofintuition
houseofintuitionla.com

TRUSTED PRACTITIONERS

IIIIIIIIIIIIIIIIIIIIIIIIIIIIIIIIIIIIIIIIIIIIIIIIIIIIIIIIIII

ASTROLOGY AND TAROT

Francesca Oddie
Expert in astrology, cartomancy, and host of an insightful podcast, *The Astrology Oddcast*.
@francescaoddieastrology
francescaoddie.com

Lucy Porter
Astrologer offering birth chart readings and teachings in astrology and tarot.
@thelucyporter
lucy-porter.com

Chani Nicholas
Podcaster and creator of the Chani app.
@chaninicholas
chani.com

Anne Ortelee
Astrologer and expert in planetary influences.
anneortelee.com

NUMEROLOGY

Remington Donovan
Expert in numerology and mystical symbolism.
@themysticalarts
themysticalarts.com

GENERAL MAGIC

Amanda Yates Garcia
Witch, healer, and alchemist.
@oracleofla

Lisa Lister
Witch and author writing about how to step into the divine feminine.
@sassylister

Pam Grossman
Witch and host of amazing podcast *The Witch Wave*.
@witchwavepod

Tree Carr
Witch, dream practitioner, and death doula.
@tree_carr

FURTHER READING

IIIIIIIIIIIIIIIIIIIIIIIIIIIIIIIIIIIIIIIIIIIIIIIIIIIIIIIIIII

BOOKS

Angelo, Jack and Jan, *Sacred Healing: a Soul-based Approach to Subtle Energy Medicine*, Piatkus (2001)

Beyerl, Paul, *The Master Book of Herbalism*, Phoenix Publishing (1984)

Cameron, Julia, *The Artist's Way*, Souvenir Press (2020)

Driessen, Tamara, *The Crystal Code: a Modern Guide to Crystal Healing*, Penguin Life (2018)

Frater, U.D, *Practical Sigils*, Llewellyn Publications (2012)

Gong, Tina, *Tarot: Connect With Yourself, Develop Your Intuition, Live Mindfully*, DK (2020)

Haksever, Semra, *Big Witch Energy*, Orange Hippo (2023)

Haksever, Semra, *Everyday Magic*, Hardie Grant (2024)

Haksever, Semra, *Mama Moon's Book of Magic*, Hardie Grant (2020)

Hall, Judy, *Crystal Bible*, Godsfield Press (2022)

Harrison, Ella, *The Book of Spells: 150 Magickal Ways to Achieve Your Heart's Desire*, DK (2022)

Leek, Sybil, *The Sybil Leek Book of Fortune Telling*, Macmillan (1969)

Lister, Richard, *Runes Made Easy: Harness the Magic of the Ancient Northern Oracle*, Hay House (2021)

Monaghan, Patricia, *The Encyclopaedia of Goddesses and Heroines*, New World Library (2014)

Parker, Derek and Julia, *Parkers' Astrology: The Definitive Guide to Using Astrology in Every Aspect of Your Life*, DK (2020)

Woolfolk, Joanna Martine, *The Only Astrology Book You'll Ever Need*, Taylor Trade (2012)

Wormwood, Valerie Ann, *The Fragrant Pharmacy*, Bantam (1991)

APPS AND WEBSITES

Astrology Zone
Plan your day, month, or year.
astrologyzone.com

Astro Style
Offers astrology charts, compatibility charts, numerology and astrological insights.
astrostyle.com

Cafe Astrology
Offers personalised birth charts.
astro.cafeastrology.com

My Moon Phase Lunar Calendar
Track planetary movements and lunar cycles.
Available from the App Store and Google Play

LEARNING

UK

Avalon Academy, Glastonbury, Somerset
In-person and online events and workshops focusing on the mystical arts, spiritual development, alternative healing practices, sound healing, and ritual crafts.
avalonacademy.co.uk

The Centre for Pagan Studies, Sussex
Blog and resources for Pagans everywhere.
centre-for-pagan-studies.com

The College of Psychic Studies, London
Offers online and in-person events, talks, and courses on numerology, palm reading, scrying, tarot reading, and rituals.
collegeofpsychicstudies.co.uk

She's Lost Control, London
Offers in-person and online events and courses on tarot, astrology, and moon rituals.
@slc_london
sheslostcontrol.co.uk

US

Magickal Circle School
Free online school offering courses on Paganism, witchcraft, mythology, divination, and healing.
@magickalcircleschooltmcs
magickalcircleschool.com

The Temple of Witchcraft, Salem, New Hampshire
Online and in-person training in magical practices and spiritual development.
@temple_of_witchcraft
templeofwitchcraft.org

INDEX

ACKNOWLEDGEMENTS

The biggest thanks to Amy, for giving me the amazing opportunity to create this book. To Gaynor, for your exceptional editing skills, thank you for your patience and care.

Thank you to Kaitlynn Copithorne for bringing the book to life with your illustrations, and to Jordan at DK and Amelia and Bonnie at Double Slice for your designs.

A special mention to my friends, who are truly my chosen family: Suwindi, Ayalah, Banos, and The Tepid Fish – thank you for being my constant cheerleaders.

To my love, David, thank you for being you, I think you are magic!

To my mum, for always believing in me.

And, of course, to my fur babies, Teddy and Fonzy, who've been curled up beside me while writing this book… *The Book of Witchcraft* has been blessed with your cosmic purrs.

ABOUT THE AUTHOR

SEMRA HAKSEVER is an eclectic witch, entrepreneur, former fashion stylist, and author of five books on witchcraft including the bestselling *Everyday Magic*. She is the founder of Mama Moon Candles, an online store based in the UK selling candles, potions, spell kits, and tools for practising magic.

Semra has practised reiki, crystal therapy, and moon rituals for over 20 years, and has always held the desire to create ritualistic tools that are accessible to all.

PUBLISHER ACKNOWLEDGEMENTS

DK would like to thank Arielle Steele for additional editorial support, Chloe Murphy for proofreading, and Vanessa Bird for indexing.

DISCLAIMER

The information in this book has been compiled as general guidance on the specific subjects addressed. It is not a substitute and should not be relied upon for medical, healthcare, or pharmaceutical or other professional advice. Practice, laws, and regulations all change and the reader should obtain up-to-date professional advice on such issues.

Herbs contain natural medicinal properties and should be treated with respect. Before trying any herbs, the reader is advised to sample a small quantity first to establish whether there is any adverse or allergic reaction. Do not ingest any spells containing herbal ingredients if you are undergoing any other course of medical treatment without seeking professional advice.

Take care when burning herbs or other combustible items. If doing so inside, ensure the area is well ventilated and clear of any flammable items.

The author and publishers do not accept any legal responsibility for any personal injury or other damage or loss arising directly or indirectly from any use or misuse of the information and advice in this book.

Senior Acquisitions Editor Zara Anvari
Acquisitions Editor Amy Slack
Senior Designer Jordan Lambley
Production Editor David Almond
Senior Production Controller Luca Bazzoli
DTP & Design Coordinator Heather Blagden
Sales Material and Jackets Co-ordinator Emily Cannings
Art Director Maxine Pedliham
Publishing Director Stephanie Jackson

Design Double Slice (Bonnie Eichelberger & Amelia Leuzzi)
Editorial Gaynor Sermon
Illustration Kaitlynn Copithorne

First published in Great Britain in 2025 by Dorling Kindersley Limited, 20 Vauxhall Bridge Road, London SW1V 2SA

The authorised representative in the EEA is Dorling Kindersley Verlag GmbH. Arnulfstr. 124, 80636 Munich, Germany

10 9 8 7 6 5 4 3 2 1
001–349940–Aug/2025

A CIP catalogue record for this book is available from the British Library.
ISBN: 978-0-2417-4280-8

Printed and bound in Slovakia

www.dk.com

This book was made with Forest Stewardship Council™ certified paper – one small step in DK's commitment to a sustainable future. Learn more at www.dk.com/uk/information/sustainability

MIX
Paper | Supporting responsible forestry
FSC™ C018179